# Creative Methods in Military Studies

## CREATIVE INTERVENTIONS IN GLOBAL POLITICS

**Series Editors: Shine Choi, Cristina Masters, Swati Parashar, and Marysia Zalewski**

The landscape of contemporary global politics is complex and oftentimes violent. Yet the urgency to provide solutions or immediate practical actions to this violence oftentimes leads to inadequate knowledge. This is despite the abundance of theoretical, conceptual, and methodological tools available—much of this produced through conventional academic disciplines, notably International Relations, Political Theory, and Philosophy. But the constraints imposed on these traditional disciplines profoundly limit their ability to incorporate and make effective use of more creative and innovative methodologies found in other disciplines and genres.

This series provides a unique opportunity to offer creative intellectual space to work with an eclectic and rich range of disciplines and approaches, including performative methodologies; storytelling, narrative, and auto-ethnography; embodied research methodologies; participant research; visual and film methodologies; and arts-based methodologies.

### Titles in the Series

*Sites of Dissent: Nomad Science and Contentious Spatial Practice* by Alissa Starodub
*Pedagogy as Encounter: Beyond the Teaching Imperative* by Naeem Inayatullah
*The Lived International: A Life in International Relations* by Stephen Chan
*Tears of Theory: International Relations as Storytelling* by Sungju Park-Kang
*Creative Methods in Military Studies* edited by Alice Cree
*The Self, and Other Stories: Being, Knowing, Writing* by Laura J. Shepherd
*Feminist Practices of Knowledge Formation in International Politics: Performing the Undisciplined Subject* by Michelle Brown, Shine Choi, Cristina Masters, Swati Parashar, Saara Särmä, and Marysia Zalewski

# Creative Methods in Military Studies

Edited by

Alice Cree

ROWMAN & LITTLEFIELD
*Lanham • Boulder • New York • London*

Published by Rowman & Littlefield
An imprint of The Rowman & Littlefield Publishing Group, Inc.
4501 Forbes Boulevard, Suite 200, Lanham, Maryland 20706
www.rowman.com

86-90 Paul Street, London EC2A 4NE



British Library Cataloguing in Publication Information Available

**Library of Congress Cataloging-in-Publication Data**

Names: Cree, Alice, 1991- editor.
Title: Creative methods in military studies / edited by Alice Cree.
Description: Lanham: Rowman & Littlefield Publishers, [2023] | Series: Creative interventions in global politics | Includes bibliographical references and index.
Identifiers: LCCN 2023009803 | ISBN 9781538160978 (cloth) | ISBN 9781538160985 (ebook)
Subjects: LCSH: Military research—Great Britain—Methodology. | Sociology, Military—Great Britain—Methodology.
Classification: LCC U395.G7 C74 2023 | DDC 355/.070941—dc23/eng/20230413
LC record available at https://lccn.loc.gov/2023009803

# Contents

# Acknowledgments

This book originates from conversations at the "Creative Methods in Military Studies" workshop held at Newcastle University in June 2019. Thank you to the Economic and Social Research Council (ESRC) for funding this workshop as part of my postdoctoral fellowship, as well as the university's Military, War and Security Research Group for additional funding.

Thank you to Michael Kerns and Elizabeth Von Buhr at Rowman & Littlefield for their patience and support in developing this volume. My thanks also to the editors of the *Creative Interventions in Global Politics* series (Shine Choi, Cristina Masters, Swati Parashar, and Marysia Zalewski) for their guidance and support throughout the whole process.

My sincere thanks to all the contributors to *Creative Methods in Military Studies* for their creativity, enthusiasm, and, again, patience when developing the book—especially during a global pandemic! Particular thanks goes to Rachel Woodward for her mentorship and encouragement.

# Preface

> As usual, Rosa starts our theatre workshop with a few games. We play the mama bird game; we split into pairs, and every pair has a mama bird and a baby bird. Each mama bird walks around the space, and makes a unique noise in order to call to her baby bird. Each baby bird has to close their eyes and find their mama bird simply by listening for their noise. The game starts out being a little rigid and embarrassing, as we walk around the room each making our own animal noises, or listening for one we recognise. The scene is faintly ridiculous, and as I pad about the room making my soft quacking noise, I wonder how exactly this constitutes research. Lorraine, who so far hadn't made her animal noise, suddenly punctuates the uncomfortable atmosphere by making an exaggerated and comical "BAAA" noise. In day-to-day life Lorraine is a veteran of the British army who suffers from PTSD, a warm but stoic woman who now works for a veteran charity. But in this moment, she is a petulant mother sheep standing on her hind legs, calling to her offspring. And I am not a researcher, but a duck in fits of laughter (Fieldnotes from theatre workshop, *Women Warriors*,[1] March 2019).

In planning this introduction, I have thought long and hard about my own experience with creative methods (what do I want to *say* about this way of working; what does it *do*?), but I always circle back to the "quacking duck moment" from my first foray into theatre as method.

At the time, I had been shadowing North-East–based feminist theatre company Workie Ticket Theatre for a number of weeks, learning how they used theatre in the context of a project with women veterans. I was finding my feet with drama, trying to throw myself into the process but ultimately still feeling like an imposter. Exercises such as the mama bird game served a number of different purposes; first and foremost, they helped participants to open up and willingly engage in the process of theatre-making. Playing games was a way of building confidence among a group who could at times be quite shy and self-conscious, but also helped to loosen up their bodies like playdough being pulled and stretched ready to be moulded. Secondly, playing games as a group helped participants learn to speak, move, and "be" as one entity, an ensemble. It generated receptiveness to one another's movements and feelings and helped to establish the group as one driven by shared aims and objectives. Finally, these games helped to encourage a spirit of reciprocity that was integral for the more challenging work that came later in the process. By participating in these games and sharing in laughter together, we created the safe space for open and authentic storytelling upon which the entire project relied.

Before we commenced work on "Women Warriors," the experiential and political gap between "us" and "the veterans" seemed to be insurmountable; how could we possibly hope to understand the experiences of these women, when we are coming at them from such fundamentally different perspectives? Like many feminist researchers in military studies, I am deeply critical of the processes through which bodies are mobilised in the war-making of violent state institutions. Vron Ware put it well when she said that "I did not think of myself as someone who was able to cross that extraordinary divide between the familiar social world and the hostile apparatus of military power" (2016, 231). And yet, by the end of the project, together we had developed a new shared understanding that was liberated from our roles as "researchers," "practitioners," or "veterans," and rooted instead in playfulness, creativity, and collaboration. Rather than being a series of uncomfortable and challenging encounters with the constituent bodies of a violent state institution, our workshops were characterised by laughter—silly, uncontrollable, hysterical laughter—as well as emotional closeness and even friendship.

One of the wonderful things about theatre, both as method and as creative practice, is that it relies so heavily on silliness, imagination, and game-playing. It necessitates the suspending of our normal adult lives, and participants temporarily throwing themselves into a way of being that for many of us does not come naturally. As I came to learn, it was not only our adult selves that we were able to cast off. In the above extract from my fieldnotes, I describe a moment in which the shackles of our respective veteran/researcher identities are momentarily discarded, and we instead find ourselves in an unfamiliar realm where we are all equal co-conspirators in "the ridiculous." As the workshops progressed into image-making and storytelling around our project's themes, these formative sessions helped to build relationships of trust and reciprocity within the group. At the same time, these workshops allowed us to craft new identities that had nothing to do with our proximity to military power, and everything to do with our creative and productive relationships with one another. As Ruth Raynor puts it, in this process "collaborators gain and negotiate new insights *together* as they participate in the shared event of theatre-making" (Raynor 2019, 704, emphasis in original). In making the research space "unfamiliar" through these acts of silliness and imaginative coproduction (Raynor 2019), the civilian/military, researcher/participant binary became fractured, and we found new ground on which to communicate and understand one another. And it was from this shared ground that we were ultimately able to approach very sensitive and difficult topics around military experience.

I want to begin this book by thinking in more depth about "quacking duck moments." Although the extract from fieldnotes at the beginning of this preface is just one vignette from my research, it represents an experience that has been recurring for me in every creative project that I have worked on—and is perhaps one that many creative methods researchers will recognise. I do not want to suggest that all research which uses creative methods is in some way silly, light-hearted or ridiculous, because we know that is not the case (and indeed, chapters in this very book are testament to that). But those of us who engage in some way with the ethos and practice of creativity in our research are perhaps more well acquainted with the sensation of feeling ridiculous than the average social scientist; those moments of reflection where the minutiae of our research practice suddenly seem bizarre, surreal, sometimes even comical. These "quacking duck moments" are the points of recognition in which the gap between the exact practice of the research at that moment in time, and the subject or object of the research, is brought into stark view. In the case of military-related research, this gap might be all the bigger; padding around the workshop space making gentle quacking sounds felt like a particularly odd way to do research that is at its core concerned with the inner workings of a violent state institution.

There is undoubtedly a level of insecurity at play here about how we might justify creative ways of working as *rigorous scientific methodology*—and of course, we must push back against such inclinations. But there is an intrigue and an opportunity that emerges in the chasm between creative practice and the [military] research subject. As my experience with creative methods has grown, so, too, has my understanding that quacking duck moments come with the territory—and, in fact, they are central. Without such moments, the power of creative methods to shed light on those things that perhaps seem obscure or antithetical about military phenomena cannot be fully realised. This is at the very centre of what we should be doing as critical military studies scholars; as Victoria Basham and Sarah Bulmer argue, "CMS work queers the military, renders it strange and exposes its contradictions. As such it is not concerned with making sense of the military through the application of existing concepts but rather at unmaking common sense understandings of military power and showing how military power often makes *little* sense" (2017, 63).

# Introduction

*Alice Cree*

What does it mean to bring creativity to our work in military studies? Social scientists have long been familiar with creative ways of doing research (see, for example, Gibson 2006; Buckingham 2009; Hawkins 2013, 2015, 2019; Raynor 2019; Von Benzon *et al.* 2021). This body of work recognises that creativity in research is not just about "research methods" as we commonly understand them, but more broadly about finding new ways of knowing the world and engaging openly and actively in curiosity. Geographers in particular have been ahead of the curve in this regard; Dowling *et al.* (2017, 823, emphasis in original) argue that more-than-human and more-than-representational ways of thinking that have become popular in human geography "[challenge] researchers to *do* geography differently" (see also Benzon *et al.* 2021). Disciplinary approaches in politics and international relations have historically lagged behind when it comes to embracing creative methodologies, although notable work such as Elizabeth Dauphinee's (2016) work on narrative engagement, and Jenny Edkins's (2013) work on novel writing in international relations (among other examples) have helped to encourage greater engagement with creativity among IR scholarship. Work that is broadly conceived as being related to questions of military power and security has, however, continued to struggle to keep up with the "creative turn" (Hawkins 2019) that we have seen elsewhere. Most security studies scholars, Lana Obradovic tells us, "remain somewhat stubbornly positivist" (2017, 75), concerned with a single and empirically observable reality which is "independent of the subjective nature of a scholar, personal experiences, social contexts and relations, and does not interfere with the research process at any stage" (4).

In critical security studies and critical military studies, we are increasingly seeing theoretical and methodological approaches that are attuned to the myriad sites, subjects and practices of power and security that cannot be easily understood within the positivist framework. Scholarship in critical military studies has examined questions around militarism and militarisation through military memoirs (Woodward & Jenkings 2012, 2018), toys and video games (Martin & Steuter 2010; Woodyer & Carter 2020), sport (Kelly 2013; Cree & Caddick 2020), tattoos (Dyvik & Welland 2018), music (Cree 2020a; 2020b), as well as the everyday popular geopolitics of military video games (Bos 2018), the poppy (Basham 2016), and even food products (Tidy 2015). Recent emerging work has also begun to consider the creative and performing arts as lenses through which to explore militarised culture, including theatre (Cree 2019) and dance (Åhäll 2019; Purnell & Danilova 2018). This work gives texture to our understandings of the embodied and affective circulations of militarised cultures and ideas, serving to expose "what is otherwise impossible to reveal" (Leavy 2015, 175).

But what happens if we mobilise the arts as a way of *doing* military research? The number of researchers doing creative work in military studies has been quietly growing for a number of years. On Wednesday 5th of June 2019, the Military War and Security Research Group at Newcastle University hosted an intensive one-day workshop on "Creative Methods in Military Studies." The workshop had emerged out of an awareness that there is a growing critical mass of scholars doing "creative"[1] projects in (critical) military research—but as yet, there had not been any meaningful opportunity to get together and talk about this work. We gathered in an overcrowded and sticky seminar room (one of those taken for granted privileges of living in a pre-COVID world) with over forty-five participants from as far away as Norway and the United States. This included academic researchers of all career stages, veterans (or those who identify instead as ex-military), artists, creative practitioners, and psychologists. The range of creative approaches we heard about included military theatre, sound installations, model-making, photography, song writing, dance, fiction, creative approaches to teaching critical military studies, and more. We talked about the added value of collective creative engagement, about what constitutes "data" and how we analyse it, and about who ultimately gets to speak through creative practice (and to whom?). We questioned whether there is a distinct ethics to creativity in military research; what does it mean to render something that is inherently rooted in violence "interesting" via creative practice? As should always be the case with academic events like this, we left the workshop with more questions than answers.

## ON CREATIVITY AND "STICKING POINTS"

The knots and tangles that we have to find ways of working through in critical military scholarship are undeniably part of what makes research on military institutions and cultures so rich, fulfilling and exciting. But they nevertheless pose the question, could there be a better way to do it? How can we change our research practice in order to better tackle these kinds of sticking points? Cynthia Enloe told us in 2015 that "to be a critical military analyst is to be a sceptically curious military analyst" (3). She explains that a critical examination of military institutions is motivated by a desire to generate reliable *explanation* as well as a full *accounting* of the causes and consequences of any military's way of operating and waging war. Central to both of these tenets is a need to "[take] seriously feminist investigatory questions" (4), and as Basham & Bulmer (2017) later argue, question the often-taken-for-granted assumptions about how it is that militaries and military power function. They compel us to ask the question, "What remains hidden if we fail to get closer to that which we critique?" (2017, 68).

At an intrinsic level, "creativity" and "military" do not seem to be words that fit together comfortably. They feel at odds with one another; to be creative is to prioritise imagination, expression, freedom, messiness, failure, and intuition, whereas military power and militarisation are wrapped up in discipline, violence, and control. And yet something interesting emerges at the intersection between these two seemingly contradictory and juxtaposing practices and ideas. Creative methods by their very nature involve the creation of something new, and so to be creative is to imagine new limitless possibilities. Put another way, creativity may offer a process through which new realms of critical possibility can be opened up. Bringing an imagination to our methods and practice may therefore help produce a new space for thinking differently about the subjects and relationships that constitute our research. Harriet Hawkins reminds us that a creative orientation towards research can facilitate an attunement to the "sensory experiences, emotions, affective atmospheres and flows of life" (2015, 248). So, too, she says, can it give us the means to "grasp the messy, unfinished and contingent," while enabling a more participatory and communicative way of engaging new 'publics' and "offering the chance to compose worldly relations (between humans and non-humans, and their environments) differently." There are things about life and the world around us that traditional research approaches and methodologies cannot fully grasp; the felt, in-flux, contradictory, intuitive, chaotic, nonsensical, and this is as true of military related phenomena as it is of anything else. To bring creativity to military research is to rethink some of the common ways of understanding military power and our relationship to it. Furthermore, perhaps there is something emancipatory or even resistant that comes with working outside the grammars of war and violence as they are often understood, by emphasising collaboration, imagination and artistic co-production in our methodologies. Such ways of working might help us to think anew about the shape that military power, for example, can take, and disturb the epistemological supremacy of violence within military research.

Creativity can, however, be an object of power as much as of resistance. Oli Mould argues that although creativity has the power to resist, capitalism co-opts it for its own growth. He argues that in a postmodern sense, creativity is rooted in a neoliberal ideology of power, however using creativity in our work should "be about seeking out those activities, people, things and ephemera that resist co-option, appropriation and stabilization by capitalism" (2018, 18). In a similar vein, while it would be all too easy to think that creativity is the business only of resistance and alternative ways of knowing or being in the context of military power and war, in fact it would be a mistake to decouple military power from creative practice. Creativity has always been wrapped up with the practice of war-making; militaries prioritise creativity as a core component of effective decision-making, and war itself has long been described by those who wage it as more of an art form than a science (this is nowhere better exemplified than in Sun Tzu's *The Art of War*). Art and creative practice are also mobilised in more insidious ways as practices of war-making; for example, the creative industries of television, film, theatre, and music have all been used as vehicles for telling particular kinds of stories about military participation that reify violent armed conflict (see, for example, Martin & Steuter, 2010 Pomarède, 2018; Bell 2018). Art and creativity are, therefore, as susceptible to co-option by military power as anything else.

What this means is firstly that there is always an undeniable politics to our work when we are engaging with creativity and creative practice in military research, but secondly that the susceptibility of creativity to co-option by military power itself may give us the very impetus for working in a creative way. There is, to my mind, no better argument for using theatre-as-method in *critical* military research than the fact that theatre has long been used as a practice of war-making. There are critical possibilities opened up by the potential of creative practice to be at once sovereign and resistant, in that it gives us a common language through which to critique, to challenge, to complicate. It is not that creativity is inherently resistant, but rather that it might help give us the language and tools with which to resist.

There are specific things about militaries, military practices and military culture that creativity and creative practice can help us to unlock or encounter differently. Creativity can provide new insights for directly examining and actively embracing those aspects of military research that are difficult to comprehend, that may otherwise pass like smoke through our fingers. Creative ways of doing military research may also help us to meaningfully think through our own proximity to military violence and power. Basham *et al.* (2015, 1) argue that "the methodological plurality of critical military studies and its engagement with the politics of positionality stands out markedly from more traditional social scientific approaches to the military and security and their often atheoretical, apolitical, and largely quantitative stances." We learn something new about military power when we examine it through our own relationship with and to it, and creative practice may offer a way of doing this (see for example Hannah West's analysis of her "becoming" a critical military researcher through creative practice in chapter 11).

It is important to anchor this manifesto for creative methods not only to our conceptual concerns in critical military studies, but also more broadly to the practical challenges that arise when doing research on military phenomena. Despite the progress made in recent years towards gaining a fuller, more nuanced accounting of how militaries and military power work, there remain persistent sticking points that keep us held back at a distance. Militaries represent institutions that are opaque, secretive, and difficult to access—meaning that certain kinds of information are hard or impossible to come by, and access to military communities can be subject to strict gatekeeping and monitoring. "[M]ore than other organizations" Soeters *et al.* (2014, 3) argue, "the military is a world on its own, an island within society-at-large on which its inhabitants work and live together. Getting access, particularly if one is not a regular inhabitant of that island, usually is no easy game to play. On the other hand, if one is a regular inhabitant, it may not be easy to do research either, because the organization wants some control over the diffusion of information about itself." There are also many aspects of the practices and functioning of global militaries that cannot be understood or fully accounted for simply through objective analysis. Consider, for example, how it is that militarism in the UK operates in and through diverse spaces, objects, and bodies, such as in the stadium of the Invictus Games or the audience of the UK's bestselling Military Wives Choir; it is as much a question of affect, emotion, and feeling, as it is of empirically observable interactions between people, places, and institutions. What results is that there are many military phenomena which we cannot hope to fully understand through conventional research methods.

Not only is the "doing" of military research itself difficult but communicating this work effectively to wider audiences is at best a challenge, and at worst closely scrutinised or even prohibited (Soeters *et al.* 2014). The challenge of speaking outwards about military research may be overcome by finding creative ways of shedding light on research questions and engaging audiences, and so, too, can it help to communicate concepts and ideas that must be felt before they are fully understood. In its ability to be collaborative and generative, creativity in research has great capacity for being participatory in nature, and directed by those people who the research is about. In an area of research where access to communities is often difficult, creative projects have the added benefit of being interesting and appealing to prospective participants.

Then there is the issue of impact. "Impact" has become one of those nebulous terms in academia used to describe the contribution of a particular body of research to society, culture, the environment, the economy, and indeed wider scholarship. As academics we often trade in impact as currency, in that effectively demonstrating the positive consequences of our research for beneficiaries and stakeholders is integral for gaining competitive research funding and advancing our careers. But for critical military researchers the question of how to achieve "impact" is a challenging one, because not only are militaries typically slow to effect social and cultural change, but there is also the ethical issue of whether it is right to effectively help a violent institution work more efficiently. As a result, we often find ourselves caught in a political (and practical) dilemma regarding what kind of change, if any, we want to affect, and whether we can truthfully say that it is possible. Creative ways of communicating research findings can help to achieve that often sought after but difficult to achieve goal of helping to shape public debate and change societal understanding.

## ABOUT THE BOOK

In this edited volume, we are animated by a concern with a few key questions; how might a turn to creativity in military studies help us to get closer to that which we critique? What can the creative arts and creative practice more broadly help to reveal, that we might struggle to approach otherwise? And how might we engage this creativity in our own research methodologies and practice? The volume explores path-breaking new research at the intersection of military studies and creative practice. It draws on a range of disciplinary approaches from political geography, international relations, sociology, and the creative arts to explore how creativity and creative methods can refresh our understanding of military power and militarised cultures. It asks, Who "does" creative research on and with militaries? What are the sites of creative inquiry in this area? What methods can we use? And what can creative practice bring to our understanding of militarised cultures that other methods cannot?

Each chapter of this volume defines creativity and creative practice differently, and draws on a unique case study ranging from theatre to dance to paper making in order to do this. However, a running theme throughout is an exploration of the critical space that being "creative" can open up in military research. Through a variety of case study creative methods and projects, we explore how these new creative possibilities provide the opportunity for new forms of critique in military research. As such, this volume does not represent a "how-to" guide for *doing* creativity and creative methods in military research. Rather, it provides researchers with the tools to trouble and think anew about taken for granted concepts such as militarisation, the sites of military power, and the civilian/military binary. In this way, the collection offers an important intervention in the study of global politics, militaries, war, and security.

Part I of the volume poses the questions; what are the objects and sites of creativity? Who "does" creative practice in military research? And how do military power and creativity intersect? The contributing authors in this section all approach "creativity" in different ways; but in doing so shed light on the complex relationships that can exist between creative practice and military phenomena. In the opening chapter, authors Rachel Woodward, Chloë Barker, K. Neil Jenkings, and Michael Mulvihill consider the value of creative research practice for bringing into recognition the myriad embodied and material encounters and relationships that constitute nuclear deterrence and space monitoring. Through an examination of their research practice at RAF Fylingdales, the authors explore creativity not as a means of producing new representational forms, but rather as the means of differently investigating and thinking anew about military phenomena. In chapter 2, Sara Matthews uses the example of a recent exhibition *The Cultural Life of Drones* to consider first how visual culture is *already martial*, but second how aesthetic engagements can nevertheless help us to differently encounter the critical politics of militarization. Next, Charlotte Veal offers an important intervention by reflecting on how militaries themselves mobilise creativity and the arts in the practice of war. By examining the British military's solicitation of dance-led methods, Veal calls for caution over the labours deployed when practicing creative methods for military research. In the final chapter of this section, Michael Mulvihill turns our attention to more-than-human creative forces and argues that creative practice can shed light on the role that such forces play in nuclear and military complexes.

Part II turns to the specific question of method, using four diverse examples of creative practice at work in military research. In chapter 5, Laura Mills discusses her research encounter with *Combat Paper*, a US veteran art project transforming military uniforms into handmade paper. Next, James Robinson reflects on model-making as a means of enlivening archival research on civil camouflage. In chapter 7, Alice Cree and Hannah West explore the critical feminist ethics of participatory research in the example of their online theatre-as-method project with military spouses. Finally, in chapter 8, Susanna

Hast walks us through the practice of spoken word as creative method, drawing on her work examining the emotional effects of synchronised movement among Finnish cadets. This section of the book offers a selection of creative methodological case studies for thinking through some of the questions and challenges we encounter as researchers in military studies.

In Part III, we move to the issue of positionality. The four chapters that constitute the last part of the volume consider, in different ways, how can creativity and creative practice help us think differently about our own positions as researchers? How might it allow us to rethink what constitutes "insider" status in military research, and how could it help military communities to "speak outwards"? In chapter 9, Alex Smith reflects on how he uses creative non-fiction writing to better understand the impact of the Second World War on his grandfather and his life and family post-service. In this deeply personal account, Smith considers how his project "Last Op" made him confront head-on his own personal entanglements with the themes of war, trauma and memory. Next we turn to Rebecca Steel's work on a fictional storytelling project with service families, which used arts-based research methods to help participants "speak outwards" about their lives and experiences. In discussing this project, Steel poses the further question of who has the right to speak in military research. In chapter 11, Hannah West leads us through another very personal exploration of how creativity and creative methods opened up a much-needed space for her to reflect on her own experience within the military, and subsequently helped her to find her critical voice. In the final chapter of the book, David Jackson discusses his experience contributing to the documentary play *Minefield*, as both a veteran of the Falklands/Malvinas war and a researcher in critical military studies. Jackson's work provides an important intervention, in that it asks us to think in more plural terms about the "skins" we wear when we approach critical research, arguing that the ultimate value of creative methods lies in their ability to harness the complex, textured, often contradictory natures of our positionalities as researchers, human beings, and artists.

In this volume, several chapters discuss a specific creative method for doing research, such as spoken word (chapter 8) or model-making (chapter 6). However, others help us to complicate our understanding of creativity in military research, either by showing how particular creative projects can shed new light on military related phenomena, or by exploring how militaries themselves actively engage in creativity to further their own goals (see Charlotte Veal's work in chapter 3). There are a number of commonalities across the chapters, for example many of the contributions are reflexive and concerned in some way with positionality, asking difficult questions about our proximity to militaries, militarism, and military power. In a similar vein, relationships emerged as a common theme; relationships between academics and practitioners, between academic-practitioners and audiences, with militaries and with different types of audiences, which can be civilian, or military, or both. In other ways though, the constituent chapters of this collection do not marry comfortably together, and new questions emerge at the intersections between them; what constitutes creativity and creative practice in military research? What do we consider to be our "data" in these creative works, and how do we analyse them? Who gets to speak, and for what purpose?

Finally, it is important to draw attention to the limited scope of the book, and the voices and experiences that it does not account for. The contributors to this collection are working within European and North American contexts, which in turn shapes how their chapters approach questions of military power, violence, and experience. Issues of power and positionality for researchers from different academic backgrounds and traditions, and working in different military and state contexts beyond that those of Europe and North America, will give rise to other foci and ways of working. These may in turn engender very different kinds of conversations on creative methods in military research. It is for these reasons that *Creative Methods in Military Studies* is not framed in terms of an "agenda," and instead represents the start of a conversation; one which, it is hoped, can be subject to constant re-examining, reframing, and reimagining in the future.

# PART I

1

# Turning RAF Fylingdales Inside Out

## *Using Creative Practice to Understand Ballistic Missile Early Warning and Space Monitoring*

*Rachel Woodward, Chloë Barker, K. Neil Jenkings, and Michael Mulvihill*

RAF Fylingdales is a ballistic missile early-warning and space-monitoring station located on the North York Moors in northern England. The station is part of the US-UK nuclear deterrent and watches space for warning signs of nuclear missile attack. RAF Fylingdales also tracks around 1,700 operational satellites and 43,000 pieces of space debris. Yet even in expert circles, the multiple roles of RAF Fylingdales are not well understood, and in the absence of wider public understanding, fictions and fantasies about the station dominate. This chapter introduces a research project at RAF Fylingdales that centres creative research practice from a range of disciplinary perspectives as a means of unlocking the histories and present of ballistic missile warning and space monitoring. Overall, we conceive of RAF Fylingdales through theories of assemblage, which prioritize materialities, processes, and more-than-human creativities in order to understand social phenomena. The chapter describes how arts engagement and curation, creative arts practice, ethnomethodologically informed ethnographic sociology, and human geography each draw on ideas of creativity in different ways to explore how nuclear deterrence and space monitoring are constituted by a myriad of embodied and material encounters and relationships at the assemblages present at RAF Fylingdales.

In this chapter, we consider how creative research practice and creativity in research methods enables understanding and analysis of two military or military-related practices—ballistic missile early warning systems (BMEWS) and space monitoring—which take place at RAF Fylingdales. Ballistic missile early warning, as the name suggests, is the set of practices by which the military forces of nation-states monitor space to warn of the imminent arrival of nuclear-armed ballistic missiles. This is a practice that is resolutely military in origin and purpose, commencing in the late 1950s in response to the nuclear threats of the Cold War. Space monitoring is a set of practices that have evolved in tandem with ballistic missile early warning, and involves watching satellites in a range of orbits in space for the purposes of national intelligence and defence, and to ensure continued operation of civilian terrestrial services and networks reliant on satellites. As well as military observation, space monitoring is key to deconflicting satellites' orbital patterns to avoid collisions. Both ballistic missile early warning and space monitoring originate with the launch of the Soviet Union's Sputnik satellite into space in 1957, which placed two objects into orbit—the satellite itself, and the final stage of the launch rocket. Space monitoring is both military and non-military as a practice; although undertaken by global space surveillance networks for military purposes, it is also a practice with civilian infrastructural, academic, and amateur practitioners.[1] As we go on to discuss, our approach to both ballistic missile early warning and space monitoring is to see these as assemblages of practices and materialities, such that exploring the organisation and operations that make these practices possible cannot be divorced from an understanding of the materials through which these practices come into being. Our understanding of creativity is of novel material and social transformations that occur as a result of actions and activities within assemblages. These do not necessarily need a human agent such as an artist, but rather they can result from technical innovation, embodied encounters, or more-than-human events occurring in the environment. It is the making visible of these ongoing material processes of change, processes that would otherwise remain intangible, that is important to our approach.

This chapter considers how ballistic missile early warning and space monitoring at RAF Fylingdales can be rendered visible through creative practices using different research and disciplinary approaches. In this chapter, we introduce RAF Fylingdales, our rationales for close scrutiny of this site, and our use of assemblage theory to inform creative research approaches. We then discuss the four different research foci around which our research revolves and through which creative approaches have been applied. These are: explorations of the Fylingdales Archive, creative practice using sound, creativity's use in ethnomethodological analysis, and walking as a creative research practice. We conclude with brief suggestions about the broader application of creative methods in military research.

## RAF FYLINGDALES

RAF Fylingdales is a secure military installation of around eight hundred hectares located on the North York Moors in northern England. Dominating the upland landscape from certain angles and visible in the distance from roads across the peaty heather- and grass-clad moors is the Solid State Phased Array Radar (SSPAR) building, commonly compared to a truncated pyramid. Here, Fylingdales' two core functions of ballistic missile early warning and space monitoring take place, enabled by a range of organisational, managerial, and practical activities located across the site, and beyond. Over one hundred RAF personnel and civilian contractors work here. Grouped around the SSPAR are some modest low-rise administrative, accommodation, mess, and security buildings, a large power station that supplies the radar that emits a perpetual machine hum, the canine patrol kennels (the sound of barking competes with the generator hum), and a large low structure that looks a bit like a warehouse and was built originally as a store and supply unit (Building 319). Here sits the Fylingdales Archive.

The Fylingdales Archive comprises a collection of thousands of photographs, documents, objects, and machines.[2] These date back to the original development and construction of the site in 1960, its first iteration with its three iconic "golf ball" radomes that housed three radars (removed in 1994), and the subsequent and current SSPAR "pyramid" building, which became operational in 1992. Michael Mulvihill worked in the archive from 2015 as its first artist in residence,[3] whilst also completing his PhD in creative arts practice (Mulvihill 2019). Michael's accounts of the archive's contents and stories piqued the interest of research team members Chloë Barker, K. Neil Jenkings, and Rachel Woodward. The combined team's expertise across creative arts research practice, arts curation and public engagement, military sociological and workplace interactions, and the geographies of military power and landscape, led to the award of funding for a project with the explicit intention of *turning Fylingdales inside out* to make the practices of ballistic missile early warning and space monitoring visible.[4] The idea of turning the base inside out stems from the ideas and suppositions that surround it. The base itself is highly visible as a prominent feature on the North York Moors, and its function over the past half century, tracking everything in low earth orbit, is very explicit and a matter of public record. Yet there is an invisibility that surrounds it too: there is no mention of RAF Fylingdales and the significance of its function in the 2021 UK integrated review of security, defence, development, and foreign policy, and it is barely and rarely mentioned in current UK space policy consultations. RAF Fylingdales is also often misunderstood, as a silo for nuclear missiles as part of a ballistic missile defence system, for example, or as a hangar for alien technologies. In turning the base "inside out," our aim is to explore and render visible its functions as a node in a particular form of infrastructure and thus accountable to civilian scrutiny. As we go on to discuss in this chapter, the research has been shaped by an argument that creativity in research practice can provide new and original approaches to socio-material phenomena, and our research does this by exploring the materialities and practices of the base. Using the resources of the archive and engagements with personnel working on site, the project (in progress as we write) is about opening up to scrutiny the history and present of the assemblages that constitute the site's core practices. At the heart of the project is the aim to demystify and make transparent Fylingdales' functions, as part of a wider objective of generating informed debate about those functions. Ballistic missile early warning and space monitoring affect us all, and there is a moral imperative underpinning this research about widening the public conversation about these activities and this site, not least because of its ongoing significance with the standing up of UK Space Command in April 2021.

But there are also more specific logics to our scrutiny, which in turn speak to the value of creative research practice in military research contexts. The first of these concerns is its contribution to critical geopolitics. RAF Fylingdales is a small site, but it is unique to the western part of the northern hemisphere; the only other two sites with similar function in the northern hemisphere are Thule Air Base in northern Greenland, and Clear Air Force station in Alaska. Together, Fylingdales, Thule, and Clear monitor the northern hemisphere for incoming intercontinental ballistic missiles (understood as most probably originating from Russia, or the Soviet Union in the past) with communication feeds to the North American Aerospace Defense Command (NORAD) located at Petersen Airforce Base in Colorado Springs, Colorado, USA. An old telephone handset stored in the Fylingdales archive speaks materially to this international connectivity developed in response to the threat of nuclear war, with the NORAD telephone number handwritten on a scrap of paper and taped to the telephone console. Here, then, is a place where the materialities and practices of geopolitics as the small, iterative actions of individual actors within much larger global power systems were—and are still—played out. As many commentators have observed before us, geopolitics cannot be understood as the sole preserve of political elites and their public statements, but rather needs to be studied with reference to the embodied, material, affective, and lived practices and experiences of its assemblages (for an overview, see Sharp 2020). Similarly, Fylingdales' role as a node in global space-monitoring networks reminds us of the functions of the satellites in orbit ranging from military surveillance, to the facilitating of global information and communications flows, to the global navigation satellite systems that facilitate the GPS functions used daily in the mobile phones of so many of us. Display boards in many of RAF Fylingdales' buildings, showing reproductions of very high-resolution satellite imagery for environmental monitoring, speak to the observant practices underpinning geopolitical imaginaries, which, in turn, shape state responses to the very things those images of environmental change depict. Understanding global power relations concerning and within space itself requires an understanding of the connections between these systems and their scales of operation exemplified by Fylingdales' functions. Our contention in this chapter is that creative practices in research are essential for teasing out these connections.

Second, RAF Fylingdales is an illuminating site to study because it exemplifies the limits of binary modes of thinking about military phenomena, which identify "civilian" and "military" as distinct (and potentially oppositional) categories. This is evident, for example, when we consider space monitoring, through which materialities, organisation, and practice are both simultaneously military and civilian in origin, maintenance, use, and intent through the investment of time, materials, and labour from military forces of nation-states, private corporations contracted to provide services to military forces, and purely commercial enterprises. Indeed, the history of subcontracted military functions, now ubiquitous and transformative of most advanced capitalist economies' military forces (see Berndtsson and Kinsey 2016 for an overview) was evident from the very start at RAF Fylingdales.[5] The subcontracting to Radio Corporation of America (RCA, the company from which the multinational government services subcontractor SERCO originates) of the task of building the first radars at the base illustrates this. Separating out "military" and "civilian" components, whilst ostensibly possible, does little to inform a clearer understanding of the dense webs of connections through which state and international military objectives, commercial imperatives, infrastructural support for social life, environmental monitoring and cultures of leisure of swathes of the global population are connected because of their reliance on space monitoring. The creative practice approach informing much of our work on the Fylingdales assemblage (see p. 8) is explicitly orientated to the connectivities between functions, materialities, processes, and embodied practices, rather than the social codes that construct boundaries between categories such as "military" and "civilian" (see, for example, Mulvihill 2021).

Third, our explorations of RAF Fylingdales bring to debates on creative practice in military contexts an example of the complexities associated with close engagement by academics and practitioners with military forces. As we argue elsewhere (Woodward *et al.* 2020), the idea that critical military studies can be pursued without conversation with military practitioners is limiting and short sighted and the idea that academic "purity" of purpose is somehow tainted by association with military institutions is, in our view, misguided. This is not to say that military engagements with academics are straightforward, but rather to assert the necessity of at least making the effort as critical friends (Wright *et al.* 2019). In turn, as our RAF Fylingdales experience shows, military institutional efforts to engage with wider publics, including academics and arts practitioners, can be a deliberate strategy. At RAF Fylingdales, an acute awareness of the need for greater public knowledge and understanding of the site prompted its first forays into public engagement (and we discuss this below). In the absence of wider public understanding, as we have noted, fictions and fantasies about the site had emerged—that it hosts nuclear weapons for example, or that it has privileged insight into extraterrestrial life-forms, or is involved in electronic communications monitoring. RAF Fylingdales instigated Project VIGILAMUS with the intention of addressing this lacuna and expanding public engagement with this highly securitized space and its functions. This engagement objective has facilitated their being open to our research and allowing our access and deployment of creative methods on this highly secure site.

## THINKING THROUGH THE ASSEMBLAGE

Our work at RAF Fylingdales is predicated on an observation that existing modes of conceptualising military installations through established strategic, international, or historical studies paradigms are increasingly inadequate for generating understanding about their functions, effects, and affects. These established approaches focus on how installations and networks operate through the abstract rules and procedures of international systems and relationships. The assemblage perspective that we take on RAF Fylingdales, following Deleuze and Guattari (2000, 2013) suggests that we look past the representational modes through which rules and procedures are established, and instead give ontological priority to lived experiences and material interactions between human, non-human, organic, and inorganic beings. These interactions constitute the practices through which social realities are produced. Rather than focusing on elite debates and the strategic politics of statecraft to understand ballistic missile early warning and space monitoring, we argue that informed understanding can be generated instead by foregrounding the geographically situated cultural, material, social, and embodied interactions and practices that materialise RAF Fylingdales through social and socio-technical interacting assemblages. These practices and interactions take place continually between the station's workforce, the technologies that facilitate the station's capabilities, the materialities of the site, and its infrastructure, including the invisible energy beam that extends three thousand miles into space, the national and international military strategies that require and constitute the station's capabilities, and the landscape and communities within which the station is situated.

Our focus on these myriad interactions and practices that constitute RAF Fylingdales as a complex, interacting, socio-cultural entity has, in turn, prompted our use of creative research practice and creativity in research methodologies to explore the assemblages of ballistic missile early warning and space monitoring. This research is framed explicitly around the argument that creative practices, including but not limited to the production of art works, can provide insights into how the materialities and practices of the social world are assembled and interact. Creativity can be an analytic tool for apprehending the invisible, because of the focus of attention onto the practices of doing rather than theoretical abstraction (DeLanda 2016) and guides analytic attention to transformation and emergence, and the "concrete yet complex materiality of bodies immersed in social relations of power" rather than the obscuring stasis (or even repressive regimes) of representational approaches (Braidotti 2012, 21). Furthermore, assemblages are multi-scaled; in this research, we can consider assemblages ranging in scale from the sub-atomic (such as the photons in the radar beam emanating from the SSPAR) through to the scale of the galactic as the domain into which the radar beam is projected, and from the daily workplace interactions in any of the office buildings on site through to the larger assemblages of Fylingdales itself, and that composed with its two sister sites in Greenland and Alaska. RAF Fylingdales, then, is approached as an array of material assemblages of unique emergent practices, materialities, and socio-technical interactions that give these assemblages their various localised experientiality and temporal meanings, both in the moment and over time.

In the remainder of this chapter, we give a taste of the ways in which creative practices have informed our exploration of the assemblages at RAF Fylingdales and the Fylingdales Archive. We consider in turn the curation of the Fylingdales Archive and plans for public engagement, the generation of insights into the relationships between radar and electronic music technologies through creative arts approaches to the radar technologies at Fylingdales, the development of techniques for understanding workplace practices in places where researcher access is limited, and the utility of walking as a way of conjuring up the complex of geographical connections between an idiosyncratic building on the North York Moors and the rest of the globe. Creativity as method and practice is evident across all four aspects of the research, but with different meanings and purposes.

## CREATIVE METHODS AND CREATIVITY IN PRACTICE AT RAF FYLINGDALES

### Creativity in the Archive

As Stuart Hall observed, "No archive arises out of thin air. Each archive has a 'pre-history,' in the sense of prior conditions of existence" (2001, 89). The Fylingdales Archive originates in the prior conditions of its inception and development, through which this unique and technologically futuristic site came into being via the prosaic day-to-day practical and administrative activities of first building, then running, a system to warn of nuclear attack. The archive's pre-history lies with the steady collection and organisation of over one thousand objects and documents relating to the development and operations of the site. One of our tasks has been to use practices which are open to these prior conditions of existence and the creativities prompted by assemblage thinking. These practices can be challenging, because they both literally and materially co-produce new and actual social assemblages from matter, rather than inscribing meaning or re-codifying the world from a singular, colonizing point of view resting on claims of objectivity. In the Fylingdales Archive, this is achieved with an attentiveness to the multiple voices and lived experiences traced in the materialities of the archive. Our aim has also been to avoid capture of the archive by practices of rarefied taxonomic objectification and re-inscription, and by notions of technological heritage or military exceptionalism. In turn, this allows more complex and nuanced stories to emerge, including stories that enable us to question, for example, the negotiated and constructed boundaries between military and civilian, the public and the private.

The creativities of the archive can be witnessed very clearly in its photographic collection. As well as comprising a collection of thousands of photographs of the site's construction and evolution, the photographic collection also depicts members of staff in the exhibitions and displays they curated on the site, including the first museum at the base. These early exhibitions (1992–1994) took place inside the decommissioned BMEWS II building (one of the golf balls) when the radar was upgraded in 1992 to Solid State Phased Array Radar (SSPAR). The BMEWS radar was to be demolished, but during this period of decommissioning and preparing the site for demolition, the staff on site began using the buildings for parties, held in the Missile Impact Predictor room, which housed the IBM 7050 computer used to track incoming missiles. In Figure 1.1, Wing Commander Mike Speed (left) and Flight Lieutenant Paddy O'Hanlon stand in front of the rope barrier and interpretation panel of the BMEWS II radar exhibition. These creative practices by station staff in developing the exhibition give the objects, in this case a large antenna radar and geodesic dome, very different meanings.

The exhibition in the radar building shown in Figure 1.1 can be seen as a specific assemblage, articulating the materials and their multiple relationships. For example, it makes visible the vastly diverse connections between the architectural practices of Buckminster Fuller, who designed the radomes, and the radar hardware designed and built by Radio Corporation of America in Moorestown, New Jersey, USA (known today for its record label division RCA records and the public service company SERCO). The combination of these two objects together exemplifies the cultural assemblages inherent in the site and how these complex connections highlight the specificity of the design and technological developments of the 1960s.

These emergent technologies of radome and radar are no longer visibly present on the site but exist in Fylingdales Archive's collection of RCA *SCAN* magazines (1960–1976). *SCAN* documents the lives, history, and technological development of the company and the many staff who developed and worked on its programmes, including radar, record distribution, television, video, sonar systems, satellites, broadcast equipment, and sound systems for cinemas. The magazines also tell us about the visual culture of the organisation at that time. One of the images from 1960 shows the interior of the RCA Missile and Surface Radar Division headquarters at Moorestown, New Jersey. Two employees read a newspaper, and in the centre of the image is a black and white table, designed by Lewis Butler for the Knoll International design firm as part of the Planning Unit, a design consultancy devoted to office interiors. These connections further illustrate to us RCA's involvement in wider activities of design and development, present in the spaces in which people in the company worked.

Back at RAF Fylingdales, after 1994 and the demolition of the old BMEWS site, the collection of archive materials was housed in the US Army Airforce Exchange Services (AFEX) building 338 and repurposed. Figure 1.2 shows how the paper archive was contextualised within wall-mounted exhibitions of images from the old BMEWS site alongside some of the old site's computer hardware used in missile detection.

The archive continued to be housed at RAF Fylingdales until 1996, when the collection began to be accessioned to the RAF Radar Museum at Neatishead, Norfolk. From 2003 until 2006, the whole RAF Fylingdales Archive was kept in storage there and never exhibited to the public. Then in 2013, the then station commander at RAF Fylingdales, Wing Commander Rayna Owens, made the decision to bring the archive back to RAF Fylingdales and wrote into the base orders the continued location and preservation of the archive in its current home, room 319 in the store and supply building at RAF Fylingdales.

From February 2020, work started on the digitising of the Fylingdales Archive, to make its materialities and histories fully available to the public as a digital archive for research. The processes of sorting and cataloguing the archive during 2020 revealed the already existing outcomes of creative practice in organisation of the materials of the archive in its previous homes and iterations. In turn, the process of collecting together the photographs into date order, of collating a large collection of photo albums with annotations, and of organising the collection of trade magazines such as RCA's *SCAN* magazine and RAF Fylingdales' base magazine, *Triball*, have enabled us to develop a much greater understanding of the technological, military, and cultural assemblages and their cultural legacy today.

Using Rosi Braidotti (2012) to think through the Fylingdales Archive has prompted engagement with the people it depicts and who have left traces of their presence there. Braidotti's argument for creativity in neo-materialist methodology stresses a focus on the materialities of bodies situated within social relations of power. For us, this has meant making space to look for histories and personal stories, particularly those that are not currently visible. For example, although UK military institutions have been traditionally white and male-dominated, a more diverse workforce emergences when we examine the RCA engineers working on the development of the radar, and across the assemblage constituted by the partnership between the US Air Force, the UK's RAF and RCA, through which the site and its functions came into being. Stuart Hall prompts us to consider whose heritage is present in archival collections, and what these presences and silences say about the visibility or otherwise of histories of postwar, reconstructed, and multi-cultural Britain (Hall, 2001). Through this theoretical framework these histories have begun to make themselves present. We see Hal Walker, an engineer of African American heritage employed by RCA whose work was instrumental in BMEWS operations at Clear in Alaska; Hannah Duncan, who at the age of twenty-six, when working at RCA developed the Satellite Information Programme for RAF Fylingdales' Ballistic Missile Early Warning System; and Jane Yates, who at the age of twenty-five in 1983 became the first woman Space Operations Officer at RAF Fylingdales. We see Wing Commander Nicky Loveday, the first commanding officer to initiate practices to open RAF Fylingdales to the public, and Wing Commander Rayna Owens who as commanding officer wrote into RAF Fylingdales' mission the intention to keep the Fylingdales Archive on base and who opened a dedicated visitor centre on site.

The creativities deployed at Fylingdales, with their focus on complex materialities, are ultimately about making entities and relationships visible. In addition to the documents and photographs in the Fylingdales Archive, it hosts a number of material objects central to its ballistic missile early warning functions. The next section discusses how creative arts practice has been used as a method to make visible this complex materiality. Sound and music

**Figure 1.1 RAF Fylingdales, interior of Ballistic Missile Early Warning Tracker Site I (building 302) with radar antenna, museum display c.1992.**

*Source:* Reprinted with permission from Fylingdales Archive.

composition have made concrete and embodied the more-than-human noumena of BMEWS and electronic warfare operations over Fylingdales Moor.[6]

## Creative Practice as Method

Beyond the human-designed codes of representation that guide anthropocentric perception, we are interested in this research in how more-than-human creative forces reconfigure new and different social assemblages, even in the hyper-mediated spaces of Cold War geopolitics and military electronic sensing. In this section we explain how sound has been used in creative practice explorations of electronic warfare operations at RAF Fylingdales.

For philosopher Christoph Cox, sound is immersive and embodied. Cox explains that unlike the spatial juxtaposition of text and image, sound involves constantly changing temporal fluxes in which elements interpenetrate one another (Cox 2018, 148). These are intensive forces that generate constantly emerging assemblages, which self-organise and are independent of human creative "genius." For electronic music composer Edgard Varèse (1883–1965) these intensive forces are composed of the more-than-human material flow of electrons running through filters and modulators of electronic instruments. Deleuze and Guattari incorporate the modulations of electronic music synthesis into their ontology, observing that "a synthesizer places [. . .] all parameters in continuous variation [. . .] making [. . .] heterogeneous elements end up turning into each other in some way" (Deleuze and Guattari 2013, 111). Engineers at RCA designed the world's first music synthesiser in 1957. Indications that disparate parts of this company's activities turned into each other are evident in the fact that several components of the RCA Victor II music synthesizer were built to USAF specifications, and several of the controls from this instrument appeared to have been reused on the AN/FLR-4 Interference Analyser, used in the original ballistic missile early warning station and now held in the Fylingdales Archive (see the equipment on the right-hand side, Figure 1.2). This equipment had been used to detect attempts to jam the radar at Fylingdales (Mulvihill 2019) and offered clues to the way sound could be used to materially actualize electronic warfare engagements over the North York Moors.

Before RAF Fylingdales became operational on 17th September 1963, North American Aerospace Defense Command (NORAD) began expressing concerns that the BMEWS radar could be blinded by Soviet electronic warfare operations taking place in the Arctic circle and the North Sea.[7] Electronic warfare operations and tactics impede an opponent's ability to utilise the electromagnetic spectrum where radar and communication systems operate. RCA Missile and Surface Radar engineer Hal Walker in an oral history recounts his experience of Soviet Union heavy bombers equipped with radar equipment attempting to disrupt the BMEWS radar beams at Clear, Alaska.

**Figure 1.2 Fylingdales Archive, AFEX building, main collection area c.1992-1994.**
*Source:* Reprinted with permission from Fylingdales Archive.

> They had aircraft flying trying to jam us. They had these T90, 192 bombers carrying heavy radar systems, flying as close as they could to turn those beams on and see if they could jam us. We were continuously getting word from the Distant Early Warning (DEW) system that they were coming [. . .] we would then switch frequency to start to use counter measures [. . .] We kept rotating our frequencies, yes yes. Every day was a challenge because we were part of a dynamic defence system that was under threat.[8]

RAF Fylingdales, still under construction, was part of this dynamic defence system. NORAD feared Soviet Trawlers operating in the North Sea could also be equipped to jam the radars at Fylingdales. NORAD's concern was that military engagement with naval or air forces could lead to nuclear conflict in the North Sea. In 1962 NORAD commissioned RCA to design and build Electronic Countercounter Measures (ECCM) for BMEWS.[9] Two years later, in 1964, ECCM facilities were installed at RAF Fylingdales. These facilities consisted of a tower topped by a 3.6 metre dish antenna enclosed in a radome, locally known as the lollypop. The dish rotated four times per minute and was operated from the AN/FLR-4 control console (Figure 1.2) in the Missile Alert Room. A real-time graphic display on a cathode ray tube monitor represented the frequency and bearing of a possible electromagnetic threat. The AN/FLR-4 filtered known electro-magnetic emissions, such as television transmissions from the nearby Bilsdale television antenna. But unidentified electro-magnetic interference triggered an environment alarm to alert the operator of electronic attack on RAF Fylingdales, signalling evasive action by switching radar frequency.[10] RCA Missile and Surface Radar electrical engineer Ed Nossen in an oral history for *The RCA Heritage Program* described how he developed an ECCM system for BMEWS from an off-the-shelf spectrum analyser built by the Polarad Electronics Corporation of Long Island, New York.[11] The Polarad spectrum analyser set was used by engineers for a variety of applications including sound engineering. A contemporary equivalent of the Polarad analyser is the equalisation (EQ) analyser functions on Digital Audio Workstations (DAW) such as Apple's Garageband. Like the Polarad and AN/FLR-4, it is used to investigate frequency profiles on sound recordings, so offered a way of actualizing electronic warfare operations over Fylingdales Moor by indexing the practices of the AN/FLR-4 operators.

To do this, Michael Mulvihill formed a band with music producer Chris Tate, called One Key Magic. Over the spring and summer of 2020, they worked collaboratively using DAWs and file sharing applications to build a collection of music emerging from electronic warfare operations. The starting point was a series of soundscapes constructed from an imaginary point of view near Fylingdales on the North York Moors. The soundscapes began as a single pulse-wave drone digitally built in a DAW, based on the beam frequency of Fylingdales' radars. To make these sounds audible, the ultra-high frequencies (425–440 Mhz) of the radars needed to be transposed down through twenty-four octaves into the audio frequencies bands (425–440 hz) of the electromagnetic spectrum. Modulation was added to the sound that simulated various environmental effects on the radar such as the panning of the AN/FPS-49 radars inside the "golf ball" radomes, scatter produced by the sea, clouds and weather, aurora and electrical interference from the sun, and noise produced by electronic warfare attacks. They then improvised melodic compositions using electric guitar and synthesizers over the soundscapes. This presented a challenge. The soundscapes were tuned to frequencies of the radar beam and not exactly to the frequency of standard musical tuning (440 hz). In the end, the musical key and relevant melodic scales were determined by the intersections in harmonic frequencies between the beam and standard musical tuning.

Other more-than-human influences shaped the compositions by the use of an electronic bow (EBow) to play the guitar. The EBow utilises electromagnetic fields to vibrate the guitar strings without the need for direct human contact, resulting in perpetually changing textures and emergent forms. The result is an immersive sound and music composition assembled from processes of human and more-than-human creative forces. They actualize what Rosi Braidotti calls the "sounds of the molecular and quasi-inaudible" (Braidotti 2011, 105), in this case the environmental interactions and frequencies of electronic warfare operations over the North Sea. This approach is not a representation modality because, as Braidotti observes, sound is less codified by powerful structures such as the performative operations that project definitions of military identity. Using sound to make audible ECCM operation has provided a way to listen through monolithic representations of military phenomena, in order to make audible the fact that military operations are dependent upon a variety of non-military actors such as the RCA engineers and the multiplicities of the technologies they produced. What is also revealed is how military operations are affected by the more-than-human environments that assemble new kinds of hybrid spaces.[12] Notions of military should not be rarefied into an object but understood as a "multiplicity of frequencies that structure possible worlds," folded with lived materiality and the physicality of the universe (Braidotti 2011, 109).

## CREATIVITY AND ETHNOMETHODOLOGICAL DESCRIPTIONS

The RAF Fylingdales site is dominated physically by its huge futuristic SSPAR building. It first appears as an almost alien presence on the seemingly barren high North York Moors. Little in the way of human activity on the site is visible to the passer-by on the main road, other than the security gate with its armed guards. This dehumanised and sterile looking (if iconic) perspective is of course deceptive. RAF Fylingdales is a working military base peopled by military and civilian personnel going about their daily work. That work, the skill sets that members have and the practices they engage in are hugely varied even if the same technologies are being used, whether analysing radar-generated digital representations of space on computer screens or maintaining the gas turbine power station that powers the radar. These practices, materialities, and technologies produce the interlinked and overlapping assemblages that constitute the larger assemblage of RAF Fylingdales as a whole, which in practice reaches out beyond the perimeter.

These assemblages are varied not just in the materiality of their structures, but in both form and function. Even the pure dominating form of the giant pyramidic SSPAR and its operations buildings are a complex of socio-technical sites of multiple activities and technologies. These resulting assemblages are contained within not just the physical site, but also the operational and organisational practices of the RAF Fylingdales assemblage as a whole.

RAF Fylingdales, and its sister sites in Greenland and Alaska run by the USAF, constitute assemblages in their own right, but jointly also form parts of yet further assemblages, both military and civilian orientated. Each are material assemblages of unique emergent practices and socio-technical interactions giving the assemblages their various localised experiential and temporal meanings in the moment, and over time. The challenge faced by sociological investigation is to in some way capture these heterogeneous phenomena and describe and represent them in meaningful ways. In particular, we have been interested in the workplace practices carried out at the site. A description of the Fylingdales site, including the interior and its main buildings, can be found in Mulvihill (2019) based upon his experience on the site whilst artist in residence. This includes a description of the interior of the SSPAR in which the artist's exhibition was held and necessitated guided tours and site inspection to locate a suitable site, a process Mulvihill describes in detail considering not just the exhibition space but also those sites that were not chosen, and the rationale for this. The day-to-day activities of ballistic missile early warning and space monitoring require both individuals tasked with activities which directly constitute this function, and other equally necessary individuals and teams tasked with a plethora of support functions, from safety, to site maintenance, to catering.

Other assemblage sites with similar attributes, however, have been investigated by ethnographers; a significant example for us is Janet Vertesi's (2015) investigations of the collaborative production and interpretation of digital images of the surface of Mars by NASA scientists. In many ways, this is similar to the fundamental job of the Fylingdales assemblage, albeit undertaken by military rather than science personnel and in a different context: to interpret images of space objects and collaboratively decide on their meaning. Vertesi (2020) reports on further ethnomethodological and science and technology studies, comparing the space mission assemblages and activities of NASA's Mars and Jupiter missions. Whilst she does not frame these as assemblages they can be interpreted as such, with her analysis showing how the two mission assemblages, through their different technological environments and their members' practices, produce both different outcomes for "science" and experiences for their scientists. The means by which she does this is through the creative use of the artefacts produced by and constituting the assemblages she describes and represents. This research involved observation from within the assemblages and the ongoing production of artefacts of their work, their situated meaning-making in these socio-technical mission environments, supplemented with interviews about their "work" and its meaning, using where appropriate the artefacts of their work. These artefacts were themselves used by other overlapping assemblages of NASA's multiple operations and ended up in an archive maintained by NASA and accessed by others beyond that organisation. A relevant example of the creative use of such archive materials is given in a podcast series by ethnomethodologist Philip Brooker analysing NASA's Skylab 3 project archives.[13] Here he uses textual and audio-archive materials to create new descriptions and understandings of astronaut and mission controller collaborative practices thereby revealing the socio-technical production and maintenance of space station assemblages, and indeed NASA's space exploration programme, which were not available in formal accounts.

The creative practices of the assemblages are to be seen in the work of Vertesi and Brooker as forming both focus of investigation and the means by which the investigation proceeds. Ethnomethodological ethnographies can focus in depth on practices, and the details of specific activities such as workplace studies of aircraft control centres (Harper and Randall 1992) where—not unlike satellite monitoring—similar space monitoring activities are undertaken for both military and civil aviation purposes. They are situated in airports, which like RAF Fylingdales, are socio-technical assemblages of separate—and shared—material structures, with dense informational infrastructures integrated with and peopled by various task requirements.

In the research on RAF Fylingdales, our sociological aim is look at the multiple assemblages across the site to understand the larger one of RAF Fylingdales itself—not from the perspective of a formal reified account, but from those who constitute and produce it. This includes therefore not just the radar operations assemblage, but electricity generation, security, maintenance, catering and accommodation, administration and the collecting activities that constitute the archive itself. These are not understood as isolated assemblages, because they are dependent on each other both in terms of material technology and in terms of their shared personnel and interdependent work.

Flt Lt Richard Weeks, the officer responsible for the Fylingdales Archive and the creative practice it supports, for example, was once a permanent duty officer in the BMEWS operations and satellite monitoring control room. In turn, he became the archive's curator through an assemblage of processes including the re-acquisition of the collection from RAF Neatishead. Research participants thus both inform and transform our knowledge and understanding through their participation in the assemblages and the creative use and archiving of its artefacts. Through ethnomethodology, traditional ethnographic practice, the creative practice use of the archive materials and those creative practices enabled by the project itself, sites can be turned inside out through hybrid sociological representations and descriptions.

In this way, the focus of military research becomes not the explosive spectaculars of "shock and awe" and the extremes of military conflict, which designate the military as 'other' to everyday life. Rather, the military assemblage here is situated within, and wholly integrated into, the ongoing production of everyday life which includes the scripts of state security measures developed to secure specific forms of social organisation, the communications networks that facilitate this, and the many and various assemblages of everyday living that are facilitated by them. Thus, whilst visually within the landscapes of the North York Moors the SSPAR may appear as unusual, what is interesting to this research is its presence as an assemblage of materialities and socio-technical practices which function daily and routinely through the work of military and civilian employees, potentially normalised to the unique building, the SSPAR, that appears so differentiated from its surroundings. The archiving of the artefacts and the accounts of the creative practices of the base's members created as part of that assemblage's ongoing work requirements, as well as the methodologies of the research team, reveal it be to largely understandable within the frames of reference of the workplace, and the socio-technical interactions generic to many other workplaces. RAF Fylingdales is undoubtedly a specialised assemblage, yet it is also a set of assemblages of everyday military practice, past, present and future. The research task in turning Fylingdales inside out is to make the assemblage truly visible, and ethnomethodological engagement enables understanding of those practices.

## WALKING AS A CREATIVE RESEARCH PRACTICE

Creative methods, in part, are about the creation of new spaces for thinking differently about phenomena (Cree 2020). Although as we have discussed, human agency is not necessary for creative production, in this section, we want to consider the wholly human practice of walking as a creative practice generative of insights into landscapes.

Walking, that basic practice of human mobility involving the placement of one foot in front of the other, is a methodology of long-standing for geographers. Older ideas about the utility of observation in the field are increasingly complemented by more recent arguments about the utility of fieldwork observations derived from self-conscious and explicit awareness of the sensory, haptic, affective, and emotional feedback generated by walking across ground and through space (O'Neill and Roberts 2020). Critiques may question who walks, and where, and remind us that geographical knowledge is always produced from a specific positionality (Mason 2021). But walking can also be a creative practice generative of new insights through sensory engagements elicited by mobility through geographical space. This is not a novel observation, nor one unique to geographers; the notion of the "archive of the feet" consolidates historians' engagements with paper archives (Gange 2017).

Walking through and around RAF Fylingdales has been fundamental to conjuring up the spatiality of the ballistic missile early warning and space monitoring assemblages at the site. Travellers along the main Whitby to Pickering road outside the station gates, the A169, are most usually mobile in a vehicle. The site is seen, but because of the ground's contours only the SSPAR is fully visible, the truncated pyramid rising, almost unworldly, from the moor. The administration buildings, staff car parks, and internal roadways are hidden from view, the sounds of the generator and kennels inaudible, the humps and bumps of terrain smoothed over by the road's tarmac. For the passing motorist or the visitor to Fylingdales, B.C.F. Wilson's 1983 description of the site in his *History of Fylingdales* rings true: "The poorly drained peat and bare rocks of the upland support only heather and scrub; what few trees there are grow in the valleys" (1). The moor's height, weather, and incised valleys give the location a "wild, unspoilt beauty."

But to park the car, leave the road, and walk, actively diminishes this representation of unwanted, productive moorland with every step.[14] Public rights of way follow old established paths across the moor, associated with extractive industry of ironstone working from an extrusion sill. Bronze age barrows visible on higher ground surrounding the site indicate a ceremonial landscape of unknown meaning constructed by people leaving no written archive (Spratt 1982, Hudson 2020). An eighteenth-century boundary marker on the site's remoter eastern perimeter indicates the limits of a parcel of enclosed land, signifying changing forms of agriculture and the emergence of what would become global mercantile economies, founded on the assertions of ownership, the exclusions of others and the extinguishing of rights in common to agriculturally productive ground. The Lilla Cross, visible on the horizon, sits as a marker-point in a network of tracks across the high ground, connecting religious houses such as that at Whitby Abbey and initiated fifteen centuries ago. The cross itself, a vestigial stump, bears a plaque attesting to the efforts of the Royal Corps of Engineers in its repositioning on (we assume) an excursion from their usual base. Way-markers for the Lyke Wake Walk, a route completed as a feat of endurance from west to east across the moor, and the imprint of mountain bike tyres in the mud and sand of the tracks signify a leisure landscape to which people travel in order to travel. All these things are accessed only by walking the ground outside the perimeter fence, and all point to other assemblages, their spatialities, and their temporalities.

Thinking of walking as a creative practice, rather than solely as a mechanism for mobility through space, reinforces something significant for military research in that walking is generative of a way of understanding the category of "military." Understanding ground in terms of these simultaneous multiple assemblages renders problematic textual and cartographic designations of ground as "military," in ways that reinforce our observations (see above) about the limitations of binary thinking around categories of "military" and "civilian." To sit at the height of the moorland watershed at Lilla Cross and look at RAF Fylingdales a couple of miles distant is to position the infrastructure enabling ballistic missile early warning and space monitoring, from the SSPAR to the power station to the staff car park, as merely three points amongst many in that view. Multiple land-uses are rendered as equally significant; hiking, agro-forestry, moorland regeneration, archaeology, bird-watching or human dwelling take equal place in that assemblage. The military/civilian binaries through which ideas of militarisation come to be constructed gradually collapse through physical, sensory engagement with this visible assemblage.

## CONCLUSIONS

Our efforts to turn Fylingdales inside out, to untangle the assemblages therein, and to make sense of ballistic missile early warning and space monitoring, in turn speak to wider assemblages and connections which show the value of creative methods in military research. A wider tradition of engagement by visual artists with military sites shows how representational visual art outputs prompt new ways of thinking about these often enigmatic sites; just in the UK, examples include the work of artists including Shona Illingworth, Gair Dunlop, Melanie Friend, Simon Norfolk, Louise K. Wilson, and Matthew Flintham. At Fylingdales, our focus has not been on creativity as means for the production of new representational forms (although we may also do that) but rather on creative practice as a means of finding new ways of investigating and thinking through military phenomena.

At first sight, the idea of creative methods and creative practice as tools for investigating nuclear phenomena can appear far-fetched. But the Fylingdales work sits alongside that of other researchers of the military-nuclear assemblage who look to find better ways of researching, thinking, and communicating than existing orthodoxies allow. For example, Peter Singer and August Cole's 2015 novel *Ghost Fleet: A Novel of the Next World War* takes the knowledge of these two defence analysts to outline exactly how emergent contemporary technologies might shape a future global conflict. Jeffrey Lewis's 2018 novel *The 2020 Commission Report on the North Korean Nuclear Attacks Against*

*The United States* imagines a future nuclear war, as a means of promoting new conversations about disarmament. The US-based progressive nuclear policy network NSquare[15] and the UK's Project on Nuclear Issues (PONI)[16] both explicitly advocate creativity in research and thinking about the nuclear threat. They point to the limitations of traditional nuclear analysis training and to the need for analysts to develop the creative skills and abilities. These are required to synthesise information about possible futures that could arise from complex material and embodied socio-technical interactions in and beyond the traditional boundaries of nuclear weapons complexes and thought. This extends to consideration of the intersections between nuclear deterrence and the emerging climate catastrophe, or the way the pursuit of nuclear deterrence intersects with citizens' rights and social justice (NSquare 2019). Creative practice as a tool is emerging as central to contemporary nuclear debates. Assemblages assemble through creative processes that are both embodied as individual experience, or reside in materialities of the more than human material environment, such as the electromagnetic fluxes of radar operations. By their nature these lie beyond apprehension by representation or objective analysis. Creative research practices that explore actual embodied experiences or material interactions have the potential to make these phenomena apprehensible to critical thought.

# 2

# Visualizing Drone Ethnography in the Shadows of Distributive War

*Sara Matthews*

One of the questions this volume explores is how the "creative turn" in military studies opens an encounter with both the material and ephemeral qualities of martial cultures—how they are embodied and affectively felt. Consider, for example, how militarization is lived in the body, as gesture or as touch. The affective hauntings of militarization similarly press our understanding of how the spectral calls upon the living in relation to the dead. A common argument is that the creative arts—visual media, performance, narrative expression—invite a rethinking of normative claims to knowledge and experience. The creative work of cultural mediation offered by aesthetic methods, it is proposed, might teach new ways of feeling, apprehending, and intervening into militarized projects of world making. From this perspective, aesthetics and creativity are positioned as outside of military studies, as a methodological lens or creative mediation. In this chapter I take a slightly different tack, suggesting that contemporary visual culture—in this case, photography—is already imbricated in martial ways of seeing even as it offers a method for visualizing that implication. By suggesting that visual culture is *already martial*, I explore how aesthetic engagements can nevertheless provoke different ways of encountering this knowledge and the implications for a critical politics of militarization. To do this, I discuss a recent exhibition, *The Cultural Life of Drones*, that employs installation and social documentary practice as a way of making evident the perceptual regimes that underlie drone vision, itself a form of ethnographic looking.

## THE CULTURAL LIFE OF DRONES

What does it mean to think of drones as culture? If culture is the range of social practices by which one comes to know and engage the world, then drone cultures might be the myriad ways in which drones are embedded into everyday life as well as ideas about what kinds of life (and death) that drones make. The term *drone* refers to a diverse range of systems, from palm-sized quadrotors to solar-powered aircraft that fly at seventy thousand feet for weeks at a time. But drone systems are not just technologies. They also animate particular ways of knowing and being known. These orientations are evident in everything from the practiced gestures of the workers who produce them to the algorithmic applications that interpret the patterns by which drones see and apprehend. Military drones such as those deployed in sovereign wars[1] have extensive cultural lives: the local economies supported by their manufacture; the networked infrastructures and logistics of assemblage; the evolution of analytics such as machine learning, artificial intelligence, and algorithmic warfare; the training of pilots and maintenance personnel; the organized resistances to drone surveillance and strikes; and the academic drone research industry, to name a but a few. The cultural infrastructures that underlie drone systems in the civilian sphere are similarly diverse—ranging from domestic privacy and airspace laws; applications in the agricultural, scientific, and humanitarian sectors; and the burgeoning field of drone photography. In his text *Drone* (2015), Adam Rothstein queries what we talk about when we talk about drones: Are they physical objects, technological inventions, existential projections? One way of parsing the drone, he suggests, is through the sum of the narratives used to describe it. The drone is, he claims, "the way that we work with, think about, and respond to technology" (xiv). As Bloomberg (2015) describes, drones are a "constellation" or assemblage of historical and political statements that energize our contemporary assumptions about social labor, politics, and bodies (6). This is one understanding of drone cultures—a set of propositions that express the intimacies between technology, militarization, and social and political life.

My approach to drone study is in conversation with other critical scholars (Parks and Caplan 2017) who analyze drone systems as integral to the processes of late modern capitalism in which technological development extends governmentality (9). It is in this sense that drone cultures are biopolitical: they "make live and let die" in the service of sovereign projects (Foucault 2011) but also compel the necropolitical relations of colonization, empire (Mbembe 2016), and racial capitalism (Bhattacharyya 2018). Bhattacharyya (2018) urges us to consider the processes of racialization occurring in the "shadows where capital meets other histories of dispossession" (xi) and how "capitalist formations create by default the edge-populations that serve as the other and limit of the working class" (5). To think of drone cultures in this way is to consider the exercise of power not only through weaponry, but also through the domestic relations of labor, technological developments, and legal frameworks that support the logistics of global capitalism and militarization. Kapadia (2019) adopts the term the *forever war* to describe the durational reach of these dynamics, providing an apt description of the United States as a nation "not "at war" but "as war" (5). The linked projects of empire and nation-building, he suggests, are not merely "a series of geopolitical and military conflicts, but also an ongoing archival project, structure of feeling and production of knowledge for interpreting and acting on the geopolitical alignments of the US in the broader 'post'–Cold War era" (8). If militarization is a process of continuance, it is also deterritorialized, existing in multiple spatial registers as suggested by Gregory's (2011) articulation of the "everywhere war." Drone cultures are part of this nexus of militarization that extends power far beyond the discrete actions of the military strike to the logistics of preparedness that support it. Discussing these dynamics in the context of the aeromobility of drone platforms that promise their widespread accessibility, Grewal (2017) suggests that drone power "threatens the sovereignty of the imperial state by breaking down the distinction between empire and colony, even as it adds to the securitization of everyday life that extends state power" (344).

Operational logistics systems are a key aspect of military power that depend increasingly on drone cultures. The following passage from a recent 2020 briefing by General David H. Berger, commandant of the US Marine Corp, to the US Senate Subcommittee on Readiness and Management, expresses this reality. When asked to comment on the challenges of sustaining warfare distributed across vast geographic regions and how these dispersed networks of operational logistics are made vulnerable, Berger expresses concern:

> First of all, we've got to be able to distribute laterally at the tactical to the operational level sustainment supplies, equipment, people, in a way we have not been challenged to do in the past, and we've got to do it in [. . .] a contested environment . . . So, we have [. . .] everything from the surface craft to the aircraft, and probably in the future, I would suspect a fair portion of that being unmanned.[2]

Berger's comment reveals the deep layers of interplay between culture, technology, and logistics that support military power. Drone platforms, he suggests, are the future of this nexus of distributed relations that undergird operational efforts. I adapt the term *distributive war* to critically signal the domestic networks of supply chain management, technological development, classification, dispersion, and administration that support the global biopolitical relations of securitization and militarization. What would it mean to think of distributive war as extending the battlefield of operations to the civilian sphere, where drone technologies are funded, developed, tested, and commercialized? Furthermore, how does the increasing ubiquity of drone platforms in our everyday worlds alter the ways in which we learn to see and apprehend? My argument is that drone vision normalizes modes of ethnographic looking and interpretation as a logistic of distributed war. To map these distributions at the local level, I engage a creative cartography of drone cultures.

When it comes to the study of drone platforms in relation to distributive war, there is a reason to start with the local. The academic study of drone cultures is tied up in the biopolitical relations of empire even as it attempts critique. Indeed, as Daulatzai and Ghumkhor (2021) observe, current military drone scholarship reflects an extractive relationship to research inquiry in which those who are "surveilled, droned and documented—that includes Somalis, Yemenis, Iraqis, Pashtuns, Afghans, Libyans, and Syrians" are positioned as objects to be studied rather than interlocuters of knowledge production. When the gaze does shift to the home front of Western wars, the focus pulls to the individual plight of the drone operator caught up in the nexus of military relations. What both attentions miss, Daulatzai and Ghumkhor argue, is an analysis of "the larger war economy and [. . .] the liberal, imperial, racist forever wars in Afghanistan and elsewhere." I endeavour to heed this call for accountability, approaching regimes of visuality as *already implicated* in drone cultures via their enmeshment with distributive warfare. How research methods are implicated in the dynamics they intend to explore may be one of the unexamined aspects of military studies that a creative approach can emphasize. An aesthetic orientation holds open the ambivalence of these various implications while revealing the structural conditions that produce drone cultures as asymmetric violence. By exploring the vocabularies and social practices manifest in local drone ecologies in the shadows of distributive war—as capital, as invention, as visuality—the intimate ties between everyday life and the military-industrial complex can be mapped and explored.

I use the term *ecologies* quite deliberately to acknowledge the social embeddedness of drone systems. From the Greek *oikos* meaning house or dwelling, the term ecology entered common usage in the natural sciences in late nineteenth-century Europe to describe relationships between living organisms and their physical environments. While it may seem odd to bring this term into conversation with drone systems, ecology captures the embodied relations in which drone technologies circulate, including those of corporeality, space and place (land, sea, sky), and governmentality. Words such as *predator*, *reaper*, and *swarm*—which describe common drone systems—are meant to evoke their various characteristics that draw seemingly innocuously on natural science discourses. Drone ecologies include logistics, gestures, vocabularies, social practices, perceptual regimes, and soundscapes. This is the terrain of drone study, and it requires, I suggest, a particular kind of methodological approach that can sustain an ecological complexity.

The work of scholars concerned with visual politics shapes my approach to investigating drone ecologies through the distinct locales of governmentality and empire. Gil Hochberg's (2015) study of the asymmetries of violence expressed via the conditions of vision that underlie the Palestinian-Israeli conflict explores how visual rights are unevenly distributed as a legacy of the changing spatial arrangements of occupation (4). Shifting the focus from visual representations of the conflict to how the visual is caught up in its making, Hochberg asks critical questions about "what or who can be seen, what or who remains invisible, who can see and whose vision is compromised" (5). Raising similar questions with her film *The Prison in Twelve Landscapes* (2016), director and critical geographer Brett Story turns the lens of her film camera to the subject of carceral power in the United States, producing a documentary in which the inside of a prison is never seen. Story's insistence that the spatial dimensions of the prison industrial complex matter to our understanding of carceral power allows for her intimate study of the contours of racial capitalism. In one of the film's vignettes, the audience is invited into the economic realities of small-town life turned from coal production to prison land, offering a human geography of the carceral that reveals how the prison shapes much more than what happens inside of its walls. Exposed are the intimate stories of how prisons emerge from the social relations that govern and organize carceral politics, including its visual regimes. What these and other scholars (Cowen 2014) point out is that visualizing empire begins with the local where the everyday gestures of governmentality (including those of resistance and refusal) are made. I am interested in how an aesthetic approach can hold the space for such an inquiry, illuminating the contours of experience that might not otherwise be seen while remaining accountable to who is seen, how, and why.

## ON CREATIVE METHODS

In his extensive exploration of the emerging genre of drone art, Stubblefield (2020) poses a provocative question: "What happens when a drone enters the gallery or appears on screen? What thresholds are crossed as this weapon of war occupies everyday visual culture?" (1). I read Stubblefield's question as suggesting that everyday visual culture is not *already* an occupied space of war but rather a separate threshold to be crossed. I propose the opposite—that drone systems reveal the porosity between war and visual culture. Furthermore, the conditions of encounter and interpretation provoked by the heuristics of the art gallery may allow for a creative rather than normative approach to this revelation. What then might happen is a shattering of the pretense that war and visual culture are separate spheres. I use the term creative to gesture to the interpretive qualities of aesthetic experience; an ability to symbolize, through aesthetic language, the dilemmas of knowing and not knowing. A creative approach might disclose the permeability of the threshold between militarism and the everyday, exposing the degree of enmeshment between distributive war and our taught ways of seeing and perceiving. Stubblefield provides some guidance on this approach, suggesting that "*drone art* is not simply a descriptive term, but a methodology. It speaks to a mode of inquiry that begins within a conflicting field of symmetry in which military doctrines such as network-centric warfare are read as aesthetic programs, and everyday social media platforms are analyzed as weapons of war" (11). Crucially for my project, such a methodology takes drone vision as a starting point for exploring how modes of seeing are already militarized. Can these same methodologies of vision illuminate the shadows of distributive war, introducing interferences and potential disruption? This is the gamble that my aesthetic project takes. In what follows, I describe my aesthetic aims and how I work with different cultural forms to denaturalize drone vision, drawing the viewer to their own implication in modes of seeing, sensing, and believing.

## THE CULTURAL LIFE OF DRONES: KW DRONE DIALOGUES

In 2019, I was approached by the Grebel Gallery at the University of Waterloo[3] to produce a site-specific installation based on my research. The invitation was to create an exhibition that would provoke dialogue about the proliferation and use of drone systems in the Kitchener-Waterloo (KW) region of southern Ontario. Developing my methodology for the project, I was inspired by the work of cultural theorist Raymond Williams. Williams had direct military experience: during World War II, he completed a four-and-a-half-year tour of duty with the British Army before returning, in 1945, to conclude his studies at Cambridge University. He found the adjustment to civilian life difficult, musing that "the fact is, they just don't speak the same language" (Williams, 1976, 12). As a scholar of history and cultural materialism, Williams observed the rapid changes that characterized postwar Europe and became curious about the capacity of language to reflect these transitions. "Culture" was a new way of thinking about social experience, and Williams was fascinated with what the term might reveal about the transformations he was witnessing. His *Keywords: A Vocabulary of Culture and Society* (1976, 1983) grew out of this interest, investigating how, in the evolution of a vocabulary, "certain words, tones and rhythms, meanings are offered, felt for, tested, confirmed, asserted, qualified, changed" (12). Vocabulary, Williams attests, is a profoundly social practice, particular to time and place; its close study enables a detailed kind of telling of experience as variable and dynamic, open to revision and debate. This invitation to language as both reflective and generative of experience was crucial to my thinking about the exhibition. Because I had been asked by the gallery to privilege dialogue as a heuristic for the installation, I settled on the central conceit of exploring local drone vocabularies as a way to inventory the cultural life of drones through the regional languages and discourses they produce.

To begin building a local drone vocabulary situated in the experiences of those directly involved with drone systems in the KW region of southern Ontario, I reached out to various individuals and organizations: four people volunteered to be involved in the project,[4] and over a four-month period I made myself an apprentice to their work. Birgitta[5] is a senior researcher with a locally based non-governmental organization that investigates emerging security technologies, advising policymakers on ethics of autonomous weapons systems. Cathy is a cartographer and geospatial specialist who flies drone missions and produces scientific data for a regional university. Kent is a flight instructor and coordinates a training program for remotely piloted aircraft systems at the regional airport. And lastly, Adam is the founder and CEO of a local aerospace engineering and manufacturing company that develops flight control systems and airframes for the drone industry. The ensuing exhibition, *The Cultural Life of Drones: KW Drone Dialogues* (November 11, 2019–April 24, 2020), was comprised of four elements: portraiture, documentary photography, drone data sets, and life-size silhouettes of UAVs[6] (Figs. 2.1–2.2).

Entering the exhibition, one encounters a large, two-dimensional, silhouette of a General Atomics MQ-1 Predator drone that covers the east wall of the gallery almost entirely (Fig. 2.1). Reproduced at 75 percent of its actual size, the digital vector drawing provides a tangible sense of the Predator's imposing size. The scale of the Predator stands in contrast to the life-size reproductions of three smaller drone platforms—the Avidrone 210TL, eBee SenseFly, and DJI Phantom—each corresponding to the specific work of the four project participants. My decision to work with drone silhouettes was twofold. The first was a signal to the drone's materiality. The second was a formal consideration: a shadow is a contour, a gesture to a presence affectively perceived before it is cognitively understood. A key aspect of my creative approach is to exaggerate the distance between perception and understanding and thus denaturalize the interpretive process. In the gallery setting, what emerges are viewer's local knowledges and experiences. Indeed, the ability to recognize a drone from its silhouette tells a story about one's implication in drone cultures. This tension is similarly explored by artist Ruben Pater, whose *Drone Survival Guide*[7]—a free, downloadable infographic identifying the silhouettes of common military drones—instructs users on drone spotting and evasion (Pater, 2013). His project pointedly reveals the inequities of life under the shadow of the drone, suggesting that for some, recognition is a matter of life or death.

Moving to the west wall of the gallery, one encounters photographic portraits of the four project participants whose work I shadowed in preparation for the exhibition (Fig 2.2). Drawing on the written notes, interviews, and images I collected over the course of this fieldwork, I set myself the task of creating a visual narrative of these encounters, mounted in a 5x5 grid of twelve-inch-square black-and-white photographs printed on archival paper. I also asked each project participant to donate some drone sensor data associated with their work and reprinted this data on panels hung through the centre of the exhibition space. With this element of the installation, I reference how visual data collected by drone sensor platforms are used in mapping and interpretation. The translucent material on which the data sets are printed harkens to the vellum used by cartographers. The scale and clarity of the images are dependent on the amount of visual data captured by each drone sensor. These differences are important when thinking about the precision by which various drone platforms can "see." Here, too, the viewer is compelled to construct

**Figure 2.1 The Cultural Life of Drones: KW Drone Dialogues.**

**Figure 2.2 The Cultural Life of Drones: KW Drone Dialogues.**

an interpretation of what the visual image represents. This process mirrors the interpretive work that goes into understanding the visual data that drone cameras can produce—partial aspects of a larger story are drawn together into meaning that is situated and context dependent. Before a more detailed engagement with this aspect of the exhibition, I first discuss my methodological approach, situating my work in conversation with scholars who theorize visuality in the context of ethnography.

## DRONE VISION AND ETHNOGRAPHIC LOOKING

In their special issue of *Visual Studies* exploring how ethnographic practice travels between disciplines, editors Horst and Hjorth (2014) consider how the visual becomes naturalized in methodologies that promise a kind of deep learning of experience. This is evident in everything from approaches in art history which narrativize human experience according to a canonical past, to current technological advances such as machine learning and artificial intelligence which normalize interpretation as a necessary vicissitude of big data representation and processing (125). The naturalization of the visual as a mode of truth telling within disciplines such as anthropology, art history and documentary photography has a long and troubled history (Poole 2005, Said 1978, Tobing Rony 1996, Mirzoeff 2011). This trajectory of visual mystification also influences the development of how and what drone systems see, including the gathering and interpretation of visual data, producing a distinct version of ethnographic looking. I am struck by the parallels between the immersive expectations promoted by ethnographic orientations to vision and the kind of looking that drone systems engage. Berg's (2008) articulation of the positivist trend in visual ethnography makes this apparent:

> ethnography is a methodology that involves a researcher immersing himself or herself into natural settings, either covertly or overtly, over some prolonged period of time. During this effort, the researcher will watch, listen, ask questions, and generally collect whatever data are available in an effort to better understand the issues and questions that are the focus of the research endeavor (936).

While this definition of the qualities of ethnographic research is quite normative (leaving out, for example, questions of power, subjectivity, and self-reflexivity that characterize contemporary conversations about ethnographic practice), the assumption inherent to ethnographic looking—that immersion (whether clandestine or apparent) for the purposes of data collection and interpellation will produce empirical data—is similar to the promise of drone vision. What happens when we bring these two seemingly disparate ways of "seeing" into conversation with each other? What critical questions might be raised? Reflecting on these prompts with respect to the development of the exhibition, I decided to centre the dilemma of how vision is normalized in ethnographic approaches to the gathering of information, including the practice of social documentary photography. Documentary photography is often encountered by viewers as a mimetic representation of experience, missing the subjective quality of interpretive visual work. My hunch was that a creative approach might denaturalize ethnographic ways of seeing and allow for their critical examination.

If one could think of drone systems as producing a form of ethnographic looking, what is the point of view of the drone and what stories of experience does it tell? Several scholars have engaged these questions from the vantage of scopic regimes. Greene (2015) investigates the broader political and technological networks of drone warfare, situating the apparatus of seeing within a constellation of practices targeted towards the killing of terror suspects as part of the global war on terror. "Drone vision," he writes, "as a particular technique of control, monitors subjects' movements and habits, calculating the probability of their becoming a 'threat' and tailoring the solution based on that probability" (235). Greene's emphasis on the drone as a technology of control positions vision as an apparatus of surveillance, but what his argument lacks is a theory of visuality—an understanding of how technologies of vision are implicated in militarized ways of seeing and conversely how martial politics organizes what or who is seen, how and why. How surveillance orients vision is a more complicated story, as argued by Browne (2015) who traces surveillance as a fact of black life, linking the discourses and practices of vision to the ongoing processes of racial capitalism. Caplan (2018) is also concerned with the "storyline of visual culture in modernity" (3), exploring how aerial views from above organize certain bodies as targets while others remain obscured. And yet it is just this view from above that is naturalized when it comes to the images captured by drone sensors, expressed perhaps with banality in the field of drone photography, where expansive, aerial views of denuded landscapes or difficult to access locales provide the viewer an aesthetic encounter with a god-like vision of discovery and wonder. Is this, too, drone vision? And if so, how is the aesthetic tied up with militarized modes of seeing and sensing?

Drone technologies have enabled remote forms of sensing (the gathering of light as data translated via imaging), that extend the range and scope of visual capture and therefore the human field of perception. Arguably, the sensor arrays developed for drone systems have also changed the capacity for vision—what or who it becomes possible to see, when and why. Take, for example, the Gorgon Stare video capture technology developed by the Defense Advanced Research Projects Agency (DARPA) for the United States military (Michel 2019). It has a visual range of up to fifty square kilometres resulting in detailed real-time video capture of several gigabytes per minute. Of course, these kinds of innovations require other new technologies to aid in the management and interpretation of such massive amounts of visual data. In April of 2017, reports from the media and the military and intelligence communities announced the creation, by the Pentagon, of an "Algorithmic Warfare Cross-Functional Team." The premise of the initiative is the maintenance of a qualitative edge in warfare via the algorithmic systems that underpin artificial intelligence and machine learning (Lewis, Modirzadeh, Blum 2017).

But developments in visual capture techniques have long been associated with innovations in industrial technologies, particularly those related to military applications. Bousquet (2018) comments on the ubiquity of militarized vision in his thorough genealogy of military perception technologies from the telescope to the drone. Noting the visual expansion of the battlefield of armed conflict, he develops the concept of the "martial gaze" to capture the logistics of military perception, including those of perspective, sensing, imaging, mapping, and hiding. The martial gaze has relevance for civilian imaging applications as well. For instance, the development of the twin lens reflex camera was apparently inspired by the imaging problems posed by World War I trench warfare, when exposing oneself above the parapet meant certain death (Parker 1993). How one sees, what is perceived through the camera lens, as well as how that visual information is organized, is ultimately influenced in some way by the martial gaze. I am very cognizant of this troubled history of seeing with respect to my choice of representational practice for the exhibition. To interrogate the logistics of the martial gaze as expressed in the local drone ecologies on the KW region, I adopted an installation design that would prompt the viewer to reflect on the ways in which everyday attitudes of seeing are implicated in the martial dynamics of looking.

## PATTERN OF LIFE ANALYSIS

I now return to the exhibition in detail considering the above claims. While social documentary photography is the anchor for this project, I have noted that the documentary form is itself not innocent of the dynamics of looking. As a researcher trained in ethnographic methods, I am aware of how documentary techniques (participant observation, recorded interviews, field work) repeat the dynamics of imperial knowledge production. Documentary photography might be able to challenge these normative forms of knowledge making if it elicits accountability to the structures that inform ones' modes of seeing and interpretation. Indeed, the unknowability that may be part of an encounter with art (what am I looking at? what does it mean?) can interrupt claims to certainty. A creative approach could potentially destabilize the ways in which documentary practices enter the University as research and as pedagogy. Indeed, with the aesthetic invitation, failure, ignorance, implication, and resistance are part of the process of coming to know. This then, is the ethics that social documentary practice might offer. As an investigative method, ethnography involves the study of experience, a kind of deep learning that attends to the nature of phenomena as it is lived. I am not so interested in rescuing the innocence of an ethnographic position because I don't think it can be accomplished, but what does interest me is the methodological problem of how to disentangle the visual from the everyday and make it political. By this I mean attention to the biopolitics of vision that organize the apprehension and interpretation of experience as part of the project of governmentality. To achieve this within the installation, I moved against the promise of conventional ethnography by privileging the unfinished encounter: the attempt to know experience is always fragile, partial, and necessarily fragmented. This orientation to interpretation is exactly the opposite of the approach taken in the analysis of drone data, which is one of certainty and veracity, whether that data is mobilized to plot drone strikes or to make efficient farming decisions. The ambition of drone vision is to present a full picture, mystifying the processes by which meaning is made. My way of confronting this naturalization within the installation was to juxtapose four very distinct elements: portraiture, documentary photography, data sets, and dimensional drawings, creating a discontinuous engagement that compelled the viewer to fill in the gaps.

How one moves through the exhibition and the various associations that are made, exposes the process by which one is drawn to create a story from a sum of the parts. These concerns were central to my production design: less interested what the drone might see, I privileged instead the interpretive modes I brought to my own experience of encountering the subjects of my exhibition.

To illustrate this approach, I turn to a specific aspect of the installation that was informed by my research into "pattern-of-life analysis," an information gathering technique developed to index and map physical activity for a wide variety of purposes, such as the US military's tracking of the movements and daily habits of terror suspects (Franz 2017). Utilizing surveillance technologies such as the Gorgon Stare that capture raw visual data, the intent is to combine the visual with other regimes of representation—for instance, the sonic or the thermal—to create searchable, three-dimensional documents as the basis for engaging what Gregory (2013) calls a "cartography of lives." Mapped out is a possible future in which supposed terror targets deviate from their lived norms and so reveal themselves as suspect. The goal is to identify a person's day-to-day interaction with their environment, including family and social interactions, frequented locations, and personal habits through geospatial referencing. This data is then available for pattern-of-life analysis, an algorithmic approach to identifying individuals not by their identities but rather how their behavior fits a particular profile. As one Air Force intelligence analyst states about the practice: "You're now getting into culture study . . . you're looking at people's lives" (Weinberger 2021, 43). It is this "looking," the specific scopic regime of the drone, that anticipates—in fact, *creates*—the subject of violence and that manifests, in Mbembe's (2003) terms "the power and the capacity to dictate who may live and who must die" (11). Pattern-of-life analysis is an interpretive orientation to social movement itself—who belongs, who does not, and who gets to decide. A hallmark of the CIA's covert counter-terrorism practice of drone signature strikes, pattern-of-life analysis is what Gregory (2012) calls an example of "militarized rhythmanalysis" or "weaponized time-geography" in which the bio-political terrain of the proposed enemy is epistemologically mapped.

This orientation to documenting and interpreting experience influenced the social documentary work that I created for the exhibition (Fig. 2.3). Each row of images corresponds to one of the project participants and represents my visual rendition of their work with drone systems in the KW region. The narratives are necessarily partial, gesturing to the interpretive nature of ethnographic work while inviting the viewer to engage an active process of meaning making; it is not immediately obvious what is being depicted. I argued earlier that drone research should be accountable to its local biopolitics, an effort I undertake with my study of regional drone vocabularies. I want to describe one example of how this is manifest in the work that the installation

**Figure 2.3 The Cultural Life of Drones: KW Drone Dialogues.**

performs. The second to the top row of photographs (Fig. 2.3) represent my encounter with Birgitta's research into emerging security technologies and their policy implications. Because her work is principally investigative and involves data driven research, her primary place of work is the office cubicle, depicted in the first three images. Birgitta's office is in the same academic building as the exhibition: indeed, one must walk through the installation to enter her workplace. The image taken from inside of Birgitta's office looking outwards onto a parking lot is through the same window depicted from the outside of the building in the fifth image of that series. While this may seem banal from the point of view of content, it is less so when one realizes the perspective—her office is located on the top floor of a three-story building, which raises the question of how this image could have been obtained. In fact, it was captured during a drone mission flown by one of the other project participants who generated visual data of the entire building (Fig. 1.2). The significance of a photograph of the window, therefore, is it's situated knowledge—only Birgitta could experience the drone's eye view as surveillance because only she could recognize herself as the object of its gaze. This import is missed by the casual observer of the artwork because of the ways in which the photographic document naturalizes perspective. It is only with an interpretive guide that viewers can understand the various linkages between the elements of the installation as well as their own implication in what they imagine that they are seeing.

Another example might make this aspect more apparent. I led quite a few tours of the exhibition with a variety of groups—both academic classes and members of the general public. One of my hopes was that these mediations would provoke a deeper exploration of the narratives presented in the exhibition. Indeed, new information about local drone vocabularies emerged through this process of re-interpretation. One student recognized a local farmer's field as the location of the demonstration drone flights undertaken by the project participant who operated their own drone system development firm. A more remarkable finding came about because of the knowledge shared by another gallery visitor who drew connections between the image of the General Atomics MQ-1 Predator and the drone data set provided by Birgitta. The data is video of a drone strike in northern Waziristan, released by Wikileaks and uploaded to YouTube by an independent news organization. But what I didn't realize was that the sensor attached to the Predator likely responsible for this strike was produced by WESCAM technologies, the Canadian subsidiary of U.S. defence giant L3Harris, one of the world's leading producers and exporters of Electro-Optical/Infra-Red (EO/IR) imaging and targeting sensor systems. WESCAM's manufacturing operation is located just a hundred kilometres away from the exhibition, another example of how the everywhere war is integrated into local drone ecologies. Canada is currently under scrutiny for their compliance with UN Arms trade treaty for their export of WESCAM sensors to Turkey (Gallagher 2020).

My initial intent with this exhibition was to explore the vocabularies and social practices associated with drone systems in the Kitchener-Waterloo region of southern Ontario and to begin the work of mapping local drone cultures as distributive war. A secondary aim was to consider how an aesthetic engagement might open an inquiry into how martial politics naturalizes our ways of sensing and seeing, including those methodologies common to research practice. What I have learned is that this work is just a beginning. As the project unfolds, I want to consider gesture, an embodiment of militarization that remains unexamined thus far. Grasseni (2004) describes one aim of observational documentary as calling "the audience itself to witness the rhythms of everyday activity, the significance of repetitive but skilled action and of what has been described as 'embodied technical knowledge' (Angioni in Grasseni)" (12). An "apprenticeship of the eye," she suggests, might educate the researcher to ways of knowing inherent to repetitive skill and their gestures. Drone ecologies have their own gestures - from the practiced labors of WESCAN manufacturing workers to the physical dance involved in calibrating the compass of a DJI Mavic before flight. A creative approach might bring these otherwise unnoticed gestures into perception and offer a critical field within which to give them new meaning. It also, I have argued, privileges interpretation as mode of political intervention, returning the possibility for implication, resistance, and revision. New questions are raised: what, in research, do we think of as "data" and how do we apprehend it? When does the data leave ethnography and become art? Creative methods not only represent the ineffable qualities of experience they also privilege that ineffability as a productive intervention into normative ways of knowing and perceiving distinct to both ethnographic research and drone vision.

3

# Notating War, Choreographing Soldiers

## *Dance Methods as Military Stratagem*

*Charlotte Veal*

There is a long history of the enterprising, open approach of the military during periods of conflict. At a time when the promises and possibilities of creative methods for military studies are gaining traction, it is worth reflecting critically upon the litheness of the military in putting diverse creative knowledge, techniques, methods, and practices to work in the pursuit of geopolitics. This chapter examines the British military's solicitation of dance-led methods and embodied knowledges in the furtherance of vertical warfare. It draws upon an experimental partnership between RAF Ringway and dance theorist Rudolf Laban in the immediate aftermath of World War II. First, the chapter traces movement ethnography deployed during preparatory training for informing the "art of falling." Second, I examine dance notation as an artful method for systematically recording martial efficiency during three-dimensional warfare. Finally, I turn to movement training as a method for cultivating elite bodies for war. Against much interest in the theories and methods of creativity, I call for sustained scholarly enquiries into the historical geographies of military coercion and enterprising solicitation of artists in the service of statecraft. Military's willingness to employ artful knowledges and practices during periods of war and peace also warrants caution over the labours deployed when practicing creative methods for military research.

## DANCE AND STATECRAFT

Dance has a long and profound relationship to statecraft. When Hitler seized power, Rudolf Laban, an Austro-Hungarian dancer, and choreographer, was serving as the director of movement to the Prussian State Theatres. Although he became an employee of the state by default, he shared much of its ideology. In September 1934, Laban was appointed director of the Deutsche Tanzbühne, effectively cementing his role at the forefront of dance in Nazi Germany. Under Goebbels, his role was to direct major festivals of dance. Delivered as large movement choirs, these events explored the possibilities for German modern dance to cement Nazi policies and a German national aesthetic (Karina and Kant, 2003); namely its pursuit of Aryan 'purity,' anti-Semitism, and political unification. Amidst growing international distrust, Nazi organisers employed the 1936 Olympics to spotlight the achievements of National Socialism. The popular medium of dance was central in showcasing the prevailing body culture. As a master of choral dancing, Laban's brief was to deliver mass propaganda to the twenty-two thousand spectators attending the Opening Ceremony. The event was a choreographing in propaganda, and a choreography of propaganda.

*Vom Tauwind und der Neuen Freude*, was performed by forty-one movement choirs. Dress rehearsals took place on the 26th of June with Goebbels in attendance. *Vom Tauwind* retold the story of Germany's transition toward unity (Dörr, 2007). Beginning with choirs of defeated soldiers, the choreography progressed through to the joy of creating a new state and concluded with groups forming a large Germanic sun wheel. Aesthetically, it undermined the regime's ideology. It depicted the terrible consequences of war, and in Goebbels's mind, the disenfranchisement of the German people. Mass movement had been solicited to convey martial strength and synchronous action, not German weakness. Furthermore, Laban's choreographic philosophy foregrounded individualism, diverging from the Nazi vision of *Volksgemeinschaft* and catchphrase "you are nothing; your nation is everything." *Vom Tauwind* was cancelled. Laban was placed under investigation and his theories and notation system declared anti-German. He escaped to Paris in 1937, traveling onwards to Britain in 1938.

Laban's entanglement in the 1936 Olympics provides a compelling account of the enterprising collaborations between statecraft and the cultural industries. Softer forms of power have long served state interests (Nye 2008). This chapter does not review the performing art's *aesthetic* complicity in statecraft. Such work has received lively critical enquiry (Breed 2014; Croft 2015). Rather, it addresses an absence of sustained scholarship on the complex methodologies, knowledges, pedagogies, and training regimes that artists have drawn upon to serve the state. Here, I focus on the pedagogic and practice-led collaboration between Laban and the British military in the aftermath of World War II. I trace the movement theorist's provision of movement ethnographies, documentation techniques, and movement training to respond to the RAF's identified lacuna of knowledge in air-to-ground warfare. Central to which is the provision of corporeally rich knowledge for the training of paratroop bodies, and for the increased efficiency of bodies for war. As the promises and possibilities of creative methods for critical military studies gain traction (Cree 2020), it is worth reflecting critically upon the litheness of the military in putting diverse creative knowledges, techniques, methods, and practices to work in the pursuit of geopolitics.

First, the chapter surveys research at the intersection of the arts and militarism. Mobilising archival research from the National Archives, the next introduces RAF Ringway. Third, I draw upon archival research from the Surrey Special Collections to examine Laban's enterprising collaboration with the RAF.[1] I trace three methods from dance studies solicited for improving martial efficiency; movement ethnography, dance notation, and movement training. I conclude with a note of caution for scholars of militarism and war in their solicitation of creative methods in the study of military phenomenon, practices, and processes.

## ART, MILITARISM, WAR

Art and creativity have been gaining momentum across political geographies, critical military studies, and geopolitics, backstopped by calls to read the political as always cultural. Such research has been endorsed, in part, through the sub-field of popular geopolitics and its consideration of dominant cultural objects (comic books, video games, spy films) as offering insight into the ways in which geopolitics operate and are generated (Dittmer and Gray 2010; Pinkerton and Benwell 2014).

Non-Representational Theory's influence has also been felt through the language of affect, aesthetics, and performance (Carter and McCormack 2010). Within geopolitics this includes tracing how affects are produced and put to work or how affects operate in spaces of geopolitical instability (Closs-Stephens, 2016; Fregonese, 2017). Literature on affect sits alongside an escalating "aesthetic turn" in critical IR. This comprises the aesthetic dimensions of targeted killing (Grayson, 2016) and of how aesthetic sources provide "creative" ways of reading the international (Moore and Shepherd, 2010). Performance meanwhile has served as metaphor for geopolitical activity, and more recently, performativity has helped to interrogate the production and circulation of narratives around violence, war, and peace (McConnell et al., 2012). Aesthetic, affects, and performance have collectively offered a means to examine how militarisation is normalised, and thus, potentially useful for resistance (Åhäll, 2019).

This flourishing body of research has strengthened calls to take seriously artworks themselves. History books are littered with examples of creative responses to war. Goya's *Third of May 1808* and Picasso's *Guernica* testify to the horrors of war, while dance choreography's including Jooss's (1932)' *The Green Table* and BalletBoyz's (2016) *Young Men* have explored the futility of peace negotiations and the fragility of bodies. Twenty years on, the 9/11 terror attacks and subsequent military campaigns continue to be powerful sources of inspiration for artistic-led critique. Scholars of art have traced artistic responses to torture and targeted killing, advanced theorising of how creative products operate politically, and introduced art as a means to make visible the bodies and voices of the dead (Arndt et al., 2009; Bharucha, 2014; Gregory, 2010). Nevertheless, artworks emancipatory possibilities cannot be taken as given. Nor should artworks be read uncritically. Artist's efforts to expose or unsettle practices and processes of war are imbued with ambiguity. Foregrounding arts' resistant qualities risks creating a one directional relationship where art merely subverts war and militarisms violent effects. This can mask arts contested, often complicit, relationship to statecraft. Taking inspiration from Rancière, Ingram (2019) proposes thinking artworks as not only commenting on geopolitical processes, practices, and events, and rather as embedded in the geopolitical dynamic itself. Two considerations emerge.

First, I argue for sustained critical examination of the enterprising collusion of artists within wider processes of statecraft and of the litheness of the military in putting complex knowledges to work in the service of the state. Political geographers have discussed how geopolitics operate at 'thresholds,' between categories such as state/non-state, un/official diplomacy (McConnell, 2017; see Horvath et al. 2015). So too, performance scholars have argued liminal performances can have an effect on the political because they work at the edge of new possibilities (Broadhurst 1999). Art's entanglement in the matrix of war (Rogers 2018) is illustrative of such threshold encounters. Creative collaborations with artists might also testify to those efforts to calve out in-between spaces precisely because of their ambiguity. Liminal spaces are ripe for experimentation. The liminal promotes encounters of great intensity where structures of power are suspended to facilitate new pedagogic or documentation regimes and/or to experiment with bodies (Veal 2020). Interrogating liminal encounters is especially prescient as state and militaries continue to engage the cultural realm; from artists and zoologists in camouflage development to music in interrogation and torture (Cusick 2006; Forsyth 2017).

Second, where knowledge, pedagogies, and bodily doings have been mobilised for martial endeavours, it is imperative to reflect critically on our own labour in the doing of creative military methods. Here I focus explicitly on arts-led methods which I understand as interdisciplinary, multi-sensual approaches to research that marshal arts practices, processes, and products in the generation of new knowledges and insights (Veal and Hawkins 2020). As interest in arts-led methods, and embodiment more broadly, mounts (McSorley 2013; Wilcox 2014), we must remain mindful of how our own labours may buttress military agendas. The arts have an important role to play in research on geopolitics and violence (Pratt and Johnston 2014), but I caution for the embodied and embodying experiences of doing creative military methods. Exemplified through the case study of RAF Ringway is the reminder to reflect, in situated and empirical ways, on how we as researchers are entangled in militarism and war.

## AERIAL SUPREMACY AND RAF RINGWAY

With the declaration of war in 1939, Britain faced the looming prospect that warfare would be waged in ways for which it was ill-prepared. *Provision of an Airborne Division* explains, "We are on the threshold of a new era and of new methods of warfare."[2] The integral role of air power in maintaining terrestrial security and "enforcing national policy" (see Lambeth 1999)[3] was solidified following the aerial ascendency achieved by Hitler's Fallschirmjäger in spring 1940. Falling bodies performed a new covert form of air-led warfare at heightened speeds and scales (see Adey, 2010; Kaplan, 2006; Veal 2021). In response, on June 21st, 1940, the Central Landing School, Ringway, was formed. Its objective was to identify the pedagogy and principles for an "art of parachuting" and to deliver five thousand parachute troops.[4] The credence placed on raising an airborne division is affirmed in *War Cabinet Chief of Staff Committee Production Programmes*; "We should bend all our energies, regardless of cost, to accelerating our production and training programme."[5] With no preparation time, and fewer resources, much of the early work into designing principles of falling was conducted on the "trial error principle."[6] Experimental in its outlook, parachute training developed as "a distinctly hazardous act," associated with high levels of injuries and fatalities.[7]

Improved training and aerial knowledge, including an increase in jumping parameters, brought a reduction in fatalities. In 1943, this stood at "one fatal accident in approximately ten thousand jumps."[8] Injury rates were a more significant concern. November 1944 saw fifty-four hospitalisations.[9] Injuries reduced the total number of bodies available for vertical warfare, but also raised questions of the RAF's aerial knowledge and the efficacy of its training syllabus. That the military lacked corporeal proficiency in aerial mobility had been the subject of much debate. A 1941 report queried, "if it were possible to enlist the services of professional tumblers or those specially acquainted with the art of falling, this injury rate might be still further reduced."[10] Militaries have long embarked upon enterprising collaborations during periods of war and peace (Barnes, 2008). Artists, filmmakers, and park designers are just some of those individuals considered to possess unusual skills to develop practices and technologies that meet military needs (Forsyth 2017, Graham 2010). With victory in Europe and Japan, the future role of the Parachute Regiment remained uncertain. Total warfare had shown however that three-dimensional combat would play a prominent role, and therefore, fine tuning parachuting technique remained a priority. Rudolf Laban was approached by the RAF in autumn 1945.

## CHOREOGRAPHING AERIAL WARFARE

Rudolf Laban was not unfamiliar to partnering with the British military during periods of war. From as early as 1942 he was collaborating with management consultant Frederick Lawrence, observing and advising on efficiency in aviation factories.[11] Time and Motion Studies (TMS) was popular at this time. Amalgamating Frederick Taylor's Time Studies and Frank and Lillian Gilbreth's Motion Studies, TMS emerged as a scientific study of human movement, aimed at increasing efficiency in industrial output. Contrary to the prevailing school of thought that blamed waste on inefficiencies in materials, the trio foregrounded the human body. While Taylor incorporated detailed observations with timed recordings, the Gilbreths focused on work motions, filming worker's activities and analysing bodily postures throughout these activities.

Backstopped by these wider business efficiency techniques, Laban and Lawrence were developing an approach that integrated "the study of movement, motion, effort and the activities of human beings."[12] The enterprising pair levelled a scathing criticism of TMS, arguing that it failed to "study human movement" and its recommendation provided for a comprehensive reduction in human movement, leading to "unrest and dissatisfaction amongst the workers."[13] Laban-Lawrence Industrial Rhythms (LLIR) was their response. As the title suggests, LLIR stressed the fundamental importance of the inner impulse of rhythm (later effort) in motion, whether that was individual rhythm in movement or collective rhythm in teamwork. It brought together movement observation and notation with training.

Special methods of movement ethnography were deemed to yield "exact characteristics of the capacities needed for each job."[14] They could be used "for selection and assessment of effort" and "to determine the best cure for personal deficiencies."[15] Laban explains, "rhythm and the shape of a movement is what really matters, (. . .) speed and the overcoming of distances are no more than by products."[16] Movement is framed less in terms of its mechanics, nor as a mechanism to achieve an output, and rather, according to individualised rhythmical characteristics. Where TMS spotlighted the speed and quantity of movement, LLIR prioritised quality of movement, capturing its flow, energy, shape, rhythm, and grace. Deficiencies in documentational practice concurrently hindered the accurate assessment of movement in/efficiencies. The movement theorist writes, there has been "insignificant time" and energy given to developing techniques for recording movement "quickly and accurately."[17] Developing methods for assessing human effort graphically was paramount to the ultimate success of any movement observation technique. Yet surpassing these concerns was the complete "lack of appreciation of rhythm" in training.[18] Existing analysis failed because of its preoccupation with the type and quantity of movement, rather than its feel, quality, energy, and inner impulses. Rhythm for Laban was "the essential nature of movement."[19] Executing a task effectively depended on identifying and crucially training bodies in the *correct* rhythm. LLIR radically reconceptualised movement as the solution to efficiency and the production of competent bodies. The military appeal is evident.

On December 18th, 1945, Wing-Commander Winterbottom wrote to Laban-Lawrence to express his interest in the principles and results of LLIR and raised the question of its application for parachuting.[20] Correspondence between Laban-Lawrence and Sir John Slessor affirms the RAF's openness to novel partnerships in response to military training needs. Laban replied, "the present military requirements will demand a new form of physical and mental training and it occurred to me that some of the techniques which I have developed (. . .) may be applicable for this purpose."[21] Laban visited Ringway on February 25th, 1946. His *Visit to Ringway Aerodrome* report, reflects on three core elements. Foremost, he was invited to conduct movement observations of synthetic training and practical parachute jumping.[22] Evident here is Ringway's attempt to set out its accomplishments in the physiological dimensions of falling, demonstrating techniques of working on the body and the achievements of a competent drilled paratrooper for Laban to assess and preferably affirm. The second objective was to discuss with Squadron Leaders training methods in use, parachute jumping techniques, and the "proceeding methods of selection and training."[23] Here, the consideration is in outlining the pedagogy and theories shaping existing parachuting philosophy and possible points of intersection with other embodied systems and philosophies. The final, and most compelling objective was to report on "the technical and education implications" of "applying the LLIR methods of assessment and training to this job."[24] Ringway's open-mindedness to the theories and pedagogies of dance studies insinuates an awareness of its sub-standard knowledge in the field of human movement and willingness to calve out experimental spaces through which to fine tune its syllabus. A lacuna of knowledge was reiterated in September 1946, when Lawrence continued discussions with the future head of the RAF, Sir John Slessor. "Sir J. expressed his conviction that close order drill and P.T are important, but he thinks that new forms appropriate to the needs of a R.A.F squadron should be developed."[25] Barracks have been widely conceived as laboratories for bodily experimentation (Foucault 1977), but what this collaboration demonstrates is the multidisciplinary approaches imbued in military preparation. Spaces of military experimentation reiterate the need to take seriously liminal encounters and to trace the sophisticated knowledge and labour that goes into the art of war.

The remainder of the 1946 report charts out the application of movement ethnography, notation, and training for military parachuting. A follow-up report dated March 18th elucidates; "Laban came to the conclusion that there were quite a number of problems in selection and training in which we could offer some advice."[26] It is here that the contentious relationship between dance methods and militarism takes on profound direction.

## MOVEMENT ETHNOGRAPHY

Proficiency in movement for Laban foremost depended on establishing comprehensive knowledge of the moving body. Laban and Lawrence write, "the study of movement, motion, efforts and the activities of human (should) be of paramount interest to (. . .) those responsible for the effort and actions of others."[27] As producers of highly scripted movement, the military have long held a vested interest in studying human motion (Woodward 2000). Parachute training manuals detail the RAF's expanding knowledge of the mechanics and functionality of vertical movement. What it lacked, the dance theorist surmised, was the technical know-how for interpreting human motion. Instructors had prioritised making bodies at the expense of understanding the bodies produced. For the dance theorist, this pedagogic gap could be addressed through the combined science and art of ethnography.

Laban differentiated his movement ethnography by foregrounding problems with existing methods which he argued were expensive, distractive and time consuming.[28] TMS failed to capture the intricacies and complexities of motion, and their multiple variations. Laban's visit also noted the absence of a comprehensive approach to movement; one that did not study an individual act in isolation, but rather, the interconnected frameworks of aerial practices.

Discrete movement tasks needed to be analysed in conjunction with P.T, synthetic training, practical training, the wider body cultures nurtured at the aerodrome, and crucially, prior to selection. This was to recognise the cultural and temporal forces that shape subject formation. In response, Laban promoted thinking movement holistically, tracing the dynamic forces that shape bodies. LLIR was put forward as an effective technique of movement ethnography. It could offer "observations of all variants of movements and efforts" during training and practical jumping and could yield "exact characteristics of the capacities needed for each job."[29] Movement efficiency was the object of study, but its aim was efficiency of movement through the scientific study of the art of movement.

As instructors demonstrated parachuting technique, Laban concentrated his energies to showcasing his ethnography in practice, focusing on two components. Foremost were the *general movements* executed during a parachute exit, descent, and landing. That is to say, the quantitative features of movement. The 1946 report is a study of body parts moving, whether arms and head, or shoulders, elbows, and wrists.[30] Directionality of body parts in space is detailed, whether high, medium, or low. And the study traces duration of movement, including sustained body positionings. Although dismembering the body, Laban insisted upon interrelationships. Ethnographic observations recorded connections between body parts, such as spine alignment, as well as the initiation or sequencing of movement, such as an off-balance landing. Army P.T solidified recruits' physical fitness and Ringway's synthetic training programme had made noteworthy strides toward building aerial proficiency. Yet this success had been achieved at the expense of *knowing* the falling body. Laban's ethnographic intervention provided a statement about the general organisation of the body during the execution of multiple components of parachuting.

The second component stressed movement-effort relationships. Whereas the objective of observing general movement was to assess quantitative features of a parachute descent, effort highlighted its qualitative features. Apparent here are the dynamic structures of movement whilst falling. *Visit to Ringway Aerodrome* subdivides this into muscle conditions and movement. The former refers to the inner impulse, whether thought, feeling, or emotion from which movement originates. Effort patterns result from inner attitudes of accepting or resisting the physical conditions influencing movement, such as whether landing is accepted with a relaxed quality. It constitutes the mind-body connection. The latter concerned itself with the dynamic structures of movement, such as direct, flexible, sustained, or quick.[31] Laban's approach is marked by the premise that movement is dynamic, not static, and whereby all movement components (body, weight, flow, time, space) are interdependent. For Ringway, effort analysis foregrounded the various qualities of mind-body movement involved in elite aerial practices ("jibbing"). It also outlined possibilities for knowing bodies in radically new ways that had implication for movement intervention; "an effort is (. . .) a composite of elements which can be separately assessed, acquired and trained."[32] Qualitative characteristics of movement represented the missing step in bodily comprehension and were paramount to achieving parachuting efficiency.

Movement ethnography equally afforded practical solutions to improving bodies by making incorrect practices identifiable. "By trained observation it is possible to discover the optimum rhythms of any job or activity and whether or not a person (. . .) moves according to it." From such evidence "it can be stated where and how the fault arose, thereby enabling the investigator to correct it."[33] Greater knowledge of the body enabled for targeted interventions on it. Ethnography of movement equally had application for selection; "the knowledge of personal effort habits" facilitates instructors in the aerodrome with "selection methods before the trainees reach the aerodrome."[34] Laban offered a method for identifying those bodies most suited for the stresses and strains of vertical warfare. The implication was radical insomuch as it diverged from existing selection theories; "the psychological tests which might be excellent for general Army purposes are not applicable to such highly specialised psychological actions as indeed in parachute jumping. (. . .) the observations described in this report might be more adequate."[35]

Knowledge of what bodies do, how and when, was proposed as a contributable factor in achieving martial vertical efficiency. Ethnography could yield valuable insight into engrained faults prior to selection, or bodies ill-suited for vertical warfare, reducing wastage. To know the body was to establish the means and methods to work on it and to therefore assert power over it. Laban promoted an engagement with the embodied in profoundly new ways. But he also called for studying the body according to wider training regimes and body cultures. Bodies are not stable but iterated and practiced over time (Butler 2004). Parachute technique depended on strong bodily foundations, and ethnography provided a means to study, know, and target bodily deficiencies; "observations records would constitute valuable material for reflection and (. . .) which personal capacities are to be strengthened."[36] Laban handed RAF Ringway a technique for studying the myriad subjects and practices of military parachuting and the means to pinpoint interventions. Dance ethnography reveals how militaries have remained nimble to creative pedagogies and practices that further militarism in ways that may otherwise be difficult to trace.

## MOVEMENT NOTATION

Mastering aerial efficacy during parachuting was, for Laban, not only about the RAF *identifying* in/correct procedure during exit, descent, and landing, but also its ability to *record*, quickly and concisely, such actions. The purpose being the provision of a traceable chain of human behaviour. A written documentational account of the micro-bodily whilst falling was a prerequisite to achieving muscular automation and rhythmical efficiency. Wartime training saw the collation of photographic records of exit, and instructors were armed with loudspeakers at the dropping zone to describe incorrect landing practice.[37] However, for the movement theorist, this provided for an insufficiently complete record of the art of falling. They also failed to situate movement practices in relation to the environment in which it was executed, such as spatial pathways and patterns. Keen to extend his influence, Laban drew upon his ethnographic evidence to set out a systematic record of parachuting through his notation system. The results were attached as an appendix to his 6th March report and expressed the conviction that the "Laban Lawrence effort notation methods seems to us to be an integral part of the achievement of objective results of assessment."[38] Documenting the art of falling was to be of scientific standards, evidencing the *truth* about vertical mobility.

Unlike other systems of notation, the "written dance" that Laban had been devising dismembered body parts. Abstract symbols conveyed quantifiable anatomical features (legs, arms, head), alongside their direction and level (high, low, forward, back). Qualitative characterises such as straight, bending and stretching movements or tense, normal or relaxed quality could also be expressed. Each was recorded on a staff, that flattened the body out from the spine to convey its symmetry. For Ringway, Laban's appendix comprised a scientific, ready-to-use, transferable handbook of symbolic representation of human movement, capable of translating fleeting bodies into methodical, traceable, and crucially knowable format. He explains, the "provisional key of signs, extracted from our effort-alphabet" contain symbols "useful for the task at hand."[39] Endeavouring to solidify its military application, Laban provided simplified examples from parachuting-specific action, including the RAF's focal consideration of correct and dangerous landing position.

Mindful of the RAF's underlying efficiency agenda, section two of the appendix concentrated on the "danger points" commonly encountered by parachutists on impact. Misalignment of ankles, knees, and hips received particular attention. For Laban, injuries arose from the incorrect arrangement of body parts. Evident here is an alignment between martial integrity (injury-prevention) and Laban's capacity to record it efficiently. Broken bones were preventable if bad parachuting procedure could be recorded for subsequent analysis and intervention. Ringway were inevitably drawn to dance studies familiarity with falling and recovery techniques that absorbed body-to-earth impact. What also seems true is the artist's willingness to be relevant to the needs of militarism.

Airborne bodies could also be documented through notation. Atmospheric conditions including air currents were a reoccurring concern to those responsible for parachute instruction, and informed military parachute pedagogy.[40] Laban demonstrated how his written language of movement could incorporate external influences, reinforcing its position as an *applied* science. He reflects on "twists, turns or circular movements"[41] induced by environmental conditions, and the mechanisms through which individuals might assist in untwisting rigging lines. Full and half body turns, and isolated body parts turning in multiple direction ("turn head left and turn shoulders right")[42] exemplified the systems adaptability. What it also offered was a shorthand for recording the impact of environmental forces on bodies. Unlike photographic records that captured single movements in time, notation created a processual record, in which movement components (body, weight, flow, time, space) were shown to be interdependent; "Our symbols are variable," Laban explains, which "means changes in the level, extension, duration of the movement can be exactly recorded in a rhythmical form."[43] Notation captured an evolving picture of the dynamic falling body through vertical spacetimes.

The appendix explores the possibilities for recording "the dynamic qualities of movement" according to their "effort accents."[44] Progress in parachute training and performance became *evidencable* through repeated records. Notation recorded evolution in technique or continued errors over the three-week programme. Thus, once trained, parachute instructors would be able to cure efforts and movement habits or target weak points that required further training. Notation positioned injuries as no long unfortunate outcomes but determinable. It detailed where injuries would conceivably occur and recorded visually repeated bodily insufficiencies. Notation offered Ringway the evidence of movement training required to prevent bodily failures. Laban explains, "effort and movement habits can be *determined,* and changes of effort habits can be controlled and tabulated."[45] The application for the RAF was a systematic written account of the vulnerable body, and how it could be targeted, intervened with, and made more efficient.

Tabulated records of movement efforts and habits, collated throughout the training programme, were according to Laban, best stored as "personal control cards."[46] If introduced at selection, control cards would support instructors in their training, through a comprehensive record of individual practice over time. Movement data could, consequently, be used to fine-tune the physical components of training and identify those with the physical aptitudes to withstand landing impact. Control cards could serve as a record base of practice, evidencing the recruits' acquisition of the technique of falling. More prudently, it would display the RAF's achievement of an efficient technique of falling, absent of injuries. Notating parachuting procedure can be understood as a record of performance. But it was equally performative of aerial mastery.

Documentation methods derived from dance studies add complexity to the techniques and technologies mobilised to work on and conform bodies for warfare. Laban's notation endeavoured to scientifically write the dynamic body and offered procedures, derived from written evidence, for contributing to the embodied pursuit of aerial warfare. Foremost, it provided the written record for the translation and replication of a standardised aerial practice. Notation documented bodies moving, illustrating correct individual alignment and could extend to group formation. But it also provided the written evidence to support intervention in individual and collective bodily skill acquisition. Notation gave fleeting bodies representational substance, and thus RAF Ringway the means to choreograph bodies in airspace. Dance documentation deepens existing research into the complex physiological, analytical, and representational work that goes into making martial bodies. It illustrates how writing the body and working on it were intimately bound.

## MOVEMENT TRAINING

Movement ethnography increased understanding of the actions of falling bodies and notation helped to record aerial mobility. Epistemologically, they advantaged RAF Ringway's ability to know and write bodies. Still missing however, was appropriate movement training. Militaries have long contrived enterprising techniques to inscribe bodies with the physical and psychological attributes necessary to produce disciplined, well-trained soldiers for war (Newlands, 2014). Devising an efficient airborne training programme was a cornerstone in the Regiment's formation and Veal (2020) documents the experimental work that went into developing pseudo-operational training practices. Victory in Europe did not herald a step-back in this pursuit. Discussions between senior RAF figures reverberated calls to refine embodied training programmes for future military campaigns.

Following his February visit, Laban concentrated his creative energies to addressing the form of training interventions required. Pre-parachuting P.T and drill training produced physically fit bodies, and Ringway's synthetic syllabus familiarised bodies to gravitational forces and low-level body-to-earth encounters. Technically, bodies were proficient. They could execute the mechanics of movements required. Yet they lacked important rhythmical, qualitative features, specific to the *dynamic* stresses and strains of vertical mobility; including "the kind of effort which he does and its feel."[47] Quality of movement can be understood as the different gradations of energy used to perform a movement, whether sustained, swinging, suspended, or collapsed.

Extending the Gilbreths' work on efficiency, Laban proposed an integrated art of parachuting that placed rhythmical movement at the forefront. Even if paratroopers executed correct bodily positioning, from Laban's knowledge of movement, injuries could still materialise because of incorrect efforts or rhythms. He writes, "General effort training, where the men learn to master tension, directions, times used in movement in a conscious rhythmical sense, is strongly recommended."[48] "Conscious" movement is indicative of the imperative to engrain the physical act (e.g., exit) with the appropriate anatomical rhythm, effort, and intensity. Both needed to become instinctive for the paratrooper to react intuitively. *Notes for Meeting with Air Ministry* states; "suitable efforts can be conveyed, instilled and automised through exercises."[49]

Not content with detailing effort considerations, Laban also sketched-out tailored exercises that met the physical requirements of the falling body. His 1946 report confirmed the RAF's concern with strengthening muscles groups such as abdominal muscles, but it equally departed from this static approach, through foregrounding training of movement in sequences. Amongst his propositions was mobility of centre of gravity and elasticity training; "we will have to find suitable actions as, say, Free flow—running (. . .) along irregular stepping-stones (. . .) until their feel is automatised."[50] Free flow refers to the combination of control with agility, strength with flexibility. Further clarification is provided: "Training can be general or particular parts can be used to develop any special element of effort which is found lacking."[51] In contrast to military's long history of standardised training and collective practice, Laban encouraged greater consideration of the person. He argued that training needed to be tailored to singular weakness and therefore iterated on an individualised basis. "(B)y a suitable and methodical arrangement and combination of such efforts, certain qualities of the training can be developed. These arrangements can be built up according to the circumstances found during the observation period."[52]

Effort analysis radically recast martial bodies as different. Any threat to martial standardisation attributed to individual traits could therefore be solved by a tailor-designed training program in those efforts found lacking. Collective success in warfare has always depended on individuals, but Laban took this further through targeted interventions. He did not call for a radical overhaul so much as a synthesis of military and dance techniques. Dance movement training could be interwoven with the existing martial structures of governance; "immerged into the present form of drill."[53] Perhaps more problematically, he leveraged dance pedagogy and practice as capable of extending the physiological and the political parameters by which civilian bodies could be coopeted into becoming military subjects. If a man had the psychological aptitude to parachute, the body could be worked on until it was efficient. This had application for those selected, profoundly shifting existing recruitment discourse. Laban writes, "It is quite possible that men are turned down who would make good parachute jumpers."[54] Almost all bodies, if provided with the correct training, could become competent.

Laban's movement training also diverged from the RAF in terms of its structural considerations. While Ringway focused upon similar mediums of mobility—to jump, to roll—Laban conceived of parachuting as a fundamentally new form of movement; "to parachute is a new art. (. . .) A new form of locomotion has been found."[55] That the RAF was faced with a new art of movement, shaped by unknown rhythms, was not wholly unrecognised. But while Ringway applied known exercises to singular components of the art of falling, the dance artists viewed it as an interconnected choreography. "(T) he old form of drill and P.T. aims at precision in static movement positions (. . .) effort training places accent upon that which happens during action."[56] Motion training enables for the progression of rhythms in action, providing for efficiency in the initiation and transition between each movement and the continuation of efforts from one element to the next. Enhancing the body's capacity to parachute required training the body in *action.* Contrary to TMS, which examined phenomena in isolation, Laban's belief lay in a contextual understanding of movement principles (Cohen 2004). The result was, for the first time, to outline an integrated, fully choreographed procedure from aircraft exit to gathering parachute for immanent action, in one unified, replicable and, eventually, automised way. Laban's effort training *amalgamated* the RAF's micro-practices of exit, control, and landing to fine-tune the aerial body.

Motion training had implications for radically positioning aerial mobilities within the realms of the choreographic; an art of designing sequences of movements, of composing bodily forms, and applying repetition, canon, and variation to bodies. Aesthetic regimes have always been integral to the doing of war. But Laban's collaboration with the RAF is illustrative of the diverse creative knowledge, techniques, methods, and practices put to work in the pursuit of geopolitics. Individually and collectively, ethnography, notation, and movement training offered the pedagogic "know-how" to assess and offer recommendations on predefined micro-practices, thus targeting individual components of the body for its enhanced military application. Critical military scholars would benefit from a deeper understanding of the embodied and *embodying* micro-practices cultivated in response to geopolitical imperatives and the artful methods that comprise the art of war.

## CONCLUSION

Militaries have long embarked upon enterprising collaborations and adopted open approaches in war and peacetime, to address practical, technical, and pedagogic gaps in its knowledge. This chapter examined the litheness of the RAF in the aftermath of WWII to the creative knowledges, techniques, methods, and practices of dance studies. Despite Laban's troublesome relationship with statecraft during the rise of National Socialism, he continued to be nimble to militarism. The chapter demonstrated the movement theorist's enterprising response to the aerial training needs of the RAF, and the transferability of his theories of movement to vertical warfare. I traced his identification of movement ethnography, notation, and training as capable of supporting Ringway's pursuit of efficient vertical bodies. Much was perceived to have value. Following Laban's visit, Slessor recommended the limited implementation of a dance-based approach with "R.A.F apprentices"—boys aged around sixteen; "best during 2 consecutive weeks from morning to evening, after which my questions as to the introduction of new training methods should be made."[57] Although limited, it necessitates taking seriously the solicitation of the arts in the service of the state, but also of individual artists nimbleness to statecraft. Both tell us much about the relationship between power, cultural and the body. Two key implications are at stake.

First, I caution for sustained scholarly enquiries into the historical geographies of military coercion and enterprising solicitation of artists in the service of statecraft. Geopolitics operate at thresholds. Betwixt spaces are valued because they are experimental, ambiguous, and temporary. Laban's collusion in militarism exemplifies the contested liminal encounters that emerge at times of great need. But liminal spaces are also carved out precisely because of their experimental possibilities. Taking this example of a dance-military encounter, liminality seems to capture much about the messy in-between spaces and ambiguous power relations that characterise geopolitical phenomena. Critical geopolitics has yet to fully capture the contingency of geopolitical forces and relations, despite growing analysis of the entangled geographies of the everyday and geopolitical processes (Brickell, 2015; Pain 2015). Liminality might enrich understanding of the relationship between art, militarism and the geopolitical and provide an important conceptual language for critical military studies. While celebrating art's provocative capacity, we must remain critical of the enterprising efforts of militaries to co-opt artists and their methods, and equally, artists willingness to be agile to military needs.

Second, militaries' readiness to employ artistic knowledges and practices raises questions of bodily labour in practicing creative methods for military studies research. The arts play an important role in examining the experiences of military personnel and for responding to the horrors of warfare. But now, more than ever, we must reflect critically on how our own labours may support military practices or agendas. One element of this may be the services we offer up by working alongside and in collaboration with military personnel, institutions, and networks. Another might be the knowledges, methods, and skills we purposefully or subconsciously produce, transferable to military contexts, as with Laban's ethnography and notation system. But it also requires taking seriously the emotional labour that accompanies the doing of this work. Such work is emotionally fraught and strenuous. As critical military scholars, we must engage critically with what these methods can and do "do" in the context of military research, but also what they may enable. Asking these questions might radically redraw the parameters by which we assess such methods and apply them to future military scholarship.

# 4

# All Things Bright and Beautiful the Lord Bomb Made Them All[1]

## *More than Human Creativity and the Cyborg Geology of Nuclear Weapon Design*

*Michael Mulvihill*

### SOUTHWEST NEW MEXICO

One and a half million years ago, the Valles Caldera in Southwest New Mexico formed from a series of violent volcanic eruptions that occurred over a period of a hundreds of thousand years. The eruptions caused the surface of the earth to collapse into a vast magma chamber, spewing lava and ash over the landscape to form the geomorphology of Southwest New Mexico as known today.[2] On the northern edge of the caldera is the Jemez Mountain range and the peak called Cerro Padernal, which overlooks the settlement Abiquiu. This is where, from her studio window, artist Georgia O'Keeffe attempted to capture the flat knife-like summit of Pedernal in paint on canvas. O'Keeffe believed it to be her own "private mountain" and if she painted it enough times, then God said she could have it, even though the Pueblo people had used the slopes of Pedernal for thousands of years to manufacture tools and hunting weapons (Lynes, Poling Kempes and Turner 2005, 80). Then looking south through O'Keeffe's studio window, hidden behind the blue ranges of the Jemez Mountains is Los Alamos, home of the Los Alamos National Laboratory, one of two nuclear weapon design and production plants that maintain the United States' stockpile of nuclear weapons. It is also the production site of the world's first nuclear bombs used in anger against the cities of Hiroshima and Nagasaki. The bombs were built under the direction of physicist Robert Oppenheimer, who, following their detonation, likened himself to a passage from the Bhagavad-Gita, stating that he had become "Death, the destroyer of worlds."[3]

Georgia O'Keeffe and Robert Oppenheimer seldom share a written history.[4] Yet O'Keeffe's art practice and the nuclear weapon designer's work both took place within the solitude and isolation that resulted from the volcanic geology of the Valles Caldera. However, this chapter will not be a comparative account that attempts to draw a common thread between creative tendencies of the artist O'Keeffe or physicist Oppenheimer. Rather, I want to diverge from a common notion of creativity as a quality of individual human genius or human expression. The story I want to tell will be from the point of view of the actual matter and more-than-human creative forces that have shaped the environment of Southwest New Mexico. Here, the artist and nuclear physicist were interacting parts of a wider geological and social assemblage that spanned eons and encompassed all scales of matter from the subatomic to the vast open space of Southwest Mexico.

By decoupling creativity from ideals of individual genius and sovereign human expression, I want to show how attention to how creative practice offers new ways of making visible the flows and turbulences of more-than-human forces that shape our social worlds and constitutes geopolitical events.[5] To do this I will draw upon my own creative "art" practice, which charted the flows, metamorphic creative variations, and convergence between the embodied process of art making and the sociologies of nuclear weapon manufacturer (Mulvihill 2019). I situate my practice in the material philosophies of Rosi Braidotti, Manuel DeLanda, Gilles Deleuze and Felix Guattari, and Donna Haraway, who posit the possibility of more-than-human creativity as a force that shape social worlds. From this starting point I will describe how insights gained about the social production of nuclear weapons emerged from hands-on experience of creative activity involved in making the artwork *MM-w76-FTLP-012017* (2016–2017) (Figure 4.1). These will frame an account of the more than human forces that drew Georgia O'Keeffe and Robert Oppenheimer into volcanic geomorphology of Southwest New Mexico, to constitute a cyborg politics of nuclear war and weapons (Haraway 1991).

In this chapter, notions of what are understood as spaces that are occupied by artists, scientists and military are put into contention. By using creative activity to investigate and synthesise practices of nuclear weapon production, I show how the boundaries of military industrial complexes, such as LANL, are perhaps more porous than are commonly understood. I argue that nuclear and military complexes are, in part, constituted by more than human affects and material intensities, which are not detected by conventional objective and analytical approaches. Ultimately creative practice-based thinking provides new ways of thinking about how bio-political, or cyborg political, power coalesces and flow between social and nuclear worlds. That seeks to draw nuclear weapons out of specialist debates of STEM and International Relations and reveal how they intersect with politics of embodied experience.

## MORE THAN HUMAN CREATIVITY

In *one thousand years of non-linear history,* Manuel DeLanda observes "human history did not follow a straight line, as if everything [or anyone] pointed towards [an] ultimate goal. On the contrary, at each bifurcation alternative [. . .] states were possible, and once actualized, they coexisted and interacted with one another" (DeLanda 2000, 16). For the past thirty years there has been an increasing emphasis upon non-representational, relational, and material-based theories to account for social phenomena. These approaches have often emanated from the work of philosophers Gilles Deleuze and Felix Guattari, in particular their works *Anti-Oedipus: Capitalism and Schizophrenia* (1972) and *A Thousand Plateaus* (1980), where they introduce the notion of assemblages. DeLanda in *Assemblage Theory* explains that assemblages are complex arrangements of matter composed of interacting material and energy, which are in a perpetual state of building and transformation and constitute our physical and social environment (2016). An upshot of this material and transformative ontology is that abstraction such as the distinction between nature and culture or notions of transcendent objectivity cannot actually exist outside of the materiality that forms the universe.

To navigate this ontology of materiality and change, New Materialist thinking positions creativity as a key to understanding the way matter shapes reality, but also the multiple variations and possibilities of reality that matter can produce. For this reason, philosopher Rosi Braidotti thinks that creativity has potential as a methodology for breaking regimes of representation that police and reproduce certain patterns of thought and repressive social construction. This offers an escape from what Braidotti terms the melancholic post-structural linguistic discourses that offer no line of escape for subjects trapped by immovable textual master codes. Braidotti explains that thinkers such as Judith Butler or Jacques Derrida omit to understand that the universe is not made of human language alone. Rather, language is an effect of matter and more-than-human process that constantly remake social worlds through material turbulence (Braidotti 2011, 3). Philosopher Christoph Cox, drawing upon the writings of Friedrich Nietzsche, observes that human symbolic life is only a single instance of multitudes of transformation taking place throughout nature. Cox quotes Nietzsche when stating that matter itself is "creative and transformative without external agency, a ceaseless becoming and overcoming that temporarily congeals into forms and beings only to dissolve them back into the natural flux, an eternal self-creating and self-destroying monster of force" (Cox 2018, 26).

Each ceaseless becoming and creative transformation leaves a trace, which leads DeLanda to state that every structure that forms reality, whether animal, plant, human language, social organisation, or mountain range, are the products of concrete historically constituted processes (DeLanda 2000, 11). In *Anti-Oedipus,* Deleuze and Guattari explain that these emergent spatial and temporal interactions form complex schemas of crisscrossed and overlapping axes and thresholds that assemble reality and constitute all kinds of lived experience (1972,19). For DeLanda, this elaborate non-linear schema evades top-down definition and analysis because it is in a constant state of emergence and formation. DeLanda explains that schema becomes visible in synthesis and production by creative activity (2011, 18). For Braidotti, creative synthesis has the potential to reveal, "the concrete yet complex materiality of bodies immersed in social relationships of power" (Braidotti 2011, 21). This is a particular kind of power structure that theorist Donna Haraway calls cyborg politics, which will be discussed shortly in this chapter.

Consequently, a new materialist creativity places at stake the traditional position of an artist as a sovereign genus giving form and meaning to inert and meaningless matter. Instead, the artist's skills and ability to manipulate materials such as paint, clay, or charcoal are deployed as synthetic methodologies to actualise the criss-cross schema of intensive forces that produce material reality (Voss 2013). Writer Jean Fisher explains, "If there is a uniqueness in the artist expression it is in the particular assemblages [they] consciously and unconsciously construct in the selection and organisation of sources" (2003, 223). In the next section, I want to discuss how I used creative practice as a methodology that selected sources and constructed assemblages that made visible the affects and complex social schema produced by nuclear weapon manufacture. The creative research under discussion in the following section took place during my three-year PhD research, which set out to use creative practice to explore a notion that nuclear weapons are socially productive. The result was an artwork known as *MM-w76-FTLP-012017* (2016–2017) (Figure 4.1). Through the process of making, the artwork produces new insights into how the W76 trident warhead assembles new variations of reality.

## A1 (M) AND THE COUNTY DURHAM WEAPON COMPLEX

The impetus to use creative practice as a way of investigating how nuclear weapons can socially produce came from number of experiences and sources.[6] However, a key intellectual drive came because of resonances I encountered between two statements. The first by sociologist of technology Langdon Winner, who stated in 1980 that because of the danger posed even by the management of nuclear weapons, their social structure must be centrally controlled and closed from unpredictable external interaction. He emphasised, "The internal social structure must be authoritarian there is no other way" (1980, 131). However, because of the vast geographies that the nuclear weapon enterprise encompasses, that includes swaths of government procurement, science and technology research, and innovation, as well as the labour that is globally mobilised for their production (Alexis-Martin 2019). This led me to think that the social structure of nuclear weapons must somehow become external and impress into everyday life. The second was by critical theorist Paul Virilio, who wrote that "while the stockpiling of [nuclear] weapons that will doubtless never be used is considered by the uninitiated to be an act of madness, in military eyes is not an aberration, its magic is precisely to be without any justification, to have no other reason or existence than to be brandished and qualified in public" (1988, 9).

At the time I first read Virilio's statement, it struck me as being interchangeable with a certain view of art, that art's own existence is justification enough.[7] While the intricacies of this point of view are not under discussion here, for me at the time it raised the possibility that materialities that exist in differently defined social spaces are interchangeable, and creative practice offered a possibility to explore how they connect.

*MM-w76-FTLP-012017* (2016–2017) (Figure 4.1) started with a photograph of technicians at Los Alamos National Laboratories (LANL) performing stockpile stewardship activities on the United States' W76 nuclear warhead.[8] The technicians are dressed in regular dark blue coveralls and the workshop where the warheads is being handled was arranged with similar kinds of equipment, such as lathes and pillar drills, which are found in the metal workshops in the Department of Fine Art at Newcastle University. This suggested a material connection could be established between the two workshops, which are usually defined as being distinct. The image also told me that there is more to a nuclear weapon than lethal radioactive parts that are re-represented in popular imagination. Crucially the image suggested that the non-lethal parts such as the outer casing of the warhead could be actualised with the tools in the fine art workshop itself. For me this was a way of

**Figure 4.1 Michael Mulvihill *MM-w76-FTLP-012017 (2016–2017)* Walnut, Bronze, Wood, 3D print, Charcoal, Smoke Glaze Ceramic, Beech..**

avoiding producing a symbolic re-representation of W76, but rather produce an artefact that materially bridges the two spaces (Mulvihill 2019).

I used the photograph to deduce the W76 warhead proportions, which were used to make a digital model, then a 3D-print. This process offered a way of mass-producing the artefact. However, the warheads took over eight hours to print, and the printers were prone to blocking halfway through the process. Workshop technician Burnie Burns thought that the conical shape of the warheads lent themselves to mass-production by slip casting in clay from a plaster mould. Burnie suggested making a new wooden warhead to produce the slip casting moulds. The wooden warhead was produced from the same digital 3D model. This time the warhead artefact was milled from a block of beech using a computer numerical control (CNC) router. The wooden warhead was polished to a high finish with bee's wax that would allow it to be released from the plaster casting mould.[9]

I cast twenty-six warheads that underwent an initial biscuit firing in an electric kiln at 1180 degrees centigrade. They were different from the W76 depicted in the photograph at Los Alamos. They were a tenth of the size of the W76 and made of clay, which been transformed into a bone white ceramic by the firing process. Yet they retained some material connection to warheads by the processes and tools that actualised them. The fact that they exist made both the art and weapon workshop strange (Mills 1959). The question for me at the time was where next for these shrunken odd, anaemic, and peculiarly bodily forms.

I had a notion to lava glaze the warheads, but industrial ceramicist Helen Brown said that unless I intend to drink from them then that technique seemed too complex for what I needed.[10] Helen thought that fire glazing was more appropriate for my purposes. She explained that fire glazing was an ancient technique, used many cultures throughout history. Materials such as dung, fat, and blood used as fuel and glazing agents, which are burnt in a shallow pit with the ceramics, although a cardboard box filled with sawdust and the glazing agents would work. There is no control over the glazing process, instead the glazing patterns are shaped by the fire and smoke in the pit. However, the warhead artefact could be polished to a very high sheen with a smooth pebble. The bodily materiality of the glazing agents evoked grim imagery from W.G. Sebald's *A Natural History of Destruction*, which describes how rescue crews working during the strategic bombing of Dresden in 1945, "slipped and slid" on the fat rendered from the bodies of those caught in the firestorms (1999). In doing so, the glazing agent actualises the bio-political dimensions of nuclear weapons that fix bodies in space under a threat of unimaginable violence and death (Mulvihill 2019, 175).

The packing and preparation of the warheads for fire glazing was done in my studio at Newcastle University. This involved placing the warheads, which had been soaked in full fat milk and blood meal fertilizer into a cardboard box filled with sawdust. I drove the warheads by car to the pit-firing site established in a remote woodland. The fire glazing could not take place on university estates, so a suitably remote site needed to be found outside the gaze of institutional regulation. A colleague who owned a small area of mixed woodland in County Durham provided this site. The site was remote, but within easy drive of the university, and partially along the same route used to transport the UK's W76 trident warheads. Two sets of firing took place at this site, and neither were a complete success in that the glazing agents did not reach the temperature to undergo chemical transformation. Yet what came out of the fire, once polished, became something quite different and strange. In appearance, touch, smell, and taste, the warhead was more like an animal horn or tusk but retaining the digital patterning from the original digital 3D file and CNC milling. The crisscrossed and overlapping axes that actualise sources from which the warheads were assembled were impressed into their surface like fossils. This unsettling conglomerate evoked the "blasphemy" of Donna Haraway's Cyborg, as the warhead artefact did not follow the conventional aesthetics that code human reality into binaries such as nature and culture, or art studio and weapon workshop (Haraway 1985). A new and unsettling organic, mineral, and technical hybrid, or cyborg, had emerged from the fire, redrawing distinctions between technology and animal, and revealing what Haraway terms a new kind of political agent. Haraway explains:

> The cyborg skips the step of original unity, of identification with nature in the Western sense. This is its illegitimate promise that might lead to subversion of its teleology as Star Wars. [Strategic Defence Initiative] [. . .] modern war is a cyborg orgy, coded by C3I, command–control–communication–intelligence, an $84 billion item in 1984's US defence budget [. . .] the cyborg [is] a fiction mapping our social and bodily reality and as an imaginative resource suggesting some very fruitful couplings. Michel Foucault's biopolitics is a flaccid premonition of cyborg politics. (Haraway 1991 149).

This view obliterates textual, hylomorphic, and, for Haraway, patriarchal assumptions that nature is merely inert matter that exist to be shaped and given meaning by a transcendent mind. Haraway writes that "the cyborg would not recognize the Garden of Eden, it is not made of mud or returns to dust." Neither "do [cyborgs] remember the cosmos." Instead, the "natural world" and techno-scientific structures, while differentiated, are configurations of the same matter, producing, and synthesising independently of human mind. Haraway considers the cyborg as the "illegitimate offspring" between the military industrial complexes of advanced capitalism and the more-than-human forces that are forever reshaping the world (1991, 151).

Therefore, politics of Haraway's cyborg encompasses vastly more elaborate and extensive spatial and temporal domains than Foucault's biopolitics, which is only attentive to human bodies and the space-time they occupy. Instead, cyborg politics is a multi-scaled schema that enmeshes bodies in more-than-human social relationships of power, formed from assemblages of geology, energy, and historical juncture. In the next section, I will position the W76 warhead depicted in the photograph of stockpile stewardship, in relationship to geomorphologies that produced the conditions for the construction of Los Alamos National Laboratories. Los Alamos not only designed and built the W76 but also created the world's first nuclear weapons during World War II. By looking beyond the human minds that built the bomb at Los Alamos, I want to show how the creative methodologies, such as those I used to produce my variation of the W76, can inform a way of thinking that seeks to reveal the mechanism and schemas of the cyborg politics. In this case, I explore those more-than-human forces that played their part in constituting LANL and affected the artistic inhabitants of Southwest New Mexico.

## W76

The W76 warhead entered service with the US Navy in 1978. The weapon was commissioned in 1973 and designed by LANL and Sandia National Laboratory in Sante Fe, New Mexico, for use on the Trident Submarine

Launched Ballistic Missile (SLBM). The missile can carry twelve independently targeted warheads but under current arms treaties its payload is restricted to eight warheads.[11] The W76 is a two-staged thermonuclear weapon, where a fission bomb, like the one used against Nagasaki during World War II, is used to ignite a secondary device containing fusion fuel of lithium-6 and deuteride contained in a uranium jacket. The original design yield of the W76 was one hundred kilotons and used to fix large military complexes, such as airfields and depots, under threat. From the beginning of the twenty-first century, the W76 weapon underwent a Life Extension Programme that extended the weapon's operational life from twenty to sixty years. The programme also included innovation in the W76 fuzing components that increases the weapon's accuracy and makes it effective against hard targets such as command bunkers and ICBM silos.[12] In 2019, a new low-yield variant of the warhead rolled off the production line at the Pantex nuclear weapon assembly facility in Texas.[13] The weapon, commissioned by the Trump administration in response to their Nuclear Posture Review, is the first new nuclear weapon produced by the United States since President George H W Bush halted production at the end of the Cold War in 1992.

During the Cold War, the United States manufactured approximately 70,000 nuclear warheads of more than seventy different types (Reis *et al.* 2017). The endeavour produced a vast industrial complex that spanned the entire United States and at its height employed over one hundred thousand workers. The cost of the nuclear weapon enterprise from its beginning in 1940 until disbarment efforts that begun in the mid-1990s is thought to be a minimum of $5.5 trillion.[14] Victor H. Reis, the architect of the US post–Cold War Stockpile Stewardship programme, writes that at heart of this complex were two "fiercely competitive nuclear weapon design laboratories" (2017, 47). These were Lawrence Livermore National Laboratory (LLNL), established in 1952, and Los Alamos National Laboratory, established in 1943 to design and build the world's first nuclear weapons that destroyed the cities of Hiroshima and Nagasaki (2017). LANL under the directorship of physicist Robert Oppenheimer was the central hub of the Manhattan Project, which mobilised the military, academic, and industrial into a weapon making assemblage.

## THE MANHATTAN PROJECT

Geographer and photographer Trevor Paglen describes that the Manhattan Project as an invisible geography that grew from temporary offices in a New York City skyscraper on 270 Broadway established in June 1942. The hidden geography rapidly expanded across the country, establishing a network of engineering and processing factories of which LANL was the central design and manufacture plant (2009). In 1942 Los Alamos was no more than a remote boy's ranch school on top of the Pajarito Plateau, which was attended by sons of wealthy Detroit Industrialist. The plateau is a vast elongated mesa on the edge of the Valles Caldera in Southwest New Mexico. The plateau had been formed over a period of a million years by pyroclastic flows made of clouds of incandescent ash and molten rock rapidly moving away from explosive eruptions created by the Jemez Mountain range collapsing into an immense magma chamber beneath the earth's crust.

Author Lesley Poling-Kempes writes that to understand the geology of New Mexico is to understand the people who live within it. She explains that New Mexico is not "a static backdrop for the story of its people. The landscape, and the geophysical forces that have created and continue to re-create it, is the story of New Mexico" (Lynes, Poling-Kempes and Turner 2005, 78). Later in the passage she evokes Nietzsche's idea of nature's more than human creativity when describing the Rio Grande valley as "the very floor of the world is cracked open [. . .] that may in a few million years from now help to split North America in two" (2005). She states that Southwest New Mexico is a burnt land, a place that carries the marks of a fire-and-brimstone birth (2005).

A history of fire and brimstone in New Mexico moved into a cybernetic phase when, in the winter of 1942, the ranch school and the plateau it sat upon was chosen as the site for LANL by leader of the Manhattan Project Lieutenant Leslie Groves and physicist Robert Oppenheimer (Smith and Weiner 1980, 238). Oppenheimer first visited the Pajarito Plateau in 1922 when he was eighteen. He was spending the summer in New Mexico with friends, while recovering from illness before commencing studies in chemistry at Harvard University (Cassidy 2005, 61). Oppenheimer was the son of a wealthy Manhattan family who were prominent collectors of Modern Art. His father, Julius Oppenheimer, had made his fortune as a textile importer. His mother, Ella Friedman, was an accomplished painter, who had studied the French Impressionist in Paris before teaching art at Barnard College, New York. Between Ella and Julius, the family acquired a collection of French Post-Impressionist and Fauvist landscape paintings. By the time Oppenheimer was a young man, the collection included significant Modernist paintings by Edouard Vuillard, André Derain, and Vincent Van Gogh (Bird and Weiner 2009, 12). During this summer in New Mexico, Oppenheimer lived around the artistic communities of Taos and Sante Fe in the company of writer Paul Horgan and literary scholar Francis Fergusson (Smith and Weiner 1995, 8).[15]

Oppenheimer showed no drive to capture New Mexico in paint or literature, but he was drawn into, and spiritually sustained, by the landscape and had become an expert horse rider. One day he and a group of friends took packhorses from a village called Frijoles to the west of the Rio Grande. Ascending three thousand meters to the Pajarito Plateau, they rode through scented pine forest crossing the interior of the Valles Caldera and the remnants of the Jemez Mountain. Eventually, the group came across a canyon that took its name from the cottonwood trees that grew there; Los Alamos. Physicist Emilio Segré described the land as a "beautiful and savage country" that contained in its volcanic geomorphology patches of grazing meadows cut through by dense pine and juniper forests (1995, 28). The sensorial intensities of the Pajarito Plateau, the shimmering heat, pine scent, and hum of insects may have evoked the wild Fauvist landscapes of Oppenheimer's family's Post-Impressionist art collection.[16] Oppenheimer fell in love with landscapes of New Mexico. But, this love cast an ominous shadow formed from the "Fauvist" landscapes of Los Alamos and the world destroying techno-military-complex of the Manhattan Project.[17]

## CYBORG MOUNTAIN

The landscape that Oppenheimer fell for pulled another artistic inhabitant from Manhattan to New Mexico. The famed Modernist painter Georgia O'Keefe was drawn to the scared and bruised landscape. From 1929, O'Keeffe divided her time between New Mexico and New York City. She spent summer in New Mexico and in the winter returned to life amongst New York City social elite. In 1934, acting on the advice of David McAlpine, investment banker and grandnephew of John D. Rockefeller, O'Keeffe established a studio at Ghost Ranch run by Brownie and Arthur Pack at Abiquiu that sits on the northern edge of the Jamez Mountain range. Here the artist could work away from "unwanted interruptions and social calls" in a carefully curated solitude (Poling-Kempes 2005, 107). Following the death of her husband, the gallerist and Modernist photographer Alfred Stieglitz, in 1949, O'Keeffe moved to New Mexico permanently.

Like Oppenheimer's expedition to Los Alamos during the summer of 1922, O'Keeffe's painting practice involved a deep immersion in the intensities and sensoria of the landscape where she was exposed and responded to the more than human creativities of nature. Her painting practice incorporated weeklong hikes or packhorses rides deep into the countryside, or travel in a Model A Ford that O'Keeffe had converted into a mobile studio (2005, 109). Carolyn Kastner, curator at the Georgia O'Keeffe Museum in Santa Fe, said O'Keeffe used the converted studio to protect her from the intensity of the afternoon desert sun, and bees that would eventually seek her out and force her to take refuge in the car studio. By late afternoon the heat inside the car forced O'Keeffe to abandon work altogether and return home.[18] Even in the solitude of the desert, O'Keeffe could not escape the more than human disturbances that inevitably influenced her painting practice.

In her home at Ghost Ranch, O'Keeffe commissioned a studio that had incorporated a window that spanned an entire wall, and looked out over the desert towards the Jemez Mountain range. Central in O'Keeffe's field of view was Cerro Padernal, one of the most recognised peaks in the world because O'Keeffe re-created it in paint on canvas over and over. Padernal is distinctive in O'Keeffe's painting because of its anvil-like flint top summit. Unlike its sister peaks in the Jamez Mountain Range it was not a volcano. The mountain was shaped by material erosion and its distinct narrow top is the result of a hard basalt cap. Just as the wild landscape of the Pajarito Plateau reached out to Oppenheimer, Padernal reached out and shaped O'Keeffe. Luce Irigaray observed in her essay *To Paint the Invisible* (2004) "my inner space is thus, for various reasons modified by things and even more by others, whom I encounter," which exceeds traditional Western economies of representation and possession (Irigaray 2004, 394). Despite O'Keeffe's claim upon Padernal, and also like Haraway's cyborg, or the bees that disturbed her work in the desert, the mountain and the forces that created it did not recognise the solitary genius, nor the meaning and identity given by the gaze of O'Keeffe. In reality and following Irigaray, O'Keeffe's paintings were assemblages of Padernal, a cyborg mountain that could not recognise the artist's possessing gaze.

In actuality, and for centuries the Pueblos people have known Pedernal as Tsiping, or the Flint Topped Mountain. Its slopes are covered in flint stone, which over millennia was a valued tool and hunting weapon manufacturer (Lynes, Poling-Kempes and Turner 2005, 80). Archaeologist Alice Gorman argues that places like Padernal accumulate human meaning because of technologies, such as stone axes, produced at these sites. These artefacts required complex planning procedures in order to secure raw materials such as wood for handles, tree resin and animal fat to make adhesives, resources for fire, and stone to make cutting edges (Gorman 2021, 24). For Gorman, and as seen in the cases of O'Keeffe, Oppenheimer and my warhead artefacts, humans are in a perpetual cyborg relationship with their more-than-human environment, combining biological components with the technical innovations. At Pedernal, millennia of flint weapon-making evolved as design and construction of nuclear weapons began at nearby Los Alamos and incorporated centuries of Pueblo skills and innovation in a cybernetic schema.

## BLACK CERAMIC

Construction of the bomb at Los Alamos drew in labour from the surrounding population of New Mexico including painter Popovi Da, or Red Fox. Popovi Da was the son of celebrated ceramicist Maria Martinez. Maria had revived and innovated the Pueblo black ceramic, a highly burnished black glaze pottery that had fallen into decline at the beginning of the twentieth century. Producing the black ceramic pots was an intense process and emerged after a prolonged period of experimentation. The firing technique that Martinez developed took days and she was assisted by her husband Julian Martinez and children including Popovi. Martinez placed pots in a fire pit during the early morning on a calm day when the wind would not interfere with the fire in the pit. The pit was fuelled with cow dung and the kiln assembly was covered with a sheet of aluminium to reduce oxygen, causing a chemical reaction in the clay that turned the pots black. The Martinez black ceramic was highly sought after by major museums such as the Metropolitan Museum of Art, New York, and the Smithsonian Institute, Washington, DC. Scientists of the Manhattan Project such as Enrico Fermi also intensely collected Maria Martinez Blackware ceramics, who like Oppenheimer posed an aesthetic as well as scientific view of the world.[19] Other scientific and aesthetic intersection are also borne out by the fact that Maria's son, the painter and ceramists, Popovi Da, started working at LANL in 1944, and therefore had a significant role in the successful detonation of the weapon. [20]

Popovi Da was drafted into the Manhattan Project as a solider in the US Army's Special Engineering Detachment (SED). SED recruits did not have formal education in the sciences but did possess scientific and technical skills that could support the Manhattan Project. At Los Alamos Popovi Da was a machinist working in the Electrostatic Generator Group (EGG). This group investigated neutron yields produced by fission of plutonium 239 atoms, which was key to determine how much, and what combination of material was needed to make the bomb explode. Because of this work, Popovi was also involved in preparing the test device known as the Gadget at the Trinity test at White Sands, Alamogordo, NM. The nuclear core of the gadget was composed of two hemispheres of plutonium 239 that had been alloyed with gallium to make the metal more workable and less brittle. The plutonium hemisphere surrounded a sphere of polonium. This fitted into a machined cylinder of uranium 238 that slotted into a ball of the same material, jacketed in boron and aluminium. The assemblage was surrounded by high explosives that would implode the core to criticality initiating a fission reaction and causing a nuclear explosion.

The Gadget was detonated on top of a thirty-meter tower at 05:29 on the morning of 16th July 1945. The inhabitants of the Jemez Mountain area reported seeing the sun rise and suddenly set, while others in the town of Gallup, NM reported their window frames cracked by the shockwave travelling away from the explosion (Poling-Kempes 2005, 160). At the test site, the explosion had briefly illuminated the surrounding mountains in a lurid purple and green light that transformed into an orange ball of fire (Feynman 1992, 135). The explosion had created an eighty meter crater and melted the desert silica, which cooled into green, radioactive crystal called trinitite. A new kind of cyborg geology emerged, this time in the fire and brimstone of a nuclear explosion.

The remarkable aspect of this account of Popovi Da is the way the story "criss-crosses" with my own account of making and pit-firing clay simulacra of LANL's W76 warhead in the woods of County Durham. Popovi Da was primarily a ceramicist assisting his mother Maria Martinez producing her sought after Blackware ceramic. Yet his technical and artistic skills became adapted into the Manhattan Project and formed part of a nuclear weapon cyborg assemblage. Through creative practice, we are able to look through semiotic inscriptions that delineate reality into meaningful domains. We able to sense and synthesis material processes and more than human forces that are perpetually at work producing worlds and reconfiguring reality. For my own part insight into the extent and production of the nuclear weapon cyborg assemblage emerged from the taste and smell of the clay warheads being fired in a clearing of a remote pine wood. As with Oppenheimer's first encounter with Los Alamos, creative methods open the possibility of making visible, what DeLanda called, the ceaseless becoming of more-than-human processes that are also involved in the production of socio-technical environments and nuclear worlds.

## CONCLUSION

A month after the atomic bombings of Hiroshima and Nagasaki, O'Keeffe painted *Pelvis Series Red with Yellow* (1945), a painting dominated by a brilliant yellow orb. Art historian Sasha T. Scott attributes the painting to the impression left by Trinity upon O'Keeffe. Scott argues that the effect of nuclear weapons manufacture in New Mexico is implicit in the artist's work after Los Alamos became public knowledge, following the nuclear attacks upon Japan (2019, 106). As the end of World War II blurred into the Cold War, new nuclear weapon technologies emerged from Los Alamos. During the 1950s, thermonuclear weapons were developed that released thousands of times more energy than the bombs used against Hiroshima and Nagasaki. The launch of Sputnik 1 by a Soviet ICBM demonstrated that nuclear weapons could be placed in orbit to strike anywhere on Earth with little or no warning. Georgia O'Keeffe became anxious that Los Alamos, and Southwest New Mexico would be subjected to a future Soviet nuclear bombardment.[21] In 1960, O'Keeffe had a nuclear fallout shelter constructed in her garden, which she kept stocked with food and provisions in preparation for the aftermath of World War III.[22] In public, O'Keeffe explained that after the nuclear war she would emerge from her shelter to paint the transformed and radioactive New Mexico landscape. Yet even in this defiant comment O'Keeffe could not escape the cyborg politics of nuclear weapons and the assemblages that were reshaping the world.[23]

In telling this story, I have tried to show that creativity is not the sole preserve of an individual human genius. Rather creativity should be thought of as material processes, interactions and transformation, which constitute realities that include but extend far beyond human experience. These form social relationships formed out of more than human of creative processes and intensities of the ever-emerging volcanic landscape of Southwest New Mexico, or the nuclear forces that produced the first trinitite in the Alamagordo desert on the morning of the 16th July 1945. The trinitite is an artefact of interactions between complex assemblages that combine self-creating and self-destroying forces of natural flux with military techno science. It is a manifestation of a cyborg politics that Haraway argues exceeds Foucault's biopolitics because its scope is more than human, and is not easily apprehended by conventional analytical approaches.

On the other hand, the processes that constitute cyborg politics can be made visible by creative, synthetic, or productive methodologies, which I demonstrated in the production of my artwork *MM-w76-FTLP-012017* (2016–2017). As a result of this creative work the power of nuclear military industrial complexes are reframed in terms of a cyborg politics, which suspend human inscription of artistic and military into delineated space. Instead, we begin to understand each of them as being composed of complex intersections of matter. Consequently, creative approaches such as I describe in this chapter widen the view on how and how far military nuclear power extends beyond the conventional understanding of the domain through which they operate. It shows that the nuclear weapon complex operates very much through social domains, which they shape and are shaped by. Using creative methods to reconfigure our understanding of nuclear weapons is extremely timely. It coincides with appeals from many in the arms control and nuclear threat communities for nuclear analysts to adopt creative approaches. For organisation such as NSquare creativity is required to build and understand futures threat models, in which nuclear weapon are situated among multitudes of existential dangers including emerging Artificial Intelligence Technologies, the climate crisis and environmental damage, as well as social injustice.[24] As such, creativity challenges habitual patterns of thought, what in the policy field is known as the "nuclear priesthood" of technical specialists. Creativity produces new kinds of assemblages and introduces different kinds of open and intersectional nuclear futures.[25] This chapter has also shown that by paying attention to more than human creative forces we are able to reconfigure our understanding of our nuclear past and present. In doing so, rich and complex histories of nuclear weapons are produced that challenge the schema of conventional geopolitical narratives and materialize the human, and more-than-human, effects of all that they encounter. Great or small.

# PART II

# 5

# "These Uniforms Have Been Places." From Combat to Paper to Exchange

## *A CMS Research Encounter*

*Laura Mills*

> A uniform worn through military service carries with it stories and experiences that are deeply imbued in the woven threads. Creating paper and artwork from these fibers carries these same qualities. We have found that all of us are connected to the military in a myriad of ways. When these connections are discovered and shared it can open a deeper understanding between people and expand our collective beliefs about military service and war.
>
> —*Combat Paper* (n.d.)

This chapter explores my encounters with *Combat Paper*, a US veteran art project transforming military uniforms into handmade paper. Through autoethnographic narrative and intersecting visuals of the papermaking process from the places of these encounters, the chapter delineates my experiences of papermaking from military uniforms by/with US veteran artists. In Chicago, as part of Iraqi American artist Wafaa Bilal's project Conflict Exchange (CX) where the paper made will be sent (back) to replenish the decimated fine art library at the University of Baghdad, I engaged in the first step to "liberate the rag." To feel the politics of tearing/cutting up a uniform as non-military researcher; finding sand in the pocket; knowing, as *Combat Paper* founder, Drew Cameron, stated, "These uniforms have been places." Then in upstate

New York with other papermaking artists, to engage in further steps of the process, the rag, now beaten pulp, pressed to become paper for a new recruit. To feel the politics of this papermaking studio's art—with handmade paper displayed for Iraq Veterans Against the War and Veterans Stand with Standing Rock—rub alongside my contribution to (making) this paper as resistance travelling to Iraq on this recruit's deployment. The places that these uniforms have been are therefore multiple, (de)militarised, and (de)militarising: home front; imperial elsewhere; military body; veteran hand; artist resource; artwork. Through papermaking, these uniforms therefore *move*—geographically, physically, materially, emotionally—taking us potentially to creative, political places that unsettle militarised/militarising power dynamics. The chapter therefore ends with how this paper(making) travels (home) with me and how creative Critical Military Studies (CMS) research can open up such places. It asks—and continually pushes—what can this creative work do? For me, this work entails engaging *with* but also *in* creative practice as part of the research process, as part of the un/re-making of worlds enabled by creative work as aesthetic-political process. Such engagement builds on and contributes to a growing body of creative scholarship within global politics and, more specifically, increasingly by CMS researchers through an array of creative practice including poetry, performance, dialogue, theatre, narrative, and/or film (Bulmer and Jackson 2016; Charrett 2020; Eichler and Wiebe 2019; Hast 2019, 2020a, 2020b; Hedström 2019; Hyde 2014; Kirtley and Cree 2022; Mills 2023, forthcoming; Schrader 2014). The final encounter, therefore, is in the researcher's body, with and on which the paper, in its final dried form (now transformed into artwork), is carried and imprinted, inspiring continuing critical reflections and interactions. To feel the politics of this ongoing exchange, the ethical tensions it raises between bodies (of CMS researcher/research-military/veteran artist/artwork) and their interrelation and interplay. This final encounter's location in the researcher's body (and this body's communication of this research via autoethnography, both narrative and photographic), entails, following Ronald J. Pelias (2004, 1), "a body deployed not as a narcissistic display but on behalf of others, a body that invites identification and empathic connection, a body that takes as its charge to be fully human." By engaging with and in creative practice in this way, these uniforms therefore also move aesthetically, politically, ethically. Reflecting the opening words from *Combat Paper*, the chapter via narrative and visual autoethnography thereby mobilises these encounters as material, embodied sites that weave, thread, and carry, yet also enable us to unpick, stories and experiences (and their politics) of the military, militarism, and war that have become deeply imbued in the fabric, not only of these uniforms, but also of society.

It is early May 2019. I have just arrived in the United States for a multisite research trip, grateful to the British International Studies Association (BISA) and the funding it has provided to get me there.[1] To support my explorations of US military/veteran artwork in the context of recent controversial wars. To reflect on how(/what) this artwork reveals (about) war and its effects. To consider the multiple ways in which (the art of) war is enacted, felt, and experienced, and leaves it mark on (military/non-military/militarised) bodies. And to explore whether this artwork then supports and/or disrupts practices of meaning-making and sense-making about the Afghanistan and Iraq wars. To do so by thinking through, with, and at the intersections of aesthetics, affect, and discomfort.

As a grant recipient, I am armed with purpose. With questions. With curiosities. With uncertainties. With doubts.

About what I will find. About what I hope to know. About what this "finding" and "knowing" does. About the discomfort this engenders. About my (not yet known) encounters—as a Critical Military Studies (CMS) researcher—with this artwork and these artists, and the politics that they (will) enact. About my encounters more specifically with *Combat Paper*, a US veteran art project transforming military uniforms into handmade paper and subsequently works of art.

First, encounters in Chicago. At the inaugural National Veterans Art Museum Triennial and Veteran Arts Summit. Then in Trumansburg, in upstate New York. At the papermaking studio of two veteran artists. And finally in the ongoing, bound(ary-)less encounters with these encounters. That is, in the self-reflective spaces of their aftermath, with the traces they leave.

Each of these encounters embodies and mirrors each stage of the papermaking process.[2] The first, deconstruction. The shredding of combat fatigues into small fabric pieces. What else must be shredded from this fabric? What other pieces must be cut away? The second, reclamation. The small, shredded fabric pieces beaten to pulp and pressed into paper. What possibilities do such (un)makings hold? What is pieced together/apart? The third, communication. The paper now dry bears the markings (of print, writing, drawing, painting) as an exchange, as an encounter of its own. What discomforting yet rich realisations unfold? What pieces linger, unfurl(ing)?

Finally, each of these encounters intertwine in terms of the politics they invoke. For the places and processes of these encounters therefore place me—regarding my researcher positionality—to process, to both experience and explore, how these encounters manifest displacements, replacements, and possibilities offered by being in-/out-of-place. It is here where the aesthetic-political processes of creative practice most acutely come to the fore. As material, embodied sites, these encounters with and in creative practice demonstrate (the here multiple, specific ways) how the aesthetic is political. For aesthetics is politics.

## DISPLACE: LIBERATING THE RAG

> The story of the fiber, the blood, sweat and tears, the months of hardship and brutal violence are held within those old uniforms. The uniforms often become inhabitants of closets or boxes in the attic. Reshaping that association of subordination, of warfare and service, into something collective and beautiful is our inspiration.
>
> —Drew Cameron, co-founder of *Combat Paper*

It is late Saturday afternoon in the Garland Gallery of the Chicago Cultural Center. Its space transformed: at once social platform, store, installation, and workshop; given over as a site for Conflict Exchange (CX), Iraqi American artist Wafaa Bilal's project exploring "the equity and relationships of post-conflict" (Bilal n.d.b). CX is an extension of Bilal's 168.01 project, which invites visitors to contribute to the rebuilding of the University of Baghdad's College of Fine Arts library (following its looting and destruction during the 2003 invasion of Iraq) through their purchase of blank white books crafted by the artist (Bilal n.d.a). A series of social platforms in the format of stores, this inaugural edition of CX sees Bilal collaborating with two US veteran artists: Drew Cameron, co-founder of *Combat Paper*, and Alicia Dietz, woodworker and studio furniture maker. Dietz has designed the interior of this first CX store, where visitors encounter and can purchase paper products—what Bilal terms "conflict byproducts" (cited in Ditmars 2019)—created with paper made from military uniforms by Cameron and *Combat Paper* during the exhibition period. Combat fatigues are rolled uniformly on wooden shelves fashioned by Dietz, while Cameron's handmade paper pulped from such fatigues hang in uniform rows on either side of the space (see Figure 5.1). Wooden portfolio boxes designed by Dietz to each carry and transport twenty sheets of paper to Baghdad are stacked in uniform arrangement while nearby sits a Hollander beater to turn fabric scraps from these uniforms into pulp to make the paper to fill these. Military duffel bags crammed with uniforms are piled beside a table crafted by Dietz around which bodies—military/veteran/civilian—accumulate (see Figure 5.2). But all of us gathered are not here to browse, but work. For we are helping to make these "conflict by-products." To engage in the first stage of papermaking: to "liberate the rag."

To liberate the rag is to remove all of the non-fibre from each military garment. To tear and cut each uniform until the fibre is free from seams, rank insignia, buttons, zips. It is to dis-member, to displace. I think here of *Combat Paper* co-founder Drew Cameron's words above. For what is this rag being liberated from? What "liberty" was it imbued with previously? What imperial promise must be decloaked? What violence is ingrained in the threads and fibres? To liberate the rag involves more than simply removing the seams, rank insignia, buttons, zips. Cameron tells us that one of the most difficult things is to take the uniform apart. But this extends beyond the tangible that piles and pools at and around this table. For his emphasis on papermaking as very much about process is multiple. For it is also *to process*. To remember. Where papermaking—notably also at this stage of taking apart and deconstruction—is as much about coming together and conversation.

Such conversation (and collaboration) is creative. It generates and engenders; it innovates and inspires; it expresses and emotes. It is productive.

So, too, it is with the discipline and creative engagements. Just like papermaking, one of the most difficult tasks is to take the discipline—what has become uniform—apart, to liberate the rag of military studies through critical creative work. Both entail labour. To liberate the discipline, creative work must also remove and dismantle seams—boundaries erected, policed, enforced; rank insignia—hierarchies of knowledge and its production; buttons and zips—methodological strictures foreclosing/gatekeeping how we "do" IR/military studies. Likewise, creative CMS research, in/for this dismantling, hinges upon and invites collaboration and conversation—what can be forged together while taking apart, what can be created out of these conversations that dismantle and displace?

Cameron reminds us that day that while papermaking is, of course, about making paper, it is also always about conversation, its generative potential. It is out of such conversations he reveals that CX was born. And as Dietz and Bilal convey, it is at the heart of CX. Bilal emphasises that "Visitors are encouraged to utilize the space designed by Dietz for encounters, interaction and communication" (n.d.b). Dietz's design then overtly integrates how these three elements—cutting, collaboration, and conversation—intertwine within CX through the table at its centre.

Dietz posits that the *Cutting, Collaboration and Conversation Round Table* is "a custom table that celebrates the second life of the tree while serving as a platform to cut uniforms for their second life" (see Figure 5.2). Through its enactment of second lives, the table in turn spurs us to think about military afterlives on several fronts. The table as a site to linger enables us to confront multiple temporalities and affects on these fronts and, what is more, through cutting, collaboration, and conversation around/at it, to engage in the unmaking and remaking of temporalities and affects. This is seen most acutely when exploring the CX table's place in terms of the larger 168.01 project. For 168.01 directly links the destruction of the College of Fine Arts library during the 2003 Iraq invasion to another moment in Iraq's "long history of such cultural destruction" (Bilal n.d.a): the thirteenth-century Mongol sacking of Baghdad where all libraries were set ablaze, including the Bayt al-Hikma (House of Wisdom). The legend, Bilal relays to us, is that the invaders threw the Bayt al-Hikma's entire library into the Tigris River, creating a bridge of books for their army to cross, with the pages bleeding ink into the river for seven days—168 hours—"at the end of which the books were drained of knowledge" (ibid.). This story, Dietz emphasises, affected the table design. Inspired by images of the river, of the ink bleeding into the water, Dietz created an organic flow of lines with the grain of the wood. A wood—walnut—whose beauty, Dietz reminds us, stems from that variation in grain, in tone, that is, however, only seen in its cutting down. Moreover, the river's etching in the table is multiple, for Dietz, as a former helicopter pilot, also sees this as topographical: the variations in tone representing the mountains; encounters from above of everyday life in the valleys below; emotive echoes from a previous life realised aesthetically otherwise in the second life of the tree, of her as veteran artist, of her as wood maker.

This manifestation of afterlife, and its play on the temporal and affective through these displacements, also finds itself in how the name 168.01 represents the "first minute after grief," which becomes a "starting point . . . signalling the struggle to move forward and the beginning of a cross-cultural encounter between individuals contributing to a globally distributed effort to rebuild anew" (Bilal n.d.a). For the stark shelves of 168.01 and its incarnation through CX—which serve "as both a monument to the staggering cultural losses endured throughout Iraq's history as well as a platform for its potential rebirth"—are not only to be stocked with the paper-filled portfolio boxes and donated books aimed at restoring the lost archives but also "double[-] as a system of exchange" connecting those visiting the store physically, virtually, to those in Iraq at the College of Fine Arts (ibid.). Playing with temporal and affective parallels, this exchange enables the shelves then to "become[-] saturated with knowledge" while donors receive their own piece of combat paper in return. Bilal argues that "Most conflicts end up with the abandonment of the people on the ground while everyone else monetarily benefits from conflict—including artists" (cited in Ditmars 2019). CX seeks to subvert these dynamics and generate creative dialogue "but also concrete

**Figure 5.1** ***Combat Paper,*** **Drew Cameron, 2019.**

action on the ground" (ibid.). By using the mode of a commercial business like a gallery, CX curator Ian Alden Russell says, CX urges exploration of "equity in conflict" by "creating a framework for transactional activity to try to reclaim some of that equity" (ibid.). For the paper made in CX will then be sent to Baghdad for College of Fine Arts students to use for their work, some of which will then come for exhibition in the US before being returned to the artists in Iraq. Introducing the project to the group of us gathered here, Bilal relays the ongoing exchange in which these uniforms partake: having been made in the US and travelled to Iraq, now being unmade and remade in the US into paper to travel back to Iraq, before coming back to the US as art forms before returning to Iraq once more. The multiple moves they make, from place to place, each move an act of displacing the stories, experiences, meanings embedded in the fibre, further beyond each time. Bilal speaks to us about hope: hope as artists to do something more, the hope of possibility in this de/construction, how through this participatory form we can do so much more. The creative CMS I advocate—engaging not only with but also in creative practice—is also seeking through its participatory creative work to rebuild anew: to imagine that another military studies is possible, to allow other knowledges (drained by the discipline disciplining) to saturate, to position itself continually as a starting point to build otherwise.

A further military afterlife, its un/remaking of temporalities and affects, then spurred by this table is that of the discipline itself. About the creative cuts we must make to military studies to give it (another) life. How this is ongoing, requiring continual collaboration and conversation to ensure the disciplinary

**Figure 5.2** ***Conflict Exchange: Cutting, Collaboration and Conversation Round Table*****, Alicia Dietz, 2019.**

uniformity this dismantles and resists is not erected and buttressed in a "critical, creative" guise. This disciplinary displacement can and should never create the neat, tidy, smoothed-over, or comfortable/comforting, but retain disorder, messiness, rough edges, and discomfort. In the table, Dietz has inserted bow ties or butterfly joints in the centre to repair cracks. Such joints are used for aesthetics but also to reinforce. So, too, it is with a creative CMS that embraces aesthetics and discomfort. As CMS researchers we too join and tie together, but it is not our job to make whole—creative work enables us to leave the cracks, indeed to centre them: we need to show those fissures, that incompleteness. We also insert but leave those flaws, those fault-lines, to ensure the complexity of these encounters is maintained. Speaking of these joints and cracks, Dietz parallels how we are cracked as individuals but still strong, beautiful. How CMS can also make space for and hold beauty, while being robust through its engagement with and in creative practice, for it enables an aesthetics-politics that is not sanitised nor ordered but challenging, discomforting.

At that table, I sat side by side with artists, veterans, civilians, all three-in-one, and engaged in the first step to liberate the rag. To lift up the scissors. To make that first cut. To realise the sharpness of these blades. To move (through) this heavy NyCo so easily. To make that decision to cut then tear through that fabric—to feel the weight of this, the greater effort entailed, to hear the weight of this. To move methodically to free that fibre—cut by tear by snip by unstitch—of a COAT, MAN'S UTILITY AIR FORCE (see Figure 5.3).

To feel the politics of tearing and cutting up that most everyday of military artefacts—a uniform—as a non-military researcher. Of cautiously unstitching stitch by stitch a label emblazoned with the final words DO NOT REMOVE THIS LABEL. Of meticulously removing the seams around the pocket to then release sand still contained, trapped within. Of knowing, as Cameron subsequently stated, "These uniforms have been places."

To feel the politics of these moves, as affect, as displacement: how that sand represents US recruits displaced elsewhere, the displacement and forced migrations their presence instigated; how the sand returns in uniforms displaced out of context on/with displaced bodies and minds, a multitude of afterlives.

To reflect then on how some elements here have no afterlife—the discarded seams and buttons, insignia and zips, labels. For us to at first not know where to place these—for they have no place in the papermaking process, a threat to the next stage and the damage they could wreak on the Hollander beater. They are retained at the centre of the table in a military duffel bag for a use unknown. Displacement always carries within it the unknown; the unknown always carries within it possibility; possibility always carries within it alternatives, replacements. That another (after)life can be possible.

## REPLACE: RECLAIMING AND (UN)MAKING MEANING

> Coming home from any war, it is very hard to share your experiences. . . . You hold back. You suppress them. . . . And now we want to reclaim those experiences, by making them into something new, something different. And it's paper.
>
> We have a unique way of transforming the experiences . . . to take a uniform, to cut it up, reconstitute it, make it into pulp, make it into paper, and eventually put art on top of it . . . that is the platform that allows the veteran to feel confident and comfortable communicating.
>
> —David Keefe, co-founder of Frontline Arts and Frontline Paper (formerly *Combat Paper* NJ) (PBS Newshour 2012)

It is late afternoon, again, just a matter of days later, the Garland Gallery of the Chicago Cultural Center replaced with a papermaking studio in Trumansburg, upstate New York. The urban replaced by the rural; the public replaced by the private, for I am here by invitation of two veteran artists—Kevin Basl and Nathan Lewis—in Nate's studio adjacent to their homes. To encounter and engage in the next steps of the papermaking process, where the shredded fabric pieces of uniforms, rendered smaller still, are beaten to pulp, the sheet formed, and pressed into paper. While the first steps of the papermaking process entailed liberating the rag through various displacements, here, as Frontline Paper (formerly *Combat Paper* NJ) co-founder David Keefe's words above convey, these next papermaking stages enact reclamation through various replacements—that is, reclaiming, un/making, re-placing meaning and sense of experiences of war through the reclaiming, un/making, re-placing of the military fibres. These juxtaposed encounters reveal how papermaking itself has multiple (after)lives too. Both with their own immediacies and intimacies. In these papermaking stages of reclamation, these immediacies and intimacies both mark and are marked by the body who re-places/becomes re-placed. Here the multiple stages this encompasses—beating, forming, pressing, drying—entail the intertwined tangibility, materiality, and dis/re/embodiment of combat-/paper-/artist. For as Basl remarks while we engage in these papermaking processes, there are literally traces on you; it gets on your skin. It marks and is marked by the body. Making paper, bringing it into being, requires the *work of* the body, the subject for the reclaiming and un/making of these uniforms—these stories and experiences of war—but it also requires the body, the subject to be *worked on*, simultaneously enacting the reclaiming and un/making of these bodies, the bringing into being of subjects (otherwise).

In that studio, I was intensely conscious of my body, a body—as non-military researcher—which did, should, not fit there, and yet was welcomed to fit, in its potential discomfiture, through my own engagement with and in these creative practices—through beating into pulp, pulling and couching the sheet, pressing and drying into paper (see Figure 5.4). This not-/fitting, its circuitry of dis/comfort, impressed itself on my body as integral to these papermaking stages, to reclamation's aesthetic-affective practices of un/making, and as such, importantly, impressed itself as felt by *all* bodies, subjects, that reclaim, re-place the rag, the meanings and experiences imbued in it; bodies, subjectivities that are consequently re-placed, that is, they become dis/re/embodied through these practices as a discomforting yet generative possibility.

Via reclamation, therefore, and its aesthetic-affective practices of un/making, these multiple papermaking stages were—are—felt on/through/with the body. With its aim to reclaim and un/make meaning through its embrace of aesthetics and discomfort, so, too, is creative CMS research.

*Beating*. Reducing the rag to pulp. The thrum of the Hollander beater, the roar of the roiling water, the hammer of the breaking fibres. The noise, the dynamism, the effort, to beat these former uniforms into a soft, wet, shapeless mass that, now malleable, holds open possibility to be shaped, reconstituted, reclaimed. The stacks of military duffel bags crammed with uniforms lying opposite as a reminder that reclamation, reconstitution is ongoing, never (un) done. For CMS researchers seeking to embrace and advance creativity, such effort, dynamism, and subsequently, noise—at what is disrupted and unmade in the discipline—are also felt in the body. For this disciplinary disruption and un/making is also a form of encounter as a material embodied site, here, for/of alternative knowledge production. How creative CMS replaces this idea of sites of "production" and its extractive implications with sites of un/making and its in-betweenness, so that sites for knowing (with its suggested embodiedness, relationality, as opposed to the clinicality of "knowledge")—as thinking, feeling, sensing (with)—can emerge, come forth, be re/un/made over and again. How creative methods—like the water here—both break down and bind. How the very fibre of military studies—like the pulp—can be rendered malleable and shapeable, its fixity broken down into something fluid that can be reconstituted and reclaimed, that can in turn reconstitute and reclaim meaning(s). How the researcher's body *matters*—in its multiple senses (Barad 2003; Butler 2011)—to/in sites of knowing-making that are not sterile nor neutral (as traditional approaches would have us believe) but haptic, situated, and lived.

*Forming*. Pulling and couching the sheet. These very terms of sheet formation make the body felt.

To pull the sheet: To push up my sleeves. To place my hand into a vat of pulp, more water added. To "charge the vat." To vigorously move my hand under water to agitate the pulp, to stir, to circulate, to evenly disperse. To be emotionally charged, vigorously moved, stirred in doing so, for what stories and experiences of war are stirred up, dispersed? To take up the mould and deckle, to align these frames to hold the sheet. To dip the mould and deckle into the vat, my bare forearms coming into contact with the pulp . . . where my body touches fibre—how many bodies have touched this fibre? . . . How it sticks to my skin—what skin did it cling to previously? To pull up the mould and deckle, to shake gently from side to side, the fibres settling, the water draining. To leave the sheet to rest, further water draining out. In the discipline, creative CMS researchers must also agitate; methodologically, we must also get one's hands dirty—aesthetics necessitates this, leaving traces on/by the body, generating embodied ways of knowing. For the discipline, creative methods similarly provide a mould, but the outcome is likewise unknown; for any mould with such openness provides space for specific creations to materialise, just like the unique forms the settled fibres take in each sheet. Aesthetics is attuned to specificity. As such, it leaves room in the creative process to fine-tune, to re-place, like the papermaking process itself. To "kiss the sheet back." To return the sheet to the water; for the pulp to again

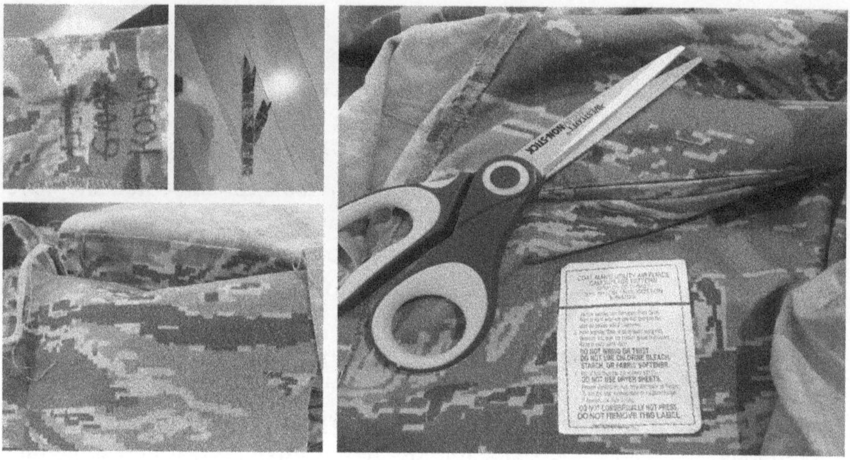

**Figure 5.3 Sand in the Pocket: 'Liberating' a Coat, Man's Utility Air Force Camouflage Pattern.**

be rendered fluid, suspended, dispersed, if, for example, I shake too vigorously, the thickness is not quite right. On the discipline, creative methods inscribe the importance of this re-placement to knowing, to understanding as a creative, careful, and caring endeavour. The importance of letting go. How making always already holds unmaking within it. How un/making always already exacts and enacts care.

To couch the sheet: To transfer a newly formed sheet of paper from the mould to the felts. To carefully remove the deckle, to carry the mould and its delicate cargo to the table with felt blankets. To "put to bed" ("couch" derives from the French *se coucher*). To gently place the edge of the mould to the blanket, to slowly lower it down, to lightly push my hands on the back of the mould, to cautiously open the mould up, out on the opposite edge. To strive for that pressure yet lightness of touch to release a sheet from the mould into the world. To strive for that gentle precision to build "the post"—layer upon layer of sheets alternated with felt to prevent their bonding during the pressing process—wary of how I lay(er) the sheets could alter their form. To feel fear in my body, tension in my hands, my arms, at the prospect of damaging this fragile form, not only because of the stories and experiences imbued in these fibres, of their meanings being reclaimed, re-placed, reembodied, but for the stories and experiences, and their meanings, yet to unfold—for this paper is destined for a recruit soon to be deployed to Iraq. Lewis was contemplative about the moves this paper will make. Paper of/in uniforms, the first he has ever made to accompany (back) a serving military body. The multiple, oscillating temporalities, geographies, bodies it encompasses. The air in the studio felt relaxed yet charged—with purpose, responsibility, and, subsequently, care. I then contemplated the moves I made to make this paper, feeling them acutely in my non-military CMS researcher limbs, being moved conflictingly, discomfortingly by what such care enacts. But the creative CMS researcher's body must always show care, care for (the becoming of) the bodies, subjects, worlds of/by these encounters.

*Pressing*. Removing water and compacting the fibres. To load the post of paper in a hydraulic press. To pump, to push, to press. To feel, hear the splash of water releasing from the sheets on, with my body. To bring to full pressure through a final lever of the hydraulic jack. To harness the strength of the body, the press to increase the strength of the paper, pushing the fibres tightly together to encourage strong bonding. To leave these sheets, pressing. To feel *pressing* in further respects. Pressing as urgent: for the paper to be made for this recruit's upcoming deployment to Iraq. Pressing as significant: for the weight of this to mark itself on the paper of reclaimed uniforms as reclaiming and un/making this recruit's new uniform, the bodies, the subjects it will contact, encounter. Pressing as imperative: for CMS to render such reclaiming and un/making as critical for the discipline, where researchers must press for aesthetics—its politics, its possibilities—to be fully embraced, where creative practice is critical practice.

To leave the paper, pressing. To ready it, ourselves, for the drying process. To know this process will occur without me due to the time required, my scheduled departure. To imagine the uniform's re-embodiment, re-placement as paper, the colour, the grain it will take on once dried. To leave the studio and wonder—what textures will the final dried sheet hold? Such textures are

**Figure 5.4 "Pulling some sheets" with Nathan Lewis and Kevin Basl in Trumansburg.**

central to creative CMS in how it seeks more textured representations of war and its experiences. These textures reveal specificity and complexity where pain, trauma, violence (discomfortingly) coexist with pleasure, joy, care. To seek more textured representations of war and its experiences means to build *relationships with* rather than *research on*. For creative CMS work, pressing, therefore, signifies in another respect: not as squeezing out in an extractive way but allowing things to pass through, with its textures, to make one's (research) encounters more meaningful, more careful, more caring. Like letting go with the pulling of the sheet, allowing to pass through demands choices—aesthetic-political-ethical—of CMS researchers.

To choose to forge connections, collaborations with veteran artists that always hold discomfort—in terms of what they conducted, what they carry, what they create—to re-place sanitised stories and experiences of the military, militarism, and war, to reclaim opportunistic, fetishising military-veteran research as careful, critical, creative encounters.

To choose not to include that interview, that comment, that story. Or not in *that* way.

To choose not to be parasitic. Reap then leave. To have these conversations openly, together. In this studio in Trumansburg. In Chicago. And beyond.

To feel the politics of this studio's art—with handmade paper displayed for Iraq Veterans Against the War and Veterans Stand with Standing Rock—rub alongside my contribution to this paper as embodied resistance travelling to Iraq on this recruit's deployment. Of Lewis declaring "Let's pull some sheets"—the politics of un/making filling the air, heavy, with purpose, significance, unrealised possibility, of where this paper will go, what this paper will do. Of Lewis imprinting each couched sheet with a paperclip, that symbol of war resistance, also tattooed on the very forearm carrying out these actions. Of working alongside artists, veterans who insist on papermaking as politics, a vocation, who press it is political not therapeutic, who unsettle the narratives of "healing" surrounding these processes—for it is safer, more comforting if healing, not safe, discomforting if political.

To feel the politics of these moves, as reclamation, as replacement: how we re-place fibres, meanings, stories, subjectivities from the beater to the vat, to the felts, to the press, to ready them for (re)place(ment)s unknown. How such replacements as art, books, pamphlets, poetry, creative writing line walls and bookcases surrounding the areas where we pulled, couched, and pressed these sheets as a foreshadowing, a resonance of potentiality. How these (re) place(ment)s mark (after)lives in transition, bodies, subjects, worlds in the process of becoming that can then—through the encounters they have with other bodies, subjects, worlds—with time and reflection, become/manifest further (after)lives, in and out of place.

## IN-PLACE, OUT OF PLACE: SITTING WITH DISCOMFORT

> *Combat Paper* workshops are veritable incubators for stories and ideas precisely because they allow contradictions to emerge and co-exist . . . papermaking is rarely an end in itself. It's a conduit. It encourages sharing, medium-mixing, and collaboration. It sparks conversations and experimentation.
>
> Drew Cameron . . . calls *Combat Paper* a "new language." This is a concept worth unpacking. . . . Is Drew proposing that papermaking could be a solution to the current crisis in the creation of truth and meaning? Papermaking as a post-linguistic information exchange? A mindfulness practice to initiate a thunderous, collective *Ohmmmmmmm*? Or maybe it's about radically rethinking the meaning of one common object (in our case, the politically and emotionally-charged military uniform) and using that new meaning as a sort of linguistic beacon—a semantic reference point—from which we might begin radically changing the meaning of other words, objects and ideas?
>
> Veterans shed off the old language (the military and its uniform) as they begin creating a new one (a blank sheet of paper, with its endless possibilities), which ideally is then used to transform self and society (what one puts on the paper matters profoundly). Ultimately . . . the new language of *Combat Paper* represents a body of words—a poem—within the language of revolution, a new way of being that will serve to transform humanity's broken superstructure.
>
> —Kevin Basl, veteran artist (2020)

It is late afternoon, again, but days, months, over a year later. The places of these papermaking processes are distant geographically, temporally, yet this paper(making) stays with me. Materially. Politically. Aesthetically. Ethically. A final encounter in the researcher's body. Through the final papermaking stage as communication.

*Materially*. For in Chicago during my encounter with Conflict Exchange (CX), where the first stage of the papermaking process was engaged in, I received a sample square of combat paper, of the "finished (conflict by-)product," of what these uniforms would become in the final papermaking stage.

My small piece of paper sits on a shelf in my office in St Andrews. Like a strange souvenir.

What encounters, bodies, subjects it materialises for/by/in me.

What languages it deploys to speak, etch these to/on me.

What an open-ended conduit it provides for communications, often multiple and contradictory, to emerge and co-exist to/by/through/between me and others.

*Politically*. For here in this office (and beyond), I reflect on how this paper in its final dried form enacts a form of encounter itself: now transformed into artwork, it carries, is imprinted with, markings—of print, writing, drawing, painting—that stimulate further encounters, exchanges, un/re/making meanings through the multiple, and potentially ever-shifting, interpretations of those that surround and come into contact with it. How they in turn carry, are marked and imprinted by this exchange, its meaning-making, its sense-making. How they are carried and turn to creative CMS research, its potential to open up political and politicising places that unsettle and contest militarised/militarising power dynamics, their hierarchies, their violences. Where the final papermaking process of communication, in its destabilising plurality (combat-paper-exchange, military/veteran-artist/artwork-researcher/research), signifies and can enact radical change. Where new languages, new forms, new worlds can be forged.

That small square of paper in my office therefore embodies, represents, engenders multiple afterlives. How creative research on/and paper(making), its aesthetics, its politics, comes full circle with this square.

*Aesthetically*. For in the multiple planes of communication comprising the final papermaking stage, communication is not reductive; it is not linear correspondence in terms of the artwork relaying meaning as mimetic representation. Like the uniforms they once were, this paper, the artforms it comprises, enacts aesthetics as openness to reimagine otherwise (Bleiker 2009); these meanings are open, unbounded regarding the bodies they generate, the bodies they touch, the bodies they encounter. Where the new languages they manifest disrupt, transform, bring forth new ways of being.

Creative CMS work also stimulates ongoing, multiple interpretations, with meanings being un/re-made. It doesn't foreclose, doesn't offer tidy conclusions but through innovative languages, registers, lets alternative ways of being emerge. Communication as aesthetic openness, reimagining, thereby manifests in creative CMS work through the conduct, creation, *and* dissemination of the research. Aesthetics of/as creative CMS work therefore materialises not only in the sites of papermaking, or in the initial research encounters, but in the places of (its) re-imagining, its continuing and unfolding aesthetic realisation in open-ended and necessarily discomforting creative forms and the encounters they mutually engender, whether in their creative formation, circulation, publication, workshopping, or conferencing.

That square of paper in my office as the embodiment of un/re-making—of new languages, of multiple afterlives, of alternative worlds—holds me accountable to push in and for these places of re-imagining, the aesthetic-political-ethical possibilities they propose.

*Ethically*. For in my researcher's body, this paper(making) in its final form makes itself felt, now transformed into sheets, artwork, communications that speak (to) the body, the subject of the researcher as agent of responsibility. The responsibility to communicate, to engage with and in the "languages" of creative forms, to commit oneself, as Basl's words above convey, to their transformative power, their radical possibility. As Basl furthers, "a person can't learn the language of *Combat Paper* from reading about it . . . you must learn by doing. To learn the language of *Combat Paper* you must come to a workshop and sit with others also learning the language. You must make paper. And you must keep coming back (as with all languages: use it or lose it)" (2020).

This entails *applying* the researcher's body to engage with and in creative practices, to feel their discomfort, to sit with that, to see what languages and ensuing transformations emerge as imperative.

This chapter claims in its opening stages that aesthetics is politics. But aesthetics is also ethics.

The square of combat paper sits in my office, urging, urgent. That this final encounter in the researcher's body *means* something, for more ethical, nuanced, difficult, discomforting meanings of the military, militarism, and war to be communicated. The final papermaking stage of communication, therefore, to draw on Basl's words above, effects the researcher's body also as conduit, with and on which the paper (dried and transformed into artwork), its multiple and contradictory meanings, is carried and imprinted, sparking ongoing critical reflections, interactions, experimentations that become integral to (the responsibility of) research as communication, to the un/re-making of worlds enabled by creative work as aesthetic-political-ethical process.

Engaging with but also in creative practice as part of the research process is not to resign oneself to comfortable modes of scholarship, to comforting ways of being, knowing, and doing (in) the world. Rather, it is an aesthetic, political, and ethical act that in turn exacts aesthetic, political and ethical demands on the researcher('s body). Creative CMS ensures we are acutely attuned to the (research) sites being explored, the (geographical) sites being inhabited, the (material) sites being un/re/made, the (emotional) sites being felt.

The discipline disciplines by trying to keep *in place*, by marking *out of place* that which exceeds this sitedness, as having *no place* there. But what would it mean to be in-place, that is, to situate oneself, with the out of place, with that which causes discomfort? Art, aesthetics, and creativity can help us navigate but not reconcile that discomfort—of the what, where, why, and how of research, the (power) relations this enacts and exacts. Engaging with and in them is not to alleviate but to sit with that discomfort, to be in place with that, to eschew retreat to the comfortable or comforting and to see what emerges critically and creatively when it takes us "out of place," just like the uniforms.

While more "traditional" forms of scholarship remain important, creative forms offer potentially more immediate, affective, potent, and perceptive modes to explore experiences of war and (non)military/militarised bodies. This is not to posit the creative as "better than" for such hierarchisation goes against the ethos of creative work to contest and challenge such privileging and universalisation. Rather, what do we risk missing, what evades us, what do these traditional forms simply fail to capture? Rather, do these creative forms offer something else—in terms of the research encounter, in terms of ethical engagement, in terms of partnership and collaboration as opposed to supposedly clinical research sites/subjects/objects? Rather, do these creative forms provide opportunities to engage in alternative ways of knowing that provide unsettling, transformative insights unprobed, even marginalised or erased by "traditional" forms of scholarship?

## Like Pelias

> Like Ronald J. Pelias I am drawn to this way of working out of a feeling of lack. I feel the lack in those critical arguments tighter than syllogism, those pronouncements given with such assurance, those judgments that name everything but what matters. I know there is more than making a case, more than establishing criteria and authority, more than what is typically offered up. That more has to do with the heart, the body, the spirit.
>
> That lack resides in my body as a wound. As I go about my business of just living and of doing my job in the academy . . . too often I've watched claims of truth try to triumph over compassion, try to crush alternative possibilities, and try to silence minority voices. Seeing the pain this causes, I seek another discourse, one that still has an edge, that could say what needs to be said but would do no harm. I want a scholarship that fosters connections, opens spaces for dialogue. (2004, 1–2)

Such spaces that centre creativity as aesthetics-politics-ethics must also be actively carved out in a discipline that seeks to keep in place. At the BISA 2021 annual conference, Alice Cree and I sought to contribute to carving out such spaces by convening an academic-practitioner roundtable on "Art and/ of Military Afterlives" where attendees—through drawing, stitching—also engaged in creative practice, sitting in-place with the out-of-place, putting oneself out of one's comfort zone in that communal place.

A key site of engagement with/in. Where the final papermaking process of communication, where a further military afterlife, a further encounter, was also enacted in my re-presentation of uniforms that went from combat to paper to exchange.

Bringing interdisciplinary scholars and artists into conversation, the roundtable sought to give texture to the multifarious, complex ways that the afterlives of war and military participation at once manifest through, and are represented in, creative practice.

Through the paper sticking with me, the moves these uniforms make marking my body, I advanced military afterlives as multiple, diverse but also contested, especially around that "after"—for the temporalities that encompass such lives and the affects that shape them are not sharp and delineated, not linear nor sequential, but overlapping, ongoing, simultaneous, never-ending, shifting, conflicting.

Creative work enables us to see military afterlives as hybrid, as "and/or" conceptualisations that like the paper hold multiple temporalities and affects within them; of

past-present-future
then-now-then
trauma-discomfort-joy

Complicating that "after" further is the term *post-traumatic*, so often aligned with framing the reclaiming of the uniform as (just) therapeutic: what does that "post" erase? In our conversations in Trumansburg, Lewis challenged such reductive temporal and affective framings, countering, "I don't buy all of it. Cos you still go through all theose same painful, emotional swings of the highs and lows of dealing with severe truama for the rest of your life."

Creative CMS seeks, to draw again on Pelias's words, to have an edge but do no harm—aesthetics demands we have a political and ethical responsibility as researchers in our encounters with these subjects, their stories, their experiences, their ongoing affects.

That contestation, that multiplicity, that hybridity of military afterlives is about maintaining a complexity and messiness to our research so that the messy actualities of military afterlives, and the complex temporalities and affects they occupy, and also do not occupy (that fleeting transience of both and how they manifest), can be explored, felt, and more ethically accounted for. Art and creative practice can therefore offer an openness, a discomforting incompleteness where multiple possibilities can manifest and be reimagined over and again. For even in those artworks that seek to render these multiple temporalities and affects in a neat, tidy, or simplistic way, the art itself with its potential always already for multiple meanings, and therefore multiple interpretations, evades such ordered or facile renderings. The excess of this openness, this incompleteness is such that radical political possibilities emerge.

Such possibilities, their ethics, arise from encounters of/with vulnerability; here in this final papermaking stage particularly requires making oneself vulnerable as a researcher.

Such vulnerability involves thinking through how discomfort can also be a method—not only are the multiple sites of research (and) encounter potentially discomforting, but how we do this work on, with, and in those sites is also discomforting—in challenging us as researchers in our positionality and self-reflexivity to have thinking, feeling, caring and careful encounters, in how creative work can re-present differently the "stuff," create different meanings, invoke different audience responses (Leavy 2009), in how such work's sense of incompleteness—contrary to traditional approaches' insistence on easy, fixed conclusions—is a strength.

To feel the politics of this ongoing exchange, the ethical tensions it raises between bodies (of CMS researcher/research-military/veteran-artist/artwork) and their interrelation and interplay. Of sensing on/with/in the researcher's body how these uniforms, having moved geographically, physically, emotionally, materially, now move politically, aesthetically, ethically. Of applying that body (of researcher/research) to communicate the politics, aesthetics and ethics of these papermaking encounters, the bodies, (after)lives and affects they encompass.

To feel the politics of such moves as the radical possibilities of discomfort, of what emerges from sitting in-place, out of place. Far from comfortable/comforting sites that render complacent, these sites and encounters of/with discomfort always keep us questioning—ourselves as researchers, our process, our scholarship—to keep that openness, uncertainty, and the possibility it holds. For messiness and complexity of the intersections of art and of military afterlives to emerge. For new languages, different meanings, other (after) lives, alternative worlds to be forged.

## WHERE TO FROM HERE?

Having focused on the places of these encounters, this chapter concludes by asking where to from here? What other places will this lead to, what other encounters will this engender? The answer is the beyond. Where endless possibility lies. Through other/ongoing encounters. Like papermaking, creative CMS is not an end in itself, but a conduit (Basl 2020) through which the fibres and threads of uniforms, of stories and experiences of war and militarism that comprise the final paper and/as artwork enable and enact encounters as material embodied sites of/for reimagining.

We should not see this as our final destination/resting place but rather an ongoing project that needs care and cultivation: we must tend and attend to the processes of displacing, replacing, and being in/out of place and the creative places of aesthetic-political-ethical possibility to which they can lead. It is vital that we continually stop as CMS researchers and scrutinise each process to ensure that creative methods fulfil their radical promise to resist discipline while also recognising (and avoiding) the risk of imposing that in other ways.

To displace—to liberate the rag of military studies: in unsettling the discipline through creative forms how certain disciplinary siloes can occur, how we do not want this form of research to become somehow "fixed," to be positioned conversely as the "right" way of doing things. Such thinking goes against and thereby curtails the very possibility that creative work holds by imposing statism on dynamism, strictures/rigours on fluidity. To address what we could—in the name of "research aims," "objectives"—leave in a pile to be discarded: the seams (those often fractiously created joins of research encounters—that refuse to break down), the "surplus" buttons (those ways we fasten together in the moment), insignia (those moments we are potentially seduced, must confront our own biases, falterings, weaknesses), that we bin as it could break the machine that is the tightly woven argument we must craft. To displace therefore entails 'thinking with,' through conversation and collaboration, no matter how discomforting or uncomfortable a process that might be. To account for the messiness, the complexity, the intricacy—to avoid neat and tidy renderings.

To replace—to un/remake meaning. Including our own earlier suppositions. With "knowledge" always in flux, "to know" is always a dynamic, never-ending process that urges us to ask questions of ourselves.

To be in/out of place—to sit with that discomfort and see what it enables. An ethical stance. But this can come at a cost. Because that work takes time. It is slow, temporal, material and embodied. It leaves its mark and we as researchers need—must take—time to process. And yet this runs into further constraints by a discipline intent on keeping in place—the rush to publish-publish-publish, the policing then to publish the "right" sort of research. As creative CMS researchers we therefore make ourselves vulnerable again in terms of the discipline. But such costs do not outweigh the costs of not engaging with and in creative practice, of leaving these discomforting yet rich encounters un(der)explored, of putting one's body on the line to provide fuller, messier, more difficult stories and experiences of war and militarism. It is only by submitting oneself to discomfort, the effort this entails, that different (non)military/militarised bodies, other military (after)lives, and alternative worlds can be reimagined.

# 6

# Modelling Military Landscapes

## *Archival Encounters, Model-Making, and Camouflage Practice*

*James P. Robinson*

Throughout history, the development of many cities has been intimately bound up with the rationales and logics of militarism and militarised practice. In his seminal work, *Cities under Siege*, the geographer Stephen Graham (2010, 10) highlights how "many of the world's cities originate, at least in part, as military constructions. The history of the imagination, construction and inhabitation of urban places cannot be told without considering the central role of such places as the critical sites of militarised power and control." Over several centuries, cities have been variously shaped and transformed by the imperatives of defence and fortification, the displaying, showcasing, and projection of military power, or acted as spaces of political violence, revolution, and insurgency (Coward 2006). Into the twentieth and twenty-first centuries, this militarisation of everyday urban space has, arguably, intensified, most notably during the First and Second World Wars, in which cities re-programmed their economies, infrastructures, and governance and mobilised their urban populations. At the same time, these trends served to heighten their presence as targets for destruction, most notably from the air (Adey, Whitehead, and Williams 2011; Gregory 2011; Hewitt 1983). For example, Britain's cities experienced their first attacks from the air in 1917–1918. This targeting of the city further intensified during the interwar period and into the Second World War; the Spanish Civil War of 1936–1939; the Luftwaffe's *Blitzkreig* of London; the RAF's area bombing of cities such as Hamburg, Dresden, Frankfurt, and Berlin; and then ultimately the dropping of the nuclear bomb on Hiroshima and Nagasaki further signalled a shift, in the words of Shaw (2003, 131) "from the selective destruction of key sites within cities to extensive attacks on urban areas and, finally, to instantaneous annihilation of entire urban spaces and populations." These trends in aerial bombardment prompted a number of concerns for contemporaries at the time: How could urban populations be prepared for such attacks? How could war-time levels of production be maintained? What could be done to deal with the threats from above?

In this chapter, I draw upon my research into one of the many responses to this projection of militarised airpower: the practice of civil camouflage. Civil camouflage was a particular set of techniques used to hide Britain's industrial heartland during the 1930s and 1940s. At the forefront of my discussion will be reflections on the intersection between camouflage practice, archival research, and creativity, with an emphasis upon models and model-making. In the following section, I historicise the practice of civil camouflage itself to contextualise the discussion and to emphasise the place of models with respect to camouflage work. Having presented this narrative, the following section reflects on the methodology of the research and how my engagements with model-making in the archives prompted me to think creatively about how these encounters might be enlivened. In the final part of this chapter, I consider the opportunities afforded by these creative encounters, both in a research and teaching context. Specifically, I discuss how the techniques of model-making allow for an exploration of the impact of militarised gazes, technologies, and practices on the transformation of our everyday landscapes, as well as the re-animating and performing of a set of militarised identities located within the archives.

## THE PRACTICE OF CAMOUFLAGE AND MODEL-MAKING

When we think of "camouflage," there are, of course, obvious connections to its uses by animals and plants, who diversely use concealment, deception, and mimicry to mask themselves from the threats of predation or to give themselves a survivalist advantage. Despite these "natural" connotations, the word *camouflage* entered the English language in the twentieth century as an adaption of the French verb *camoufleur*, meaning "to make up for the stage" or "to blind or to veil." This emergence coincided with its earliest militaristic evocation, when *camouflage* became part of the lexicon of warfare when it was initially used during the First World War to denote the application of strongly contrasting colours of paint to artillery and ships (Behrens 2002). In its earliest guises, camouflage was a practice that was clearly informed by the creative and the artistic; for instance, it has been widely acknowledged that the "dazzle camouflage" applied to Royal Navy ships during the First and Second World Wars drew upon and was variously inspired by the principles of vorticism and cubism (Taylor 2016; Williams 2001). Tracing camouflage's history uncovers not only the intertwining of its practice with war-making, but it also reveals the continuing and complex entanglement of the creative with the exercising and projecting of military power.

The focus of my own research has been the practice of "civil camouflage," a form of camouflage work that focused on the concealment and protection of Britain's industrial landscapes of the 1930s and 1940s. It was a practice that emerged as a response to those anxieties and concerns about the increasing targeting of the city from the air, which I discussed in the introduction to this chapter. For British civil defence planners, maintaining the physical and psychological well-being of the British population and protecting, where possible, the infrastructures that were to sustain Britain's contribution to the war, was of paramount importance (Robinson 2012). Civil camouflage was a response to these concerns; its objective was "not an attempt to conceal the target completely, but so to disguise it as to mystify and mislead the pilots of attacking aircraft."[1] Acting as a "passive" means of defence, civil camouflage incorporated the concealment of a number of important industrial and "key" sites that were deemed valuable for Britain's war-making effort. Among the sites to be camouflaged were munitions, aircraft, and motor transport factories, as well as the various infrastructures needed to power and sustain these sites; as such, electricity-generating stations, gas holders, and oil tank farms were also to be camouflaged. Civil camouflage was similarly applied to adjacent buildings and other important navigational landmarks that might be used by enemy Luftwaffe pilots to attack these industrial complexes; roads, railway lines, rivers and canals, lighthouses, and white chalk figures, amongst other landmarks, were therefore also concealed. Between October 1936 and April 1944, 4,074 factories and key points were treated with camouflage, along with an additional 942 navigational landmarks, at the total cost of £1.5million[2] (approximately £53 million today). In terms of the geographical distribution of this work, this was largely concentrated in the South of England and along the East Coast due to the proximity of these sites to continental Europe, though camouflage work was also carried out in other significant industrial cities beyond this (e.g., Manchester, Birmingham, Cardiff, etc.).

Most of this work was conducted by the Civil Defence Camouflage Establishment (CDCE), which had been formed under the auspices of the Ministry of Home Security in 1938. The CDCE itself was based in Leamington Spa, Warwickshire, and was a unit comprised of individuals from a wide variety of backgrounds. At its heart, this included many artists, including the chief camouflage officer of the CDCE, Captain Lancelot Glasson, who had experience of camouflage work having worked as part of the British Camouflage Section at Wimereux between 1916 and 1918. The predominance of artists within the CDCE was reflective of what was often referred to as "paint-brush supremacy," an enduring legacy of camouflage work from the First World War that had privileged paint-based solutions and adherence to artistic principles. However, civil camouflage of the 1940s progressively became a space for the inclusion of other forms of knowledge: aeronautical, biological, chemical, and structural engineering, amongst others. Combined, these various intellectual knowledges helped to foster a highly experimental, imaginative, and creative culture within camouflage work.

Crucial to civil camouflage work was acknowledging the importance of the militarised aerial gaze. The aerial gaze had long been understood as occupying a position of power, mastery, and control (Adey 2008; Cosgrove and Fox 2010). Through the occupation of this elevated viewpoint, it became acknowledged that the terrestrial world below would become uncovered and revealed in very different ways from the grounded perspective. For architects of the 1930s, the aerial perspective provided an alternative framework for "reading" and critiquing the built environment from above, uncovering and revealing grotesque, vulgar, and discordant urban development, and, thus, initiating an agenda for fostering the design of a more regular and ordered landscape (Le Corbusier 1987 [1934]; see also Matless 1990, 1998). For civil defence planners, however, the militarisation of the aerial gaze challenged and contested these discourses that architects and planners were promoting. Such aesthetics inscribed the landscape below with a series of traces and markers that enhanced and made industrial "targetable" when viewed from the air (Adey, Whitehead, and Williams 2011; Gregory 2011). These traces included regular and geometrical structural forms and layouts, smooth and reflective building surfaces (notably, glass and pale concrete surfaces were an issue), as well as other visual markers like smoke plumes or the scarred ground left by construction work. Collectively, these traces were seen to heighten the conspicuousness and vulnerability of Britain's industrial complexes.

The object of camouflaging, therefore, was to address these visible traces in the landscape. In order to achieve this, however, it was acknowledged that the camouflage officer (or *camoufleur*) should adopt the same embodied practices and viewing experiences of the enemy bomber crew; indeed, being "aerially experienced" became a marker of being a proficient camouflage practitioner and camoufleurs were encouraged to undertake regular aerial survey flights from the nearby Baginton Aerodrome (now Coventry Airport). As part of their flights, they would catalogue prominent features in the landscape and analyse and scrutinise why particular buildings might be "conspicuous" when viewed from the air. Such observations would take place in line with what was considered to be a "typical" bombing run, five miles at three thousand feet for daytime observation (these would alter later in the war following a shifting emphasis towards night camouflage, see Robinson 2013). Aerial survey flights would be repeated once a camouflage scheme had been applied to assess its efficacy. These survey flights were intended to allow the camoufleur to "become" the bomber body, performing in particular ways that "mimicked" their enemy counterpart.

When it came to designing schemes, camoufleurs would determine the level of treatment to be applied in accordance with the level of importance attached to the "vulnerable" structure. Sites of relatively low importance would be issued with general instructions advising them to "tone down" with medium or dark tones that corresponded with the surrounding landscape. For higher value targets, more intricate designs were needed and so the owner or occupier of a "conspicuous" factory was asked to provide a model. Within architectural practice, the culture of model-making has long been integral to the showcasing of architectural visions to investors, stakeholders, and the general public (Mindrup 2019). In the context of the 1930s and 1940s, however, model-making became complexly entwined with the advocacy and performance of militarism. Peter Adey's work, for instance, showcases how practices of model-making were used to help foster enthusiasm and passion for aviation throughout the 1920s and 1930s; "the youth's construction of models was designed to be constructive of them. Models could help construct *model* aerial subjects" (Adey 2010, 50), youthful citizens that would later form the backbone of Britain's future air force. Elsewhere, model construction also became progressively a part of military training; accounts by Reed (1946) and Pearson (2002), for example, highlight the significant role played by geographers in producing terrain models for military and strategic planning for campaigns such as D-Day in June 1944.

With respect to camouflage, models were integral to the trialling and designing of schemes for industrial buildings. Indeed, as one camoufleur put it, "there is danger that without models . . . designs will be clumsy, crude, and ineffective."[3] Models were seen to have many strengths, namely related to the economy of the work being done at the time. They were seen to be relatively inexpensive to construct and they enabled various schemes to be trialled and tested, without the risk of failing with a full-scale scheme (Cave-Brown-Cave 1945, 265). They also helped to ease a great deal of pressure on the rather limited flying resources available to them. Despite the formation of a Camouflage Flight at Baginton Aerodrome, there were only six aircraft at their disposal, hardly enough given the nationwide demand for survey flights to be conducted (Horlock 2018, 129). Practically, models eased these burdens as well as permitted viewing of the site under various viewing conditions; as one report put it:

> weather, pressure of work and the limitations of flying facilities make it inevitable that such factories will rarely be examined under [all] critical conditions of lighting. . . . It is, therefore, desirable to supplement experience gained in flying by observations on models in a viewing room with controlled lighting. Observations are then independent of weather [and] time . . . and schemes can quickly be subjected to the most critical tests.[4]

Models, therefore, permitted opportunities for multiple viewings, something operational flying could not. However, more significant was how models enabled the observing, experimenting, and designing of schemes to be carried out in three-dimensionality. In many ways, this was in accordance with the notion that the oblique viewing perspective of the "bomber body" could not simply be reproduced in 2-D form. Models enabled a more "realistic" simulation of the "bomber body's" viewing experience; they allowed the camoufleur to perform as their enemy counterpart, viewing the structure from all angles and under varying conditions of viewing and altitudes.

To facilitate this simulation of the "bomber body" experience, a specific room for viewing was created in which it was intended for the designer to be "able to build up and judge his [*sic*] scheme under all conditions of light and from all aspects."[5] Following his appointment as chief camouflage officer in December 1938, Lancelot Glasson requested the use of "a large and lofty room . . . in which models can be viewed from a height and distance which will enable the Camouflage officer to determine the effect of his design and tones as they will be seen from the air."[6] In Leamington Spa, the CDCE were allocated the local skating rink and began to adapt it for their purposes. "The Rink" (as it became known) emerged as an important space for camouflage design and research; it was a space of dialogue and discussion where individuals from their different backgrounds, knowledges, and experiences could be brought together to help refine the camouflage scheme. But it was also an important site of affirmation and verification, achieved through attention to detail when it came to simulating the viewing conditions of the "outside world." The model of the factory to be concealed would be placed at the centre of the room onto a revolving table, enabling it to be viewed from all angles akin to a circling enemy bomber aircraft. At one end of the room was an observational platform, set at a distance and height that corresponded with the angle of viewing expected by the "bomber body" (a fifteen-degree angle that matched viewing from three thousand feet at a distance of five miles). At the disposal of the camoufleur on this platform were several optical devices: a variable magnification telescope helped the designer to view the model from simulated distances of between one and seven miles, whilst the development of a "haze box" enabled the mimicking of the effects of light cloud, mist, and fog. There were also controls for the lighting, with a revolving "sun lamp," suspended on an arm above the model, that could be inclined and manoeuvred to "mimic" the different positions of the sun at various times of the day and season.

In addition to creating the "right" conditions for viewing the model, attention was also paid to the construction of the model itself. Indeed, it was contended that:

> it is vitally important [that] for all indoor observations . . . the models [themselves] shall reflect the light in exactly the same fashion as the full-scale camouflaged factory and its surroundings. . . . As it is impossible to simulate natural surfaces by paint alone, careful simulation of natural textures is essential, and in making models for viewing room use, care [must] always be taken to see that textures [are] equivalent to those already determined for natural surfaces.[7]

To achieve this authenticity, "natural" and building surfaces were measured using texture meters; information gathered through this was then used to match these with commonly available model-making materials. Woodland was simulated using coffee granules or painted hessian; ploughland mimicked through corrugated cardboard; and the effect of water achieved through the painting of green varnish. As for artificial surfaces, roads were created through "recycling" old roof felt or painted cartridge paper. Even the camouflage treatments themselves required scaled-down simulations; textured-based treatments, for example, were created through the use of coloured sawdust, cork granules, and painted sand or coffee grounds.

Through these creative efforts, "the Rink" was invested as a site of affirmation and verification. It was a space that facilitated the acting out of a set of simulated embodied and militarised practices that defined the "bomber body" and its encounter with the landscape below, enabled through the specific arrangement of objects, technologies and optical devices, the adoption of attentive acts of simulation and the mobilisation of model-making skills and knowledges. In animating this landscape encounter through these assemblages, it was contended that the industrial landscape could be further scrutinised and deconstructed, camouflage schemes be trialled and tested, and an "effective" solution be determined, both economically and successfully.

## ANIMATING ARCHIVES

The first part of this chapter has focused on how civil camouflage emerged as a militarised practice and how the British landscape was reinscribed through the embracing of a discourse of defence and protection. As this context showcased, creative practices and knowledges were integral to facilitating this protection, with model-making playing a central role in the designing and testing of camouflage schemes. In many respects, this narrative represents a "conventional" historical approach to the re-telling of the past. It is a set of stories about the past that has emerged from the residues and artefacts engaged with by me, the researcher, during the course of archival research at a multitude of sites. The materials for this historical-cultural geography of camouflage were wide-ranging, consisting of traditional documentary sources, such as meeting minutes and memoranda, science papers, policy documents, and correspondence, as well as a wide range of visual and cultural artefacts, from aerial photographs and technical drawings to landscape paintings, documentary film footage, and camouflage netting materials. In this section, I want to focus on the "doing" of the research and how my encounters with the archives prompted me to seek out alternative ways of bringing to life and "animating" the stories I was coming across in the archives about this militarised practice.

Across the humanities and social sciences, there have been many reflections on the influences and the "place" of the archive in historical research (Burton 2005; Gagen, Lorimer, and Vasudevan 2007). Certainly, there have been numerous appraisals of the ways in which the researcher might select, interpret, analyse, and re-present the historical materials they find within these spaces to tell a particular story. An acknowledgment of the effect of these multifarious processes has meant that rather than viewing the "archive-as-source," historical research has increasingly come to consider the "archive-as-subject" (Ashmore, Craggs, and Neate 2012, 82). This has become particularly clear within geography, where it has been contended that "the archive, like all geographical locations for methods, should not . . . be considered as lying passively in the background of the research encounter, but as an active participant in the constitution of relations" (Anderson, Adey, and Bevan 2010, 598). As such, the archival encounter has become a more critical and reflective experience, with attention being paid to the co-constitutive role of the researcher and archive in the evolution of the research and its subsequent findings.

In the context of my own encounters, there were three particular issues that shaped and defined my engagements with camouflage, broadly, and camouflaged models, specifically, but which also encouraged and inspired me to think differently about how to bring the stories about them to life. Firstly, as with other historical work, I acknowledge the site of the archives as a power-laden space; as Maddrell writes, "archives are . . . sites of power: not least power to tell a particular story from particular points of view" (2008, 128–29). As a result, it has been contended that "we need to be careful to think about how certain voices are present in the archive, while others are absent" (Edwards and Gilbert 2007, 75). In the context of my own research, I spent most of my time engaging with sites such as the National Archives, Kew and the Imperial War Museum, London, as these were repositories for organisations such as the CDCE and the Ministry of Home Security (under which the CDCE operated). However, it soon became clear that these engagements reinforced a particular vision of civil camouflage, one that reproduced an "official" and regulatory discourse; the materiality of these archives appeared to act as a tool of "camouflage governance." Accordingly, I found myself having to negotiate the politics of both camouflage work and these archival spaces to seek out "alternative" sites and so shed light on the "silenced" voices and "counter-narratives" the "official" archive hid and concealed. Such a move also served to illustrate how a nationally coordinated practice was subsequently translated from a "centre of calculation" to the local level (Naylor 2006). Visits to local and regional archives and history centres as well as university archives generated insights into the application of camouflage schemes as well as the reception of these by the industrial occupiers and their workforces.

These trips also addressed a secondary issue of archival work: the issue of "absence." The very nature of historical research is that things get lost or go missing; as Black (2010, 467) writes, "the past can never be recovered as a solid whole, as history is always fragmented. Historical research can only deal with residues or, to use a geological metaphor, sediments left over as a result of past actions." This is certainly the case if we think about the space of the archives; things get lost or destroyed in the process of archiving, judgements are made about what is worthy of preservation or not, and the very materiality of the objects that feature in the archives (paper, for instance) is subject to decay and destruction (in spite of the best efforts of the archives themselves to preserve them) (Mills 2013; DeSilvey 2007). Equally, as commentators on the "military archives" have highlighted, these "absences" can be due to the secretive nature of these spaces (Farish 2016; Forsyth 2016). Collectively, these can lead to absences in the historical record and incomplete or "obscured" recollections of the past. My own immersion in the archives gave a sense of the lost or decaying materials in the archives: damaged papers and faded typescript making for incomplete readings of documents; files related to the camouflage of specific factories missing, either on account of the secrecy surrounding such work or the unwieldy amount of paperwork that could not be preserved in full. Seeking out regional and local archives went someway to address these, but the absences still remained.

A final reflection is on the embodied encounters of the archives. Historical geographers, amongst others, have often gone to great lengths to profile the various encounters that they have had in the space of the archives and the influences of these engagements upon the interpretation and (re)presentation of the past. Such accounts of the archival experience have emphasised the significance of "autobiographical reflection," with the researcher thinking through their "affectual" encounters with archival objects and environments (Bailey, Brace, and Harvey 2009). As such, historical researchers have frequently evoked the "dramas" and "pleasures" of historical work, alluded to the "seduction" of the archive environment and the effect of archive regulations in "disciplining" the researcher (Bradley 1999; Rose 2000). Once again, my own research shared similar experiences: the repetitive and intensive working in narrow time frames, the frustration of missing documents, the excitement of the unexpected finding, the enjoyment of conversations with archivists, the feeling of strained eyes in dimly lit rooms, etc. These different encounters shaped and informed the ways in which I engaged with and utilised the materials I was finding. Positive research experiences helped facilitate the easy recall of certain camouflage stories, episodes, and the work of particular individuals, whereas archival experiences defined by dullness, boredom, and distraction distanced oneself from the material. In this sense, one's personal and intimate experiences of the archive informed and moulded the narratives I wanted to tell.

These three elements—the politics of the archives, their fragmentary and absent dimensions, and my embodied experiences of these spaces—combined in terms of my engagement with camouflage models. Within the National Archives itself, allusions were made to the presence of models for camouflage work; indeed, the stories that I've retold earlier draw upon their textual representation with the archives, largely from various research papers and correspondence. In and of themselves, these models were a noticeable absence in the archives; at 1:200 scale, they would have been simply too big to have been retained by the archives. Furthermore, in most cases, models had been sent back to the firms whose premise was due to be camouflaged. It is, therefore, highly likely that they might have been destroyed or lost following the war itself. My only opportunities to engage with them came through the odd photographic record; such encounters became particular "highlights," or moments of surprise and excitement. These opportunities only came about as I sought to negotiate the politics of the archives and seek out historical materials beyond the National Archives itself. A trip to the Julian Trevelyan Archives at Trinity College, Cambridge University, for example, allowed me to engage with the non-official organisation, the Industrial Camouflage Research Unit (ICRU), a group of artists and designers looking to capitalise on the "camouflage craze" in the late 1930s. These engagements, unlike the encounters at Kew, were defined by a wealth of photographs capturing models onto which the ICRU designers had applied their visions for how camouflage might be applied to an assortment of industrial buildings. Equally, during my visit to the National Gas Archives in Warrington, I encountered photographs of a model for St Anthony's gasworks in Newcastle-upon-Tyne.

To reflect on the emotions of these encounters, these "moments" of archival research "stood out": they were captivating; they intrigued and fascinated me. But these "moments" were equally frustrating and, perhaps, even tinted with a little sadness; my encounters with these models were defined by their physical absence. The remaining traces of them were confined to a two-dimensional medium and a largely monochrome existence. Given the very performative way in which models were utilised, their existence in a static, black-and-white representation had a slightly "deadening" effect. This prompted me to think about how I might bring these models "to life." How could I enliven my archival encounters? How could I animate the narratives of the embodied practices of the "bomber body" that camoufleurs were trying to simulate?

Since childhood, I have been a model maker, largely of military aircraft. For me, model-making has been a form of escapism, a leisurely pursuit, a time-space to switch off from everyday life. Over time, it is an activity through which I've developed and honed my creative skills, skills that require concentration, attention to detail and the unleashing of the imagination. It was for this reason that I found discussions around models (and photographs of them) in the archives as particularly fascinating. But equally, it was these creative skills that prompted me to want to do something more with the textual and visual representations I was encountering in the archives. These aspirations were also being informed by discussions that were emerging from recent debates within the literature. Across the discipline of geography, there has been much discussion around the "animating" of the archival encounters as well as exploring more "playful way[s] of working as geographers" (Woodyer 2012, 313). Sarah Mills's (2013) work, for example, provides an overview of the ways in which historical-cultural geographers have sought to "bring to life" the various "fragments, objects and ghosts" that we encounter in these spaces. Likewise, Dwyer and Davies (2010, 89) emphasise how historical-cultural geographers in recent engagements with the archives have sought to "bring the material and documentary properties of archives into play, through an emphasis on bodily performance, the mobility of materials and the interplay between generating accounts and ongoing processes of interpretation" (for example, see also Lorimer 2003). A particular noteworthy example is Kathryn Yusoff's (2007) work into the body-landscape encounters of Antarctic explorers, where she makes creative use of Action Man figures to reanimate past embodied encounters contained within archival and historical artefacts.

These more animated and playful ways of engaging with the archives have also intersected with various debates to emerge within critical military geography. Woodyer's work on "ludic geographies," for example, has prompted a more critical examination of "war play" and the cultures of militarism beyond the battlefield, particularly amongst youth (see also Carter, Kirby, and Woodyer 2017). More specifically, in the context of modelling, Richard Yarwood's (2015) focus on modelling, miniaturisation, and the playing out of military practices through wargaming has commenced discussions about the simulation and performance of militarised identities and the playing out of militarised knowledges and scenarios. It was this performative aspect that drew me to wanting to recreate the camouflage models that I was encountering in the archive. Indeed, through model-making, I hoped to be able to (re) produce and perform a militarised identity I was exploring in the archive: the role of the camoufleur. Such a role was something I'd been performing in my other archival encounters. For instance, when examining aerial photographs of a camouflaged factory, I often found myself transcending my role as a researcher to become a photographic interpreter, looking for signs and traces to discern where a camouflage structure might be or to think through issues of conspicuousness within the interwar landscape. To (re)create a camouflage model would enable me to "bring to life" a set of militarised identities that were relatively confined to the archives and, through this re-animation, allow myself as a researcher to access and perform a series of embodied knowledges and skills that embraced the aerial and militarised gazes that I was exploring in my wider research. Animating these embodied practices might also

**Figure 6.1 Photograph capturing the uncamouflaged model factory.**

grant others the opportunity to experience these militarised body-landscape encounters.

The process of model-making itself commenced with the materials found in the archives. In particular, there were two specific types of structure that I wished to replicate that were discussed in the archives themselves: what was referred to as a "typical factory," usually a single-storey building, combined with the "usual" traits, such as a chimney, a saw-toothed roof, and roof windows (Figure 6.1); and an oil-tank farm, a cluster of cylindrical structures set against a tarmacked or concrete base. For each, I wanted to showcase a "before" and "after" camouflage treatment, the former to highlight why certain structures might be conspicuous, the latter to showcase the act of camouflage itself. As such, each structure was made with duplicated sections (triple for the factory chimney to showcase "toning down" and "disruptive" methods). The structures themselves were constructed making use of "waste" or "excess" materials: chimneys and the oil tank holders were cut from an old broom handle and the factory buildings and roof constructed from off-cuts from various DIY/household projects. Pathways and roads were simulated using coloured card and old roofing felt, approaches similarly adopted by camoufleurs themselves. The effect of glass was reproduced through thin sheets of acetate cut to size to produce a "reflective" quality. When it came to the designing of the camouflage schemes, once more I sought inspiration from the archives. The use of paint was informed by a list of standardized "camouflage colours" I'd been fortunate to obtain from a colour card sample in the National Archives. These were roughly matched to matt colours that I held in my own model paint collection. A camouflage manual provided an illustrative diagram of a camouflaged chimney in a "semi-rural" setting that was used to inform the application of a disruptive pattern to model factory. A set of large, coloured plans for a scheme for a factory in Ipswich were found in a local history archive and provided the inspiration for the "imitative" patterning applied to my factory model (Figure 6.2). Finally, a series of monochrome photographs informed the texturing of the oil tank farms model; subsequently, a disruptive pattern was applied to the crowns of these tanks, making use of discarded shed roofing felt.

Like my archival encounters, the process of model-making soon became an emotive, tactile, and multi-sensory experience shaped by a series of "moments" that both inspired and obstructed my progress. As part of this process, I can recount and recall the feeling of wonder at discovering old tins of model paint that evoked childhood memories of previous modelling projects; the excitement of trying to colour-match with the standard "camouflage colours"; the exertion of hand sawing off-cuts of wood; the pain of wood splinters; the tedium of sanding or drying paint; the frustrations of "things not looking quite right"; the off-putting odour of enamel paint; and

**Figure 6.2 Photograph capturing the model factory, incorporating camouflage techniques researched from the archives.**

the exhilaration of the model itself "coming to life." In short, not only was the journey of model-making allowing me to re-tell "camouflage stories," but the experiences and the intended outcome of this process (i.e., producing a model) were both helping to address the deadening effect that their two-dimensional, black-and-white existence was facilitating.

## REFLECTIONS ON MODEL-MAKING AND ANIMATING (PAST) MILITARISED PRACTICES

Having focused on the *process* for model-making, I want to consider in this final section the *purpose* of such an undertaking: What contributions might model-making bring to a critical discussion of militarism and its impacts on space, place, and identity?

A first set of opportunities that models and model-making might present are for the military researcher themselves. What has hopefully emerged over the previous sections is how model-making, for the researcher, can play a useful role for accessing and animating past performances of militarised actions and practices that are the object of one's research. As showcased here, the production of camouflaged models helped to address "absences" in the archives, both of the material artefacts themselves (the models) and the embodied practices with which they were associated. In doing so, they enabled the re-animation of past body-landscape encounters, engagements that were shaped and defied by the logics and imperatives of militarism. In this case, these were orientated around the imperatives of defence and protection. Through this process, I contend that this can enhance critical understandings of militarism and, thus, contribute to the ongoing agenda that seeks to examine its reach and impact upon everyday spaces, places, and landscapes (Woodward 2005). Furthermore, reflecting on the embodied experiences of the historical researcher, engaging with the past through these creative means, might also serve to provide the renewed impetus in the "doing of" research, particularly when confronted by the unique and often challenging and exhausting experiences of working with and against the archives. Indeed, as discussed earlier, the military archive itself presents unique challenges due to their secretive, disjointed, and disruptive nature (Forsyth 2016), and adopting creative approaches like model-making might well present opportunities to circumvent these barriers as well as allow for the re-constitution of the militarised identities that are often obscured or hidden within them. From my own encounters, model-making helped to provide a renewed enthusiasm, prompt alternative ways of retelling "stories" in the archives, as well as uncover a distinct set of embodied and militarised practices and identities located within them. That said, there are certainly challenges to this, most notably in form of the skills required to pursue model-making (Yarwood 2015); this might prompt further opportunities for the researchers themselves, either through the acquiring of new skills or in facilitating interdisciplinary discussions with those in the creative arts.

Secondly, embracing creative practices such as model-making might be helpful in terms of thinking about how we communicate research into militarised practices to a wide range of audiences, within and beyond the academy. Given the pressures to showcase research and demonstrate research impact, the production of models might provide that space for dialogue and engagement with a diverse audience. For example, making use of models might be particularly beneficial in helping to enrich and enliven teaching and learning experiences within the academy. Gallaher (2004), for instance, has highlighted the significance of the classroom as a critical space for thinking through the impacts of militarism and political violence upon everyday people and places. In my own teaching praxis, I have often reflected on the kinds of class-based activities that might be drawn upon to help foster critical appraisals of militarism, its legacies, and its spatial impacts and consequences. Where I've led classes focusing on camouflage as an "emergent" form of military urbanism, I've often assigned students the task of deconstructing a series of aerial photographs and "reading" the military landscape. However, their material existence as a two-dimensional, monochromic representational form presents the same "deadening effect" I've experienced and discussed throughout this chapter. These photographs are limited in their performative dimensions; they fail to capture the more mobile and performative ways in which these sites would have been scrutinised by a militarised eye. Creating models and bringing them into spaces such as the classroom, and beyond, facilitates a more animated and enlivened discussion and critique, achieved through embracing the performative and the creative. Dalton (2020), for example, has emphasised the role of crafting models to initiate conversations and share thoughts on difficult and sensitive issues. From my experience of camouflage model-making, models that capture or embody military practice afford an opportunity for military researchers to interact and engage with their audiences, to encourage them to transcend their own identity and perform an alternative militarised identity. In the case of my own work, this involved inviting others to perform as a "bomber body," to occupy a militarised eye, and to immerse oneself in the critical and militarised "reading" of the landscape through circling and scrutinising the models presented before them. Adopting and engaging in a creative practice such as model-making was central to this performative dimension. In facilitating these re-enactments and performances, we might collectively begin to re-think how everyday spaces and places might be transformed to fulfil certain military objectives, but it also might encourage us to critically reflect on how militarised organisations or individuals exercise power and control over space or how certain military logics govern the peoples that occupy these spaces. This might, then, provide the start point for not only developing a critical voice, but also an opportunity to intervene, resist, and challenge this imposition of military power over space, place, and landscape in the present day.

# 7

# Theatre of War

## *Critical Feminist Research Praxis in Creative Military Research*

*Alice Cree and Hannah West*

To say that you are undertaking feminist, participatory research with members of the military community can seem like a contradiction in terms. Victoria Basham and Sarah Bulmer put it beautifully when they said that "the assumption that feminism and being in close proximity to military personnel are somehow incompatible constitutes one of feminism's most problematic fables. Yet these sentiments still haunt the feminist military scholar" (2017, 65). It is often assumed that to be a *good* feminist, you must maintain a respectable distance from violent state institutions such as the military, and that to get *too close* is to taint yourself in some way. On the one hand, we obviously disagree; we argue that creative and participatory methodologies, which by their very nature involve embracing closeness and collaboration, have a great deal to offer us in military research. As Basham & Bulmer tell us, close encounters such as these can generate important revelations and expose messiness, nuance, and contradictions in our understanding of how militaries and military power function (2017, 60, 64). And yet on the other hand, the research at the heart of this chapter shows that the practical *doing* of critical and creative feminist research often involves a decoupling of military *people* from the military *institution*, harnessing creative collaboration with individuals while maintaining a distance from the organisation itself to remove its potential to control our practice and its outcomes. That is not to say that military communities themselves are not wrapped up in the practice of military power, because of course they are. Rather, in order to engage with the military community *in a feminist way*, keeping a distance from the "military institution" is an imperative practicality.

In a similar vein to David Jackson's work on theatre in chapter 12 of this volume, in this chapter we discuss our current theatre-based project, "Conflict, Intimacy, & Military Wives: A Lively Geopolitics."[1] This research uses participatory theatre-as-method with military spouses to explore how military service and conflict impact upon intimate spaces of the home and personal relationships. At the time of writing, this project is very much live, and we are preparing for the performance of our research-based play, *Magnolia Walls*. At the very core of this work has been a commitment to critical feminist research praxis. For us, this kind of praxis really centred around three core principles; firstly, we were determined to maintain a critical distance from the diffuse people, spaces, and organisations that operate under the broad heading of "the military." This is primarily because we strongly believed the military institution[2] should not have any influence or authority over the voices of our (predominantly women) participants. This was less of an ideological position but more a practical choice. Secondly, we wanted to make the project totally participatory and shaped by the experiences, wants, and needs of the participant group at every stage. Finally, our aim was to centre domestic, intimate spaces of the home in our conversations and creative work on war and military service. In practice, there were a number of challenges we found ourselves navigating, particularly in relation to the first two of these guiding principles. In what follows, we untangle some of these challenges, and pose the question of what it means to do creative, participatory research with military communities when you are committed to maintaining a critical distance from the military institution itself, and what it is like to re-engage with the military institution with the findings.

Theatre has long been used as a way of telling stories about war to a receptive public audience, but in our research we used it as both a research method and a critical representational tool, which flips the more traditional ideas of "military theatre" and "theatre of war" on their heads. Drawing on techniques from Theatre of the Oppressed, forum theatre, and Rainbow of Desires (Boal 2019), our research sought to think anew about what it really means to "recover" from war and proposed that conflict is experienced as much by military spouses as it is by individuals of the armed forces. But in doing this more critical kind of theatre, we found ourselves actively negotiating and sidestepping the minute practices and highly "peopled" processes by which creative work on military issues can become appropriated *by* the military. We have been intrigued by how the practical challenges of doing participatory and creative military research became entangled with the parallel challenge of doing *critical* military theatre. Additionally, our research was, like countless other projects, greatly impacted upon by the global COVID-19 pandemic, which added further complexity as we tried to do all of our "data collection" via Zoom and Microsoft Teams. Amidst these stumbling blocks however, our work is premised on the understanding that there is both a challenge and opportunity offered by the bringing together of participatory methodologies, military theatre, and critical feminist research praxis. Creativity and creative methods have clear promise as critical and emancipatory tools in military research, and yet the practice of *doing* creativity when it comes to military-related topics and phenomena requires careful navigation. This, we argue, is because creativity is as much the purview of militarisation and military power as everything else.

## THEATRE OF WAR: THE ARTS AND THE BRITISH ARMED FORCES

Our research is concerned with the central question of, how do we come to "know" war? It is one that scholars of critical military studies and political geography have done much to try to answer. Work in these areas have explored examples from popular culture and everyday life, such as military memoirs (Woodward 2003; Woodward & Jenkings 2012, 2018), music (Cree 2020a, 2020b), film and television (Stahl 2010; Pomarède 2018), and video games (Jarvis & Robinson 2019; Bos 2021) as means through which publics consume military conflict. Theatre is perhaps one of those lesser-examined contemporary cultural engagements with armed conflict, despite being one of the most long-standing ways in which interested publics become exposed to war and war stories. One of the most obvious historical examples is ancient Greek theatre, which was used as a collective ritual of the polis and a way of discussing contemporary democratic, political, and cultural issues in Athens. A number of the most well-known examples of ancient Greek drama were about experiences of the Trojan War, for example Sophocles' *Ajax* and *Philoctetes*, which both depict the visible and invisible wounds of war on soldiers.

Contemporary theatrical representations of war draw heavily on participation of actual veterans and members of the military community, with theatre often being in part mobilised as a way of helping veterans to "recover" from trauma and injury. One prominent example from the last decade is *Bravo 22 Company*, an award-winning recovery-through-the-arts programme for the British Armed Forces community, and their production of *The Two Worlds of Charlie F.* Bravo 22 Company was created by Alice Driver in collaboration with the Theatre Royal Haymarket Masterclass Trust, the Royal British Legion, and the Ministry of Defence (MoD), with the aim of giving serving and ex-serving personnel new skills and experiences, improving confidence, and supporting transition into civilian life. *The Two Worlds of Charlie F* presents a serviceperson's view of injury and recovery, exploring the consequences of both physical and psychological wounds. It is performed by wounded, injured, and sick service personnel of Bravo 22 Company, and it brings to life their real-life stories of war. In 2012 it won the prestigious Freedom of Expression Award at the Edinburgh Fringe and since then has toured nationwide. In the years that followed, there have been a number of regional legacy projects off the back of the *Two Worlds of Charlie F*, all of which use theatre as a practice of "recovery" for veterans, but also a way of telling particular kinds of stories about the British military and their role in the Iraq and Afghanistan wars. We are seeing a similar trend towards participatory military theatre in the United States. Bryan Doerries's "Theatre of War" project has for the past fifteen years been using dramatic readings of classical Greek tragedies to military communities as a way of opening discussion about the visible and invisible wounds of war. Similarly, Adam Driver (of *Star Wars* and *Girls* fame) founded the charitable organisation Arts in the Armed Forces. The blurb on their website states that "AITAF honours and enriches the lives of the US military community by offering powerful shared experiences in theatre and film." Beyond simply mechanisms of recovery, these kinds of military performance projects have, like other cultural forms (see Woodward & Jenkings 2012 on military memoirs), become a popular form of communicating war stories to a receptive public audience.

While creative and theatrical approaches to exploring the lived experiences of war and recovery have great potential for helping us to think critically about how war affects military communities at scales beyond that of the nation, dominant narratives regarding the sites of conflict and the masculine experience of warfare remain pervasive. Military community performance projects typically "only partially destabilise the frame of virtuous war" (Purnell & Danilova 2018, 370), and they continue to follow the trend among cultural engagements with conflict that prioritise images of heroic masculine soldierhood enacted in spatially "far-away" wars. Indeed, in these narratives the lived experiences of military partners and families are rarely given a platform, let alone centred, despite long standing recognition that they play an integral role in upholding military practices and values (Enloe 1988; Horn 2010; Hyde 2016; Basham & Catignani 2018). Where military partners do feature, they do so reciprocally to their serving hero as military wives performing very much the "supporting" act.

So, contemporary ways of "knowing" war through theatre often replicate dominant tropes around military heroism and the idea of the "virtuous war." What is also striking is the ease with which theatre as a form of representation can be co-opted by military power itself. This is not a phenomenon unique to theatre; we already know that military power is enacted through diffuse sites, spaces, and bodies, and that includes diverse genres of war storytelling in popular culture (see Cree 2020a, 2020b). It is also not just that this is happening in ways that are insidious and difficult to trace, but in fact, the arts and the British Armed Forces are intertwined at an overtly organisational level, because of the latter's long history of engagement with the arts. Music has marked the movement of troops and advances on the battlefield from the earliest days of organised warfare (Bateson 2019). Military music is integral to the collective national commemoration of war and has influenced many a classical composer to honour military success in their works. Beyond choreographing and commemorating war, music has long accompanied military life, providing comfort and distraction through entertainment whilst also providing a means of documenting the lives of the military and their families. Meanwhile theatre has continued to have a place in providing escapism for the troops or a space to reflect on what they had experienced, for example through theatrical troopes formed amongst the men in the First World War, later continuing in the form of British Forces Broadcasting Service (BFBS) live events, formerly known as CSE Shows (Imperial War Museum, n.d.). The Royal Navy similarly has a tradition of the SODS Opera as onboard entertainment, with singing and sketches often reflecting ribald humour and poking fun at senior leaders (Tawney 2015). Such entertainments featured the ships' company themselves performing, again providing a space to let off steam after a period of intense operations.

In the British Army, the Artists Rifles were established in 1859 in response to the threat of French invasion. Comprising artists, actors, musicians, and architects, they were nonetheless a light infantry unit seeing high casualty rates but also producing countless iconic artworks reflecting on the nature of war (Gregory 2021, Haines 2019). The First and Second World Wars saw the establishment of official schemes sponsored by the government to record the conflict. The year 1917 saw the Imperial War Museum established by Act of Parliament and entrusted with commissioning and collecting materials including artwork to form a record of the war (a role it continues today). This was accompanied by government commissioning and purchasing of art to record and memorialise the war. By the Second World War, a War Art Advisory Committee had been established to coordinate the collecting of war art. This official sanctioning of war art represents a concerted effort to control the war narrative at a time before live news reporting.

War narratives continue to be shaped and controlled by the British military through the arts all the way up to the present day. For example, the British Army has established an initiative, "Army and the Arts," whose remit has been presented to the public through media reports as fostering a "close relationship between the Army and the arts" (Female First 2020), claiming to "bring [. . .] communities together using the creative industry" (Eastern Eye 2020). Representatives for the initiative state that their aim is, in part, to ensure authenticity in art about the army:

> They support work that is powerful, informed and independent. In some cases they do that by inviting artists who want to create work about the Army to come "behind the wire" and give them access to the kind of people and experiences that interest them. At other times they provide a showcase for veterans who now work in the arts and whose work reflects lived experience. Both result in an authenticity that make productions all the more affecting and persuasive whether they are addressing how families cope with death or injury, the courage of gay soldiers in coming out, women's struggle for equality or the experiences of black and overseas personnel. The result is agenda-setting art that asks tough questions about our lives and our Army—something that matters greatly for a healthy, open society.
>
> —Lieutenant Colonel Wendy Faux in *The Herald*, 2020

While purporting to be asking "tough questions," the unavoidable fact is that there are some questions that work under the "Army and the Arts" heading *cannot* and *will not* ask because of the risk it might pose to the reputation of the army itself. Furthermore, there is arguably a level of gatekeeping being undertaken by such initiatives (whether deliberate or not) that has the consequence that certain projects (those deemed to be particularly "topical," or chime with the army's concerns at the time) find it easier to access funding, participants, and equipment, as well as publicity, while others may struggle with all of these things. In "Army and the Arts'" *Army@TheFringe*, for example, projects benefit from funding and the prestige of being part of the official programming, as well as access to authentic army equipment to use as props or costumes. However, pieces of theatre that are part of this programming but found to be explicitly critical of the British military and their policies may find more barriers in their way, are cast aside, or even neutered of their critique.[3] In other examples of military theatre, meaningful critique of the armed forces can be difficult because of where the funding comes from. Public funding for projects in the arts is limited in the UK, and so for armed forces-related work, the pots of money offered by bodies for whom military issues are the central concern can seem attractive. For example in 2017–2018, Soldiers' Arts Academy CIC's stage production of *Soldier On* received £20,000 of funding from the Armed Forces Covenant Fund, a trust that "supports the Armed Forces Covenant by delivering funding programmes that create real change to Armed Forces communities across the UK" (The Armed Forces Covenant Fund Trust, n.d.). However, as Nick Caddick argues in his forthcoming book, funding of this nature is often either directly tied to the military institution itself, or serves to further its interests in other, more insidious ways. In the case of *Soldier On,* the Armed Forces Covenant Fund was still based at the MoD at the time the funding was administered, and so the play was effectively funded by the MoD. Our point is not that *Soldier On* was, because of its proximity to the MoD, devoid of critique. Nor are we suggesting that all "military theatre" is controlled in some way by the British Armed Forces. Rather, we argue that military theatre is an example of how creative practice and military power continue to be intertwined, whether in overt or more subtle ways.

In our work on the "Conflict & Intimacy" project, we wanted to use military theatre in a different way. Aware of the legacy of the British military controlling war narratives in and through the arts and creativity, and in particular the continued entanglement of the military institution with theatrical representations of military service and conflict, we wondered what theatre might do for a more critical engagement with the topic of war and military violence. In the following sections of this chapter, we discuss in practical terms how we tried to do "theatre of war" in this more feminist and critical way. But it is important to recognise there are practicalities to the very *doing* of creative work on military issues that can engender a tangled and complex relationship with "the military" as broadly understood. For example, doing anything with people from the military community fundamentally requires access to that group, but the difficulty of this and the common necessity of having to use personal contacts or "gatekeeper" figures has been widely acknowledged in military studies (see Ben-Ari & Levy 2014; Walker 2016; Hyde 2016)—and such gatekeepers often act in the interests of the military institution. To do creative work with military communities, particularly over a period of weeks, months, or years, requires a level of "buy-in" from participants that is difficult to achieve without significant support from gatekeeping organisations. In this chapter we offer an examination of how the day-to-day practices and processes that make up "creative research in military studies" can require careful navigation and sidestepping of military control. As we have shown, theatre becomes a vehicle of military influence through the kinds of knowledges and stories that are centred, but also through the diverse forms of gatekeeping that allow that centring to take place. In what follows, we explore how we have confronted and attempted to disrupt both these aspects.

## "ROLL UP, ROLL UP": ON METHOD AND PARTICIPANT RECRUITMENT

In August 2020, when our research project grant period officially commenced, it was only five months since the start of the first period of government restrictions on mobility and movement to minimise the spread of COVID-19 in the UK. We did not, at that point, know if we would be going into another lockdown or how long the pandemic would last, and so the methodological approach of the research had to be adapted to work [either in part, or entirely] online. Like many researchers facing this kind of pandemic uncertainty, the first six months of the project were dedicated to what can only be described as a period of "grieving" for the intimate, situated, tactile, in-person research project that was originally planned, as well as a state of panic as the team figured out a plan for moving forward. Eventually, a decision was made to move all the "data collection" onto Zoom and Microsoft Teams, and a plan for the research process was formulated.

Although it has been much more fluid than this outline suggests, our structure for the research process followed seven roughly consecutive stages; 1) participant recruitment; 2) theatre taster session and 1:1 interviews on Microsoft Teams; 3) introductory large group theatre workshops on Zoom;[4] 4) themed, smaller group theatre workshops on Zoom; 5) follow-up focus groups and writing workshops on Zoom;[5] 6) writing the play based on interview and workshop material; 7) performing the play onstage, and other impact and dissemination activities. At the time of writing this chapter, we are in the midst of preparing the final play, *Magnolia Walls*,[6] for performance at Northern Stage, Newcastle Upon Tyne, in June 2022. The research was designed to be driven by participants throughout, towards the shared goal of having their stories told to the public through theatre.

From the onset, we knew our biggest challenge was going to be recruiting participants. We were looking for a significant group of at least fifteen to twenty military partners who were willing to commit to weekly workshops over a six-month period, and who were not put off by them being "drama-based" and possibly quite emotionally demanding. Military spouses already represent a hard-to-reach group due to their widely acknowledged feelings of "survey fatigue," the fact that they often move regularly, and that they shoulder significant childcare and domestic responsibilities. Furthermore, the context of the pandemic meant that the carefully crafted plan of reaching out in-person via taster sessions at community hubs and family centres on married patches was thrown to the wind and replaced with the difficult process of online recruitment.

Being funded by the Economic and Social Research Council (ESRC),[7] our research project is independent of the MoD, and we guarded this independence carefully. We wanted participants to know they were entering a participatory research space that did not replicate power dynamics that might underpin their prior interactions with the MoD, and where they were free to share their experiences and be listened to. In practice, this had several implications for our recruitment strategy. To start with, we decided not to put our research before the Ministry of Defence Research Ethics Committee (MODREC) (having already been given full ethical approval from the Newcastle University Research Ethics Committee), based on their guidance that "research involving veterans and military families are not generally included" (JSP 536), although their remit is ambiguous and inconsistent across the policy. Nonetheless, we felt strongly that working with—importantly, civilian—military partners to explore their lives and relationships with their serving or veteran partners should not be subject to MoD approval. This decision did have the unfortunate effect of denying military partners who were also currently serving from taking part as their participation would have been subject to MODREC approval. We replicated this approach in our interaction with the military charity sector, where we felt that major military charities such as Help for Heroes, the Royal British Legion, and SSAFA are, in the eyes of our participant community of military partners, aligned with the MoD and we felt had become gatekeepers to the wider military community (see also Caddick, forthcoming). Large military charities often have blurred relationships with the MoD, with former (usually high ranking) service personnel acting on executive and trustee boards, and funding coming either directly or indirectly from the MoD (for example, through the Armed Forces Covenant Fund Trust). We were keen not to put our project in the position of having to get "approval" to be shared or publicised by any of these organisations, nor did we want to inadvertently align ourselves with any of the diverse organisations that in our minds still form parts of the "military machine" in the UK. So, we adopted a very personal and low-key approach to recruiting, reaching out amongst our own networks and smaller military charities with a local or specific remit.

A research team of two, Alice had prior connections with women veterans in Newcastle, and Hannah was able to draw on her connections from her own military service. Being forced to take the recruiting online had the advantage that it opened the geographical scope beyond the North-East of England, where the project was based, so we could look nationwide (and indeed beyond as we recruited one participant who was stationed with her serving partner overseas). We embarked on two main routes to recruiting in tandem. We tried emailing smaller military charities, but with little prior connection to these organisations, we had a very limited response. We recruited most of our participants by reaching out through email and direct messaging on Twitter, Facebook, and LinkedIn to former participants of Alice's earlier project with women veterans and former colleagues of Hannah's. This latter approach was much more successful, although not without an occasionally uncomfortable sense of "using" one's own contacts, and it is how we found the majority of our participants. Trying to avoid a big social media splash by posting publicly, which might draw major charities and the MoD to comment or repost, thus suggesting an association with our project, we asked our contacts to share adverts with closed social media groups. We were much more dependent on our networks of personal contacts than we had anticipated and, realistically, without being able to meet face-to-face to build a rapport with potential participants and answer their questions, we were reliant on people advocating for us based on past relationships. As such, Hannah's extensive network of former colleagues was invaluable, but it simultaneously raises questions as to how the non-veteran researcher could have achieved this access through online recruiting only.

Determined to recruit a cross-section of participants representing serving partners from different military services and ranks, as well as including participants with disabilities and of different genders, ethnicities, and sexualities, we were relatively fortunate that from our group of over thirty participants, we did find representation from many of these minority groups. It is perhaps not surprising that groups we have found the most difficult to reach such as men, members of ethnic minorities, LGBTQ+ spouses, and spouses of Foreign and Commonwealth origin, reflect that Hannah, who was leading the recruiting effort, was not from any of these groups. However, determined to increase this representation, we attempted to reach these minority groups by preparing a short video specifically requesting their participation and raising its profile slightly such that we shared it publicly on social media. This had limited impact, though, and left us questioning whether our efforts were reaching the "right" online spaces to be visible to the community we were trying to reach. Ultimately, we decided to focus our effort on reaching the Foreign and Commonwealth military community, as we did have some representation of the other groups. Our most successful effort here was recruiting a peer-researcher, consultant, and dramaturg from the Fijian military community who was able to introduce us to gatekeepers who enabled this access.

## THE MILITARY HOME AS CRITICAL RESEARCH SPACE

The second and third core tenets of our critical feminist research praxis in this project involved, as explained earlier in the chapter, making the project totally participatory and centring the domestic, intimate spaces of the home. Work in critical military studies has shown the military home is a militarised space, where gendered relations of military power play out (Basham and Catignani 2018, Hyde 2016, Pain 2015), and yet the home is rarely (if ever) represented in cultural forms such as theatre as a site of military conflict itself. In the "Conflict & Intimacy" project, we wanted to reframe the military home as a space of war and military violence by using the practice and process of theatre-making.

Our main series of workshops took place from April to September 2021 amidst ongoing pandemic restrictions and social isolation for many. In this context, "the home" took on differing and often complex meanings for all of us, as a site of safety and comfort for some, and a prison for others. There were therefore obvious ethical concerns associated with our switch to online workshops; for example, our interaction was limited to what we could see on the screen and so we could never be sure who might be listening in. We knew our creative work might touch on topics of abuse, trauma, and PTSD, and so if partners or family members were living in close proximity, this would influence what they were willing to share and how comfortable they felt participating (and indeed, the safety of others in the group). Participants were given extensive information about the kinds of topics the workshops would cover, and in signing consent forms, they gave specific agreement to ensuring they took part from a private room with a closed door, respected the anonymity of others in the group, did not capture screenshots or recordings from the sessions, and did not "tag" anyone from the group in posts on social media. We found participants to be very sensitive to these issues, making us aware if they had children who were just going to bed or if their partner was in an adjacent room. Participants were also able to use pseudonyms on Zoom or keep their cameras off if they so chose—although in the end, no one chose to do so. There were, however, a number of people who only took part in 1:1 interviews rather than the theatre workshops, and in some cases, we knew this was because they did not want their partners to know they were taking part.

The main set of twelve theatre-based workshops were split into three themed blocks of four sessions; 1) Love, Intimacy, Home; 2) Body, Identity, Absence; 3) Power, Secrecy, Control. These themes emerged from the interview material as well as the four introductory workshops, which had given participants chance to get to know us and each other better and to bond as a group. We really wanted participants to be invested in the co-creation of the play and in deciding what they wanted to be heard through this project, and so we also used these early workshops to engage with their ideas on possible themes. The themed workshops combined discussion-based exercises and theatre-based activities to engage participants in creative ways that helped them to explore some of the, at times, challenging topics we wanted to discuss in different ways. Participants were asked to create static non-verbal images which represented the different stages of their partner deploying, or they were asked to create a moving silent mime to represent the military machine. Paired exercises involved devising a short scene to represent the conversation between a military couple when separated through deployment, and then bringing in a third person as the narrator to ask questions about what they were really feeling, or to represent the military institution itself. These activities all helped to visualise the lived experience of the military partner, at once unlocking fascinating conversations between participants and pointing to how these experiences might be represented onstage. Beyond the main workshop series, we followed up a number of emerging themes with one-off workshops, including on the Iraq and Afghanistan wars, and sexual intimacy and friendship. We also conducted a "Whatsapp hour" on the subject of remembrance, which allowed participants to engage with this emotive subject in a more detached way. Participants were finally offered the opportunity to take part in three writing workshops to help them to write their own stories.

Exploring the kinds of research themes we outline above with military partners took on new meaning in the context of online working, as participants attended while sat in the very homes in which many of them had *lived* these issues. We were asking questions about the presence of the military in their lives and in their homes, and in so doing we were bringing war and the military *back into* their homes through conversation and theatre. We addressed this by creating a safe and caring space, where we offered breakout rooms for those who needed a time out, including relaxation exercises at the end of every workshop to delineate the end of the session, and encouraging participants to write in research journals we provided as a way of letting go of the conversations we had in the workshop. One of the most challenging sessions was the follow-up workshop on Iraq and Afghanistan, where one participant asked to use the breakout room to speak with one of us as she was finding the recollections of the time her husband had been deployed there distressing. Arguably, being confronted with these questions in the safe space of her home was too difficult. When tackling the most difficult of topics, such as absence or war, however, we found the online space had much to offer in decentring the personal narrative and allowing us to talk about concepts in a more abstract manner that took pressure off individuals. For example, by using an online whiteboard, the focus of the participants was on this white space on the screen as we contributed comments to the discussion, without all looking at one individual who was sharing their personal story. Encouraging participants to explore how we might "stage" abstract concepts around violence and intimacy also helped in tackling otherwise difficult subjects, as it has again shifted the focus off the experiences of individuals and onto the shared goal of theatre-making. Furthermore, the relative anonymity of Zoom calls helped participants feel more comfortable sharing their experiences with a group of women they weren't likely to just bump into in their daily lives.

Being in their own homes during the workshops meant participants were surrounded by the paraphernalia of life. This stimulated reflections on how the miliary encroaches on the domestic space, as they looked around and saw the artefacts of military service surrounding them. Asking them about their relationships in the context of military deployments whilst many of them sat in the homes where they had been alone, perhaps caring for children or carrying on their lives in the absence of their serving partners, brought into vivid definition the home as a place of both togetherness and separation. Participants were able to bring artefacts of their lives into workshops, grabbing photographs to share or using items of military uniform in drama-based exercises.

For our participants, the online space of community and "ensemble voice" we had cultivated became one that was empowering and powerfully supportive. We had group members whose partners had been posted overseas during the pandemic and found themselves isolated, but our consistent weekly workshops offered the opportunity to try something different and creative, while getting to know new people who understood, at least to some extent, the lives they were leading. Whilst there were many differences amongst participants, not least in relation to the regard with which they held the military, they were supportive and listened to one another. On playing a theatre game in which participants pretended they were being given an invisible gift and then reacted as though they had been given the most perfect present for them at that moment, one participant described being given flowers and how she never received flowers anymore as she was currently going through a divorce. Another participant was moved to contact us after the session and, through us, order flowers to be sent to this group member, which was heart-warming and an indication of the bond these women felt despite having never met face-to-face.

The workshops became creative research sites in which participants were able to find their critical voices and explore messy ideas and feelings through theatre. There was something almost resistant to military power about how the military home was mobilised; this space that was, for many, representative of the oppression and control by the armed forces suddenly became a site for imagining the world differently. In encouraging participants to create a six-word play to represent the military partner as a superhero, one participant's play read, "size one—size three—size eight," using the change in the shoe sizes of her children to articulate what is missed by her partner when they are separated, and she is alone in dealing with their children. She was using the domestic artefacts of the home to invoke the impact of military conflict on her everyday existence. And it was not just that we were able to reframe conversations about war and military conflict around domestic homelife, but, in so doing, we were attributing military partners with authority and agency on narrating the subject of war. Participants were also able to ground fundamentally imaginative and creative thinking about their lives *in* the visceral and felt the reality of the home.

## *MAGNOLIA WALLS*: DISSEMINATING CREATIVE AND CRITICAL RESEARCH ON AND TO THE MILITARY

As we write this chapter, we are turning our attention to the project's legacy through the communication of its findings. Our ambitions are to catalyse a public conversation about the impacts of armed conflict on military families and spouses, whilst also influencing both the MoD and military charities in the support services they provide for military families. Currently, the play based on the research has been written, a director and actors have been engaged, and we are working towards the staging in June 2022. Set in Northumberland, *Magnolia Walls* follows the tumultuous lives of two military wives, who form an unlikely but close relationship forged through defying stereotypes and going through their own individual personal growth. The play highlights some of the key themes and issues that emerged from the interviews and theatre workshops, tackling difficult topics such as domestic abuse, trauma, PTSD, suicide, and racism. The cast is made up of two professional actors, but the play also has a filmed "chorus" element performed by real military partners who participated in the research.

It has been an interesting challenge to write a piece of theatre based on this work. We wanted it to accurately represent the diverse experiences of the participant group, while also doing something critically interesting in relation to the research themes. It needed to be theatrically arresting, challenging to those who watch it, while also maintaining the moments of both light and shade that you need in any script. We wanted our participants to be proud of the play, and for it to depict their experiences in a way that was honest but also respectful and not judgemental. A decision was made to tell the majority of the play's story through two characters, who were effectively composite figures made up of traces of all our participants. The storyline is built around an ongoing conversation between the two of them, in which they offer very different perspectives on their lives and the struggles that they face. In structuring *Magnolia Walls* in this way, our aim was to create an open dialogue on stage about what the impacts of military service and war are on partners, and where the responsibility for these might ultimately lie. We want the play to encourage our audience to think differently, to reflect on the mainstream narratives about war, and to ask questions. It is not light entertainment to be enjoyed for a night out and then forgotten; it is written to shock and diversify understandings of what it means to be a military partner.

We want those in positions of influence to see the play, to reflect and revisit how current policies impact on military families. This is primarily because we feel a strong obligation to do something meaningful and significant with our research for the benefit of our participants. Driven by a participatory ethos, the research uncovered specific things that the group wanted "the military" to know, and to change. It is also undeniable that we feel a pressure to engage with the MoD to be able to tell a convincing "impact story" about our research. As academics, impact is a currency that we trade in when applying for jobs, promotions, and research grants. Using theatre to simply "start a conversation" with the military about the impact of war on military partners is something we feel strongly about, but the impact of this is hard to evidence. We therefore want the play to be just one component of our project's bigger engagement effort with the MoD and those in the position to effect change, while still wrestling with our own misgivings about the implications of being seen to be getting "too close" to the military institution itself.

The first step is, of course, getting the "right people" to see the play; however, this is not without its practical challenges. Where we have previously worked to foster our distance from the MoD, we now find ourselves approaching them in the hopes of encouraging critical reflection on our research themes. We have become aware of the critical influence of gatekeepers in reaching our desired audience and are increasingly resigned to acknowledging the power of the senior officer in making these connections. We have drawn on Hannah's past connections with various senior officers who were willing to make introductions to those individuals who might be well positioned to help us. It has been notable that some organisations who have been initially contacted by unsolicited email and made no response have been later willing to engage with the project as a direct result of these introductions via familiar and senior individuals. Hannah's military past has been influential in making some of these initial steps but being ex-military has perhaps led to assumptions about the type of research she is involved in, for example that it fits the military ideal for research that aims to improve the operational effectiveness of the Armed Forces (Higate & Cameron 2006). Through these initial engagements, we have had to broach the reality of the critical nature of the research project, but again here we have found that the military's understanding of critical as involving "lessons learnt" (Antrobus & West, forthcoming) has been in our favour. The testament will be their response to the play and findings report in due course.

Beyond the play, we have a nervousness about how our critical, feminist research will be received by a sector for whom qualitative research, let alone creative methodologies, are unfamiliar and easily dismissed (as demonstrated by the experiences of social science researchers engaging with the MODREC process). In thinking about how to communicate our research findings to the relevant change-makers, we have found ourselves thinking through how we might "translate" the messy, imaginative, free-form ideas and experiences that emerged from our creative workshops, into tangible and contained "research findings," which can be easily understood by high-ranking military officials and representatives. In doing so, it is hard not to feel that the nuance and potential of our work might become lost, sanitised, even neutered of its fundamental critique. Furthermore, as with much research that in some way hopes to improve the lives of military communities, we are always grappling with the question of; are we inadvertently helping the military to do fundamentally violent work more effectively?

## CONCLUSION

Theatre has long been used as a tool for communicating stories about war to receptive public audiences, and like many other forms of artistic engagement, it has been subject to significant co-option by military power. The complex relationship between the arts and the military is not only evident in the kinds of stories about war and military life that we typically see represented in cultural forms, but also in the roles that diverse military figures, organisations, and institutions play in the practical "doing" of creative work. We see this in the example of "Army and the Arts," who provide much needed support and publicity for creative projects on the British Army that they consider to be aligned with their aims and values, while removing the critique or simply casting aside other work.

Set in this context, the "Conflict & Intimacy" project attempts to do military theatre and "theatre of war" differently. In using participatory theatre-as-method, we have tried to generate more critical knowledge on the intimate sites of war and military violence in the military home, collaboratively creating a piece of theatre that questions who it is that experiences "military conflict." However, the practical "doing" of our work has shed light on an interesting tension, even contradiction, at the heart of our work. Driven by a participatory ethos and the shared goal of theatre-making, we were comfortable with the close collaboration with military subjects that this would necessitate. To return to Basham & Bulmer (2017), we take seriously the need in critical military studies to engage openly with the individuals, practices, and processes that form constituent parts of military power. And yet, the participatory and creative ethos of the project require that both critical distance and "critical friendship" (Holvikivi 2019) are maintained with the military institution. We needed to distance ourselves from the diverse people and organisations who make up the military machine to harness the critical potential of our work, but in order to do something meaningful *with* that work on behalf of our participants we have found ourselves inching back towards this military machine. This, we argue, is a tension at the centre of much work in critical military studies that seeks to engage in a critical way with military subjects.

Creative methods in military studies have the power to be critical, emancipatory, and resistant. However, we must acknowledge that the practical reality of *doing* creative research requires as much careful navigation of military control as any other form of engagement with the military (Catignani & Basham 2021). Creative practice is, we argue, subject to diverse and often minute forms of gatekeeping that can collectively work to make critical and impactful work extremely challenging. At a broader level, this is a reflection of how military power is practiced in the most subtle and unexpected of ways.

To conclude, we would like to reflect briefly on the temporality of doing and writing about creative methods. As we write this chapter, the "Conflict & Intimacy" project is still "live," an incomplete and, as yet, not-fully-knowable thing. The questions and challenges with which we are grappling now may yet give way to new feelings and ideas once the play has been performed, we have had feedback, and our participants have moved on. All research is messy, complicated, and there is a time and a place to it. But for creative methods more than other ways of doing research, ongoing reflection and the process of continually thinking anew are fundamental—and a big part of what makes these kinds of methodological approaches so interesting.

# 8

# Making Spoken Word on Combat

*Susanna Hast*

This chapter discusses a spoken word piece written and recorded in a research project investigating somatic social bonding among the Finnish Defence University cadets.[1] It illustrates how sensual and sensory experience can be modes of insight through which difficult questions around soldiering can be examined. In the spoken word piece *Hast & Cast: Ei niin pelottava asia* (2019), the text is constructed from interview data while voice, rhythm, amplification, and repetition all work to open up a space of wonder and association. This humorous and disturbing research-creation is not only meant for academic audiences, but it speaks back to the cadets in a language that is accessible and thought-provoking. This chapter demonstrates how the artistic manipulation of research data addresses the paradoxical emotional stakes of military training by tapping into the rhythmic, corporeal, and sonic qualities on which military training also relies.

## HORRIBLE NOISE

In this chapter, I explore spoken word art as a creative method in Critical Military Studies. The use of spoken word became a method in a research project that studied the emotional effects of synchronised movement among Finnish cadets (Hast 2020a). In the study I discovered overlapping and sometimes conflicting corporeal ideals of soldiers' attunement: *minded*, *machine*, and *combat body*. Minded body refers to bodily awareness that enabled cadets to respond to the movements of others. Machine body, instead, is a view of the soldier body as a self-sacrificial part of the military machine. Combat body refers to the ultimate reason why synching as a body technique matters: being able to win in combat. It was through the idea of the combat body that questions of killing emerged and became a topic so sensitive that I decided to engage with it in more creative terms.

Before you read any further, I would like you to listen to *Hast & Cast: Ei niin pelottava asia* on YouTube (subtitles available) or Spotify.[2] The vocals and text are by Susanna Hast; composing, arrangement, and guitar by Timo Rehtonen; and the flute by Hannu Mikkola.

The following is a rough translation of the piece, yet I recommend listening to it first if it is available to you. It is the sonic experience that gives the text its contradictory flavour and emotional weight. The piece is based on a text (below) accompanied by funk tunes played by guitar and a flute. The spoken word is art in its own right while scholarly in content. It is excessive, documentary, emotional, political, corporeal, and musical. It is many things, and never just one thing.

*combat makes me think of a situation where I clash with someone*
*that I would have ended up in a situation that someone is so close*
*that we are really at each other's throats*
*battle instead is something in which we fight as a group*
*team, or whatever that is, company*
*we would fight against some other enemy*
*combat, well, it is a taboo even in this organisation*
*even if this organisation is training for that*
*killing and dying is a part of combat*
*a soldier is not just some strange and peculiar thing*
*but a part of this country and society*
*some of those bodies who inhabit this country*
*are soldier-bodies*

*it is not just a scary thing*
*grenades, artillery and horrible noise*

*every soldier should be able to kill*
*this is what I have been pondering*
*but have not really talked about*
*it is a different thing to talk about these things with someone*
*I have never really thought*
*that what if I die at some point during these assignments*
*soldiering has become such a strong identity*
*that I feel it all the time in civilian life*
*my thoughts circle around it, and everything I do*
*you feel older here*
*you grow ten years older here in an instant*
*I don't see the enemy myself*
*I have screens, keyboards and then we do it as a group*

*of course, there is still the enemy on the side*
*and it is not really a humane situation*

*it is not just a scary thing*
*grenades, artillery and horrible noise*

*for example, if you have a wounded enemy soldier*
*you have to move forward; you have no time to move the wounded backwards*
*there is a danger,*
*that he will shoot you in the back, so what do you do with him?*
*do you sacrifice a patrol to move him backwards*
*or shoot him right there*
*and cover your back although you know it's wrong?*
*combat . . . firefight is such an easy perspective to it*
*you have tanks, weapons, forest, buildings*
*grenades, artillery and a horrible noise*
*I rarely think about the fact that I could die*
*you see enemies, and they die*
*but you rarely die yourself in these imageries*
*now, this is deep*
*no combat between soldiers is without deaths*

*it is not just a scary thing*
*grenades, artillery and horrible noise*

*it also says in this school book*
*that it is the last resort*
*when political decisions and negotiations fail*
*that's when you end up in armed conflict*
*combat must be in its totality then quite a mess*
*the common soldier,*
*he doesn't necessarily go to combat by his own decision*
*but by a decision from a higher level*
*controlled aggression*
*we are all vulnerable*
*hybrid wars and influencing the enemy media*
*and spreading propaganda*
*back in the days*
*they used to hit in the head with a shovel in a foxhole and shoot*
*it's not like that anymore*
*it's no longer about having two fronts*
*and then people are shooting with guns there*

*grenades, artillery and horrible noise*

## ART-MAKING

Here is a manifesto: *Art knows more.* A piece of art can make an absence known; it can describe with precision, archive with care, that which is ambiguous and non-graspable. After eight years of conducting art-based and practice-led research, after two albums and a novel, I genuinely feel that art knows more. I write this not because I want to make a distinction between art and science, but because art is so low in the knowledge hierarchy that pursuing it often requires justification within disciplines outside art itself. Sometimes creativity is seen as self-indulgent in the scholarly world, as if experimentation and creativity did not inherently belong in the realm of science. As if there could be too much creativity. As if too much creativity and expressive power was a threat. The manifesto "art knows more" is not against other knowledge. It is against art knowledge as *the other*. It is a celebration of the vital force of creativity in all its forms and materialities.

Art is for many things, but art is also for its own sake. Elizabeth Grosz (2008) proposes a non-aesthetic philosophy of art that does not assess the value, quality, or even meaning of art. What is that art for then; what does it do? Reading Deleuze, Grosz (2008, 3) refers to art that generates intensity, "that which directly impacts the nervous system and intensifies sensation." She goes on, "Art is the art of affect more than representation," something of indeterminacy and chaos. When art is considered non-representational, interpretation becomes secondary to experience. The claim of non-representational art is a political one. Such creative practice does not bend to wills; it does not bow to authorities but is monstrous, nomadic, unpredictable, unstable, and more (see Hast & Bagheri Nesami 2021). What makes art fascinating for me as a creative research practice, is the fact that artistic practice creates value in the mere happening of it. As bell hooks (1995, xvi) writes, "ultimately only our engagement with the work suffices—makes art matter."

To say art is knowledge is to make art instrumental—art becomes a portal to a deeper understanding of a phenomenon, and potentially a motor for change. As I have argued elsewhere (Hast 2020a), creative practice is not merely an interesting evocation but, more importantly, *an act of responsibility* through which boundaries can be dismantled, reshaped, and questioned. I believe creative practice produces critical insight, but it can also challenge the vulnerabilities, nostalgias, rationales, and violences generated and upheld by militarised societies. Thus, curiosity towards the aesthetic arrangement of research translates into activism—form becomes political.

In studying something so sexualised, destructive, generative, secret, emotional, gendered, and mystified as the military, what could be more revealing than exploring the workings of militaries through its own tactics? I do not mean taking up a gun, but rather taking up an embodied practice: utilising the body's conditioning, the expressiveness of the body, and the centrality of the body's performance in military training and rituals. Since militarized cultures, including military bodies, are highly performative (see, for example, Brady and Mantoan 2018), our research can make that performativity known in many different ways. The spoken word piece is very much at odds with the public image of the Finnish Military when it depicts soldiers who are confused and critical instead of patriotic and obedient. Being "out of place," the spoken word creates disorientation in others (see Ahmed 2006). It juxtaposes the soft voice of vulnerability with an imagined soldier's body made of sacrifice, bravery, and hardness. Due to the perverse soundscape, the militarising act of a recruitment video would probably turn into a critique of the military, while the spoken word still vocalises military ideals of Finnish cadets.

I have played with the quality of my voice in different academic contexts to subvert the patriarchal privileging of reason and dominant articulation, by centering the emotional body in my research. Researching the Finnish military, qualities of voice became an apparent ground for experimenting with distance and intimacy between bodies. I could not help feeling my voice was out of place, and as such it could become a tool for disorientation which taps into the more subtle qualities of militarisation, its seductiveness that does not express itself necessarily in hypervisibility but in the undercurrents of corporeal sensations. Think of the masculine shouting of commands contrasted with the seductive speech from my mouth. We associate command with the military instinctively, but we rarely think about how the seductive side of militarisation is voiced, lived, and promoted in softer qualities of voice, in softer words of care.

Taking part in a march with Finnish cadets in 2018, I felt drawn to the collective rhythm and the culture of care as it extended towards my body (Hast 2020b). At the end of the thirty-kilometre march, I was so attuned to my "research subjects" that I did not want to leave their company. I felt the "muscular bonding" (McNeill 1995) I was researching happening to me. *Seduction* was the word to which I kept returning when I tried to understand how I had transformed from feeling like an outsider (civilian, researcher, woman), to feeling like part of the military group. Voice was the means through which I could express the emotional weight of the autoethnographic moment, so I created a spoken autoethnography in which there was no room for a distant researcher-observer (Hast 2020b).

Grosz (2008, 7) writes that seduction entails becoming the other. The word *seduction* is easily attached to the feminised body, an act of transgression that centres a feminised body as culpable. Seduction, or enticement, is a use of the erotic, where erotic, borrowing from Audre Lorde (2017, 23) is "a measure between the beginnings of our sense of self and the chaos of our strongest feelings." Erotic does not mean pornographic. Erotic refers to a depth of feeling, a creative power of the body. Seduction is the quality of voice through which I can address the erotic, the military, and their entanglements. I was easily seduced, and I could have never imagined that happening. I was seduced by marching, by becoming visible, by becoming a body (see Hast 2020b). The promise of martial masculinity was summoned, and I enjoyed becoming another body, a momentarily military body. The man-to-be, the exceptional body, and the promise of inclusion, are they not seductive? What I then do in my art is make the seduction, which is often invisible and inarticulable, audible and lyrical. In practice, this means accepting the uncertainty with which a non-argumentative performance such as spoken word is imbrued.

## COMBAT

*What is combat? Does it mean killing?* This is what I asked about twenty-eight first-year cadets during my time in their company in 2018. I asked many other things, too, and combat was not on my itinerary, but once I opened that troublesome window, it was evident that the topic required special attention.

During the project, I came across a paper by Katharine M. Millar and Joanna Tidy (2017) titled "Combat as moving target." The authors were curious about combat as an empirical category. They pointed out that while critical scholarship had investigated how masculinities are constituted in relation to combat, it had not tackled the question of how masculinities constitute combat as normative imagery. This paper came to my mind when I was marching with cadets in the autumn of 2018, and I could not resist the temptation to ask the cadets what they thought combat means.

The question—What is combat?—was not the trouble to stay with, but the follow-up question—Is it about killing?—was. The responses to these questions took me somewhat off guard. I did not expect to meet silence, unease, and hesitation when I asked this question. I did not anticipate confusion, embarrassment, and a lack of language on an aspect of soldiering that appears central in military training.

There were instances when we talked about the death and dying of the soldier. When the cadets spoke of dying, they spoke of violence. However, when they spoke of combat, violence went into hiding. Perhaps I had set a trap and was being unreasonable. *Killing* is a word with much weight. It is not easily spoken of, especially with a stranger. We stayed with moral questions of injury and never discussed more practical questions such as the fact that "the vast majority of soldiers cannot kill in cold blood and need to kill in a de-subjectified state, e.g., in reflexes, rages, and panics" (Protevi 2013, 130).

When I asked about killing, time slowed down. Cadets prolonged the answering time with pauses and filler words. Physical gestures of discomfort and signs of stress were evident. I wrote in my notes, *He is smiling, but he nervously touches an item in his hand, moving it between his fingers. His legs are shaking too.* Hesitations indicated that maybe this question had not been asked before. Although claiming to be an academic institution, it appeared that at the Defence University, there was no space for questions that are unpatriotic, questions like, "A military solution is a solution for whom?" or "What is violence, whose body does it touch?"

I became interested in how cadets' bodies responded to the question, but also what words they used. As I studied the military manuals (Puolustusvoimat 2021), I discovered that the phrase *to kill* is not mentioned. Plenty of creative alternatives appear in a combat manual, such as *choosing a goal*, *centering fire*, *disabling*, *destroying*, and *conquering*. Language can erase violence; it matters what words are used. The distaste for the words *to kill* is unsurprising, considering it is not part of the military vocabulary. Yet there is another side to the coin: the interviewed cadets paid attention to their own hesitation and became aware of what it meant. They knew it was a taboo, they knew it was a topic that needed to be discussed but was not, and they knew that "guns were dangerous tools." No cadet valorised combat. Only one cadet spoke in a manner that made me somewhat concerned. They did speak excitedly about combat exercise but got serious when they remembered the times when they used real ammunition.

When I tried to figure out other reasons for the difficulty to see combat as killing, I first reasoned that it was because combat, and warfare in general, was so distant to this corner of the globe. But that made no sense considering how much remembrance takes place throughout society for past wars. We are not allowed to forget. And war cannot be so distant since the cadets do train operational skills (battle skills and motivation to win battles) as part of their bachelor's degree in military sciences. Moreover, Finland is still very much a country preparing for war, taking part in the arms race and rationalising it with traditional security threats (inter-state war). For example, the state plans to purchase sixty-four multi-role fighters (HX Fighter Programme) on a ten-billion-euro budget to replace the current Hornet fighters. In addition, Finnish cadets might experience combat if they applied and went to serve in an international military crisis management mission. According to a news report from 2014, Finnish troops were involved in forty-four firefights in the ISAF-operation in Afghanistan between 2008–2014—two died, and fifteen were injured (Moilanen 2014).

One reason for the difficulty in addressing killing in combat has likely to do with the academic side of the cadet training. Based on my interviews, the cadets' self-image was that of a peacetime soldier, an officer in a military outfit. Someone who looks like a soldier but is not a soldier who would have to go to war and kill people. I believe there is a pull between the ordinary and exceptional, civilian and soldier, when academic requirements cannot help but co-exist (or collide) with the norms, values, and practices of militarism. Jan Hanska (2015), an academic and a soldier, describes this as a tension between the academic and the officer, the critical and the obedient.

A retired professor from the Defence University, Juha Mäkinen (2019), problematizes the fragmentation of military and civilian selves, arguing that the two spheres are no longer so distinct. He writes that instead of seeing the two as opposites, we should focus on soldier-civilian relations, their conformity. Even if this is the case, it has not made the soldier any less exceptional and worthy of special praise, and so "the hierarchical elevation of the soldier over the civilian population is assured, despite changes in the 'actual' empirical practice of martial violence over time" (Millar and Tidy 2017, 150).

Of course, there is no pure civilian space to begin with, since political life is not apart from but constituted by war (Howell 2018, 6). As Maya Eichler explains,

> The military sphere is not simply militarized, but itself partially constituted by politics and by the civilian. Even military members—quintessentially militarized subjects—are not just martial subjects, but have complicated and varied entanglements with the military and civilian worlds they inhabit (MacKenzie et al. 2019, 12).

Thus, to speak of a soldier or a soldier in combat, we would have to investigate the flimsy border between the civilian and military spheres. This is where the music begins to play.

## SPOKEN WORD

I had these findings. Cadets uttering their images of combat, killing, and their soldier bodies—and I wanted to undo the erasure, speak back to them, and do what I do best, shake things up a little. I told my collaborator, Timo Rehtonen, that we would make a spoken word piece, and I travelled to Rovaniemi in Northern Finland to record it. I had transcripts with me, and in one go, I underlined intuitively the sentences that felt compelling and created a text that was nearly copied word-for-word from the cadets' interviews.

Yet even choices that seem random are often not. The lyrics are filled with artistic choices that create new meanings and feelings. For example, the chorus, which goes, "it's not such a scary thing/grenades, artillery and horrible noise," is composed of two disconnected sentences that two different cadets said in different contexts. "Not so scary" refers to soldiers as human beings like any other rather than martial bodies to be afraid of, while "grenades, artillery and horrible noise" refer to a description of what combat is potentially like, a huge mess, as the cadet in question continued. It was not intentional to combine these two, but we were missing a repetition that would make sense musically (creating a structure for the song). Rehtonen asked me to pick something compelling, and I did that in the middle of the recording session. Combined, these sentences pieced together, became a puzzle for me, creating an unintentional new meaning, an iteration that reminds me of the power of language and the power of imagination.

Decisions that were made within a day, sometimes in minutes, are not haphazard when you take a closer look. To quote hooks (1995, 126) again, "Work for women artists is never just the moment when we write, or do other art [. . .]. In the fullest sense, it is also the time spent in contemplation and preparation." There was entire research behind the spoken word that was in the making. There was also a long-term collaboration of music-making, composing, arranging, recording, and performing around the topic of war and researching war (Hast 2018) with Rehtonen and Mikkola. We had already lived through the uncanny nature of this kind of work, in which musicians who had nothing to do with my research suddenly were creating more than an expression of research—the very heart and soul of it.

Musically, we had Gill Scott Heron's "The Revolution Will Not Be Televised" from the album *Pieces of a Man* (1971) as an inspiration. Tracing the history of spoken word and rap, Alice Price-Styles (2015) begins from old oral storytelling traditions and oral performance in African cultures. In the United States in the 1920s, she continues, jazz poetry became popular, and towards the 1960s spoken word became openly political. Price-Styles (2015, 12) describes Scott Heron's "Whitey on the Moon" and "B-Movie" as "examples of how rhythm and melody can perfectly offset uncomfortable truths and deep messages." Thus, in the spoken word piece, we are borrowing from African and African American cultural and musical traditions, from an art form in which poetry and music come together, and which "emphasizes the dynamic qualities entailed in speech" (Jones 2011, 184).

Just like in Scott Heron's song, the flute plays a distinctive role in our creation. Hannu Mikkola (2021), who played the flute, describes his playing as free improvisation in the genre of soul/jazz. The flute, an Armstrong brand dating at least to the 1970s, follows the development of the piece itself: it intensifies in the middle when the key is modulated up until it returns to the original and calms down. The melody (and lack of it) was improvised, and the flute was placed in empty spots, making it impossible for me ever to perform this the way the recording goes.

Timo Rehtonen (2021), who did everything else to the very last stages of mixing and mastering, describes the piece as music dictated by the lyric and the declarative nature of the vocal performance. Spoken word in our case—and unlike rap—does not aim at articulating on the beat. Parts of the text and the feeling change according to longer sections in the piece. Rehtonen explains further that we felt the drum could be electronic, but the flute needed to be loyal to our source of inspiration. If the drum machine is punctual and precise, the flute is improvising within the limits of the key but still with plenty of liberties. We humorously called the flute "porn-flute," because there was something erotic about how it sat into everything else in the song. The flute's particular energy can also be heard as a reference to the sexiness of military and military bodies, or the seductiveness of militarisation. The background music is funk, a timeless musical genre that we have explored in our music before this. Rehtonen explains that he made a "basic riff" that stays relatively constant for a long time. The flute's improvisation is constant but shifting and overflowing to the extent that individual notes do not matter for the whole.

After we had recorded the entire thing, I was uneasy. "Are we really publishing this?" I uttered, staring at the microphone that had just taken in my voice. The whole thing felt perverse, and I was afraid that instead of expressing the problem of erasure or the uncanny ideas of combat, I had created a monstrosity that would not be understood. As this concern rose within me, I realised that I am worried because I care, and since I care, I need to trust myself and the art.

After the piece was published in 2019, I asked three cadets about how they felt about it. This is how they responded:

> The background music was positive all along, yet the text was negative and even morbid. The quotes you used sounded very familiar, part of the cadet life. I think it is easier to listen to a song than to read a black-and-white text.

> My first impressions: This is brutal text and still somehow very thought-provoking. The background music makes this chill. There's contrast! Really awakening! This is amazing! And I don't believe anyone will be offended. I am really excited about this.

I actually heard this song through my friend. It is pretty cool, and I like music.

> The quotes sound like campfire stories. I could imagine building on something similar, like freestyling by a campfire. I first felt it was somewhat confrontational, but then I realized you had used the interviews as material. Some of the staff (at the Defence University) have heard this too. They have diplomatically

commented, "Everyone can express themselves as they please as long as no names are mentioned." I thought it was bold.

The spoken word did reach at least some cadets and personnel, and it succeeded in provoking thought. Two cadets told me that, to their knowledge, no one had openly criticized my work, but they felt that some people in the personnel did not quite appreciate the art. There is something disarming about the effort to create music out of these interviews, something out of the ordinary. But it can also be too much, too bold.

The spoken word both documents cadets' views on combat and the soldier body, and also messes with them. I brought the cadets' words into a new environment and made them sound unfamiliar. I was not analysing or theorising the interviews but arranging, unsettling, uprooting, and realigning military idea(l)s and language in my own tone. Only after the spoken word was released, and I spoke with some of the cadets about how they felt about it, did I understand that because of the musical form, the research findings were accessible and thought-provoking. It provoked the question, "do we really think like that?" The cadets were my intended audience, whose critical thought I wished to excite.

Later, I performed the song at an event in which we discussed the taboos of violence and militarism with a soldier and two other researchers. This was during the COVID-19 pandemic, so we were streaming the event. I went to a shop selling old military clothes and bought a pair of "pickled cucumber salad" pants, and as I stood in front of the microphones in those trousers, I instantly felt more serious, manly, and strong. Voicing the elongated text, trying to keep my composure as I performed in clothes that were purposefully provoking while making me feel things, it all returned to where I had begun: the body—all the body—through and in the body. Music is meant to be performed, and it is in performance when again something new emerges in the moment. Something happens to me as a researcher and artist, and a new layer appears on the piece of art that was not there before.

## BACK TO THE BEGINNING

I rely on chaos in creative practice. Improvisation is a direct way to tap into the possibilities of risk and the present moment. The spoken word is not the same as the conversations I had with cadets, not the same as their thoughts, not the same as my thoughts on their thoughts. It is a shadow world of sound and words. Sound gives shape to a subject, transmuting material and changing bodies. This is a research-creation that no writing can replace. And this is where artistic creation matters and why it is compulsive—it is knowledge in the language of music, music that is integral to human cultures, music without which we could not live.

I consider sound art as a portal. It transports into the world of sound stripped of tactile and visual stimuli. I am aware of the ableism embedded in this quest: it excludes people with impaired hearing. Thick with affect and ambiguous meaning, recordings do not always easily or immediately translate into "research as we know it," which is the entire point. Plunging into the unknown, "research as we do not know it," is to take a long walk of bewilderment, awe, and messiness. The unruliness, wildness, and unexpectedness of artistic creativity is my activism as a woman artist and researcher.

With art, I make myself vulnerable and known, and this is the only way I can study militarism, or anything else for that matter. This is the research I believe in. Such research might have a small but still profound impact. The fact that some cadets and personnel have become curious about militarism and militarism, and the possibilities of Critical Military Studies, feels to me like a major achievement. Drawing attention to the question of killing by simply asking about it and then re-creating the conversations in sounds and rhythms, are minor gestures (Manning 2016) facing overwhelmingly powerful structures. Like Rebecca Solnit (2005, 6–7), "I worry now that many people never disband their armies, never go beyond what they know." At the same time, as Cynthia Enloe (2015, 8) has argued, "militaries are a lot more fragile and contingent than elites will admit," and we must believe that the minor gestures can promote non-violence. Challenging the persistence of militarism as the solution to threats requires radical acts of imagination. It is very difficult to imagine something other than a profoundly militarised world without becoming creative.

We are a singing species, and voice reveals. If you now begin to sing, you will reveal something of your life state at this very moment. Even if you would try to pretend, your voice would still expose you. Music has expressive power due to its ephemeral and experiential nature that draws me to rely on it, especially when the "data" I have at my disposal is troubling. Moreover, with art comes the uncertainty of interpretation, the certainty of misinterpretation and the irrelevance of the artist's intention, no matter how much a piece of art is explained to the audience. All these aspects are present in any kind of research, but with music, I can make them visible, tangible, and explore the paradoxes and (im)possibilities that arise with musical interventions.

The military is a rhythmic institution that relies on regulating bodies, culture, and materialities with their patterns, tactics, beats, strikes, and accents. I believe there is much to study in terms of the deep musicality of the military itself—for example, the tone and volume of command, the auditory experience of military training, the invisibility of automatic movement patterns, the role of cadence, the regulation of bodily functions, continuities and structures that become a military melody, and so on. A creative effort can open new pathways for research, and music is a metaphoric and practical companion in this quest.

# PART III

# 9

# "Last Op"

## *War, Trauma, and the Legacy of Bomber Command*

*Alexander Thomas T. Smith*

In my grandfather's wartime service file, there was a curious letter.

I had requested his records from the National Archive in Australia, to better understand the man my grandfather was when he went to war in 1941. The file contains his enlistment papers, the oath of allegiance he swore when he joined the army, his pay book and officer records. In addition to listing the squadrons he was assigned to and when—in Australia and then the UK—after he transferred to the air force, it contains details of the aircraft he had trained on and the number of hours flying experience he built up, as he qualified to become a pilot. Perhaps most poignantly for me, the file also includes a copy of the telegram that was sent to my grandmother after he was wounded during a bombing mission over Nazi Germany; his Handley Page Halifax was peppered with flak. When I was a child, she often told me the story of her panic, that warm October day in 1944, when the postman arrived with that telegram—and then her relief at learning her husband was still alive.

The curious letter, though, had little in common with the rest of the papers in my grandfather's file. For starters, it was dated 1 May 1969—over twenty years after the war had ended. It was short, from the Repatriation Department in Adelaide to the secretary of the National Department of Air, requesting "particulars of all promotions and ranks" held by my grandfather during the four years he served in World War Two.

That was all.

I asked my mother why a bureaucrat might have been seeking access to her father's wartime service records in 1969. "Oh," she replied. "That would be when your grandfather had his breakdown and was taken to the Repat [Hospital].'"

I already knew the story. I had been seventeen years old when my grandmother told me our family's secret. During a long walk, she had been talking about her marriage to my grandfather, Harold "Hank" Hancock. We, as grandchildren, knew him simply as a kind, loving, and benevolent man who had flown bombing missions in the war against Hitler and wore his medals with pride on Anzac Day. However, my grandmother now explained, this was not the whole story. Just after they married, he had left for war a teetotaller. Three years later, he came back a drunk. His life after the war—of raising a family and running his father's butcher shop—was dogged by struggles with alcoholism, depression, undiagnosed PTSD, and a violent rage. Even when she threatened divorce, he continued to drink. But in 1969, a routine appendix operation in the local community hospital turned into a violent meltdown as my grandfather went into withdrawal from alcohol following his surgery. He was transferred to the Repat and went into rehab, followed by a further three-month stint in Glenside Hospital. My grandfather came out and never touched alcohol again.

In this chapter, I reflect on my creative efforts to better understand the impact of the Second World War on my grandfather and his post-military life and family. I focus on "Last Op," an experiment in non-fiction writing that interweaves elements of the autobiographical novel and personal memoir with family mythology, ethnography, post-military history, and a psycho-geographical journey through some of England's forgotten wartime airfields. I started writing "Last Op" in 2013, when I commenced a part-time MA (and then MFA) in writing at the University of Warwick. It eventually became my MFA dissertation in 2020, finally completed after several years of false starts and interruptions to my studies. As an academic who teaches sociology, my turn to creative practice involved coming to grips with a new discipline of writing. While informed by my scholarly interests, "Last Op" forced me to engage with entanglements of the personal and wider societal themes of war, trauma, and memory that have now, in turn, reframed my scholarly interests. In the final section, I will address how my creative practice has deepened my own critical perspective on military culture and the ways in which it shaped my grandfather's troubled legacy. To begin, however, I must explain what drew me, as an academic sociologist, to creative writing and how this set me on both an unexpected and surprising—though not always painless—personal and intellectual journey. That journey continues, and "Last Op" remains a work in progress. Along the way, however, I have come to a deeper appreciation of the potential for creative practice in advancing our understanding of the role military culture plays in shaping wider society.

## SOCIOLOGY AND CREATIVE WRITING

My motivation to study creative writing had come from my growing frustration with the conventions of academic writing. After reading a review of her book in the *Times Literary Supplement*, I purchased Helen Sword's *Stylish Academic Writing* (2012). "Pick up any guide to effective writing and what will you find?" she asks.

> Probably some version of the advice that Strunk and White offered more than half a century ago in their classic book *Elements of Style*: always use clear, precise language, even when expressing complex ideas; engage your reader's attention through examples, illustrations and anecdotes; avoid opaque jargon; vary your vocabulary, sentence length, and frames of reference; favor active verbs and concrete nouns; write with conviction, passion, and verve (Sword 2012: 3).

But pick up an academic journal and with what kind of writing will you be confronted? "Impersonal, stodgy, jargon-laden, abstract prose that ignores or defies most of the stylistic principles outlined above . . . a massive gap between what most readers consider to be good writing and what academics typically produce and publish" (Sword 2012, 3).

Sword's goal was to help academics learn how to write "stylishly." A survey of seventy academics from a range of disciplines confirmed an appreciation of good writing:

> Stylish scholars, my colleagues told me, express complex ideas clearly and precisely; produce elegant, carefully crafted sentences; convey a sense of energy, intellectual commitment, and even passion; engage and hold their readers' attention; tell a compelling story; avoid jargon, except where specialized terminology is essential to the argument; provide their readers with aesthetic and intellectual pleasure; and write with originality, imagination, and creative flair (Sword 2012, 7–8).

As Sword observes, "wordy, wooden, weak-verbed academic prose finds few if any explicit advocates but vast armies of practitioners," and only by choosing to address questions of style "one publication at a time" might we improve academic writing overall (Sword 2012, 10).

I found Sword's book persuasive and inspiring. If her mission was to improve the quality of academic writing as literature, another book published around the same time set out to understand why social scientists write the way they do. In *Learn to Write Badly: How to Succeed in the Social Sciences*, Michael Billig set out not just to complain about "poor writing in the social sciences" (2013, 1). Drawing on George Orwell's classic 1946 essay "Politics and the English Language" as well as twentieth-century critiques of academic writing (e.g., Andreski 1971; Blanshard 1954), Billig argued that jargon and the invention of new terms conveys "less, not more, information about human actions":

> [The] big concepts which many social scientists are using—the ifications and the izations—are poorly equipped for describing what people do. By rolling out the big nouns, social scientists can avoid describing people and their actions. They can then write in highly unpopulated ways, creating fictional worlds in which their theoretical things, rather than actual people, appear as the major actors" (Billig 2013, 7).

Reading both books, I realised that my frustrations with scholarly writing were not simply borne of a weariness of reading academic prose that was overly abstract, unnecessarily convoluted, and "unpopulated" (Billig's descriptor) of actual people. Rather, I became firmer in my conviction that a quality—of empathy, of understanding, perhaps even of agency and authorship—had been lost as I had been disciplined into the conventions of academic writing during my postgraduate studies and then my postdoctoral career. The question was not simply whether I could improve my writing, as an academic sociologist. By elevating argument and analysis over passion and empathy, I wondered whether scholarly writing runs the risk of undermining its promise of a deeper understanding of culture and society—the kind of understanding once achieves through intuition, sensitivity, and emotional intelligence. These were the qualities I wanted to recapture as a writer.

I began studying my MA in the autumn of 2013. The first module on which I enrolled was "Non-Fiction Writing," which the American writer David Vann—the award-winning author of the semi-autobiographical novel *Legends of a Suicide*—taught. As I tried to find a point of entry into writing creatively rather than academically, he encouraged me to engage with genres of life-writing and memoir in order to explore my grandfather's story in my creative writing. This made good intuitive sense to me. In sociology, a number of leading practitioners of the discipline have turned to personal and family memoir at some stage in their careers. The French sociologist Didier Eribon revisited his working-class roots to explore themes of class, sexuality, and identity in *Returning to Reims* (2019) while Ann Oakley tackled issues of patriarchy and gender in her quasi-memoir *Father and Daughter* (2014). Stuart Hall has explored themes of race, colonialism, and the end of empire in his subversive autobiography, *Familiar Stranger* (2017), while Hazel Carby tackles class, race, and migration in her memoir of growing up black in working-class London, *Imperial Intimacies* (2019).

Memoir, it seems, continues to provide sociologists with an opportunity to explore intersectional and cross-cutting themes of identity, class, race, and sexuality while also reaching other, non-academic audiences. However, the intellectual debt social sciences owe to this genre and its close literary cousins does not end here. It has long been argued (perhaps most famously by Stocking (1984), Clifford and Marcus (1986), Marcus and Fischer (1986), and Gupta and Ferguson (1997a, 1997b) that the ethnographic traditions of social anthropology—in which I hold a PhD—emerged out of late-nineteenth-century genres of memoir, journalism, and reportage, the personal essay and travel and nature writing that became popular when the British Empire achieved its peak. This was followed by literary/intellectual movements, including mass observation in prewar and wartime Britain. More recently, ethnographers have employed literary techniques borrowed from fiction writing (see Goffman 2015, for a controversial recent example) and have even experimented with their own subgenre of literary memoir. Engaging with life-writing and memoir therefore seemed to be a logical point of departure for me, on my journey from transitioning from academic to more creative practice.

Inspired, I wondered if this refocusing of my writing might push the boundaries of my sociological imagination, the concept famously coined by the sociologist C. Wright Mills (2000). For him, the sociological imagination promised to enable the individual "to use information and to develop reason in order to achieve lucid summations of what is going on in the world and of what be happening within themselves" (Mills 2000, 5). Helping us grasp "history and biography and the relations between the two within society" (Mills 2000, 6), Mills suggested we distinguish between "the personal troubles of milieu" and "the public issues of social structure" (Mills 2000, 8):

> [To] understand the changes of many personal milieux we are required to look beyond them. And the number and variety of such structural changes increase as the institutions within which we live become more embracing and more intricately connected with one another. To be aware of the idea of social structure and to use with sensibility is to be capable of tracing such linkages among a great variety of milieux. To be able to do that is to possess the sociological imagination (Mills 2000, 10–11).

I had always been attracted to the evocative potential of Mills's writing about the sociological imagination. I now wondered what other forms of understanding—of those connections between personal troubles and public issues about which Mills wrote—might be enabled, through a spirited re-engagement with my own (sociological) imagination, via creative writing. Could we reimagine how to place our individual biographies in history, locating ourselves within the deep cultural metanarratives that shape our lives? Exploring that space which connects biography and history, how might sociologists unlock the imaginative potential of our discipline, to unearth the stories that lie buried and untold in our collective inheritance from World War Two?

## LAST OP

Once I decided to write about my family's history, I knew that my grandfather's military service would take centre stage. In addition to revisiting the foundational myths and lore of my family, I would have to do some research. Given that my grandparents passed away in the early 2000s, they were no longer available for me to interview directly. I decided to reach out to my mother and her brothers. I also wanted to track down some of the descendants of my grandfather's bomber crew, thinking that they might be able to shed some light on the man he was and their collective wartime experiences. On this, I was fortunate; my brother was already in touch, via Facebook, with the grandson of Les 'Dutch' Holland, the bomb aimer in my grandfather's crew. At this point, while I initiated contact with him, I accessed my grandfather's file from the National Archives of Australia and began to put some detail together about his military service.

Harold Hancock enlisted in the Australian army in October 1941—three months after Nazi Germany invaded the Soviet Union and a month before the Japanese attack on Pearl Harbor. He then transferred to the Royal Australian Air Force and underwent pilot training in South Australia and New South Wales. In 1943, he embarked for England, a journey by sea to San Francisco on the west coast of the USA, then by train across North America to Boston, where he was billeted for several weeks during the winter. While there, he saw snow for the first time. His ship from Boston, part of a wartime convoy, finally docked in Liverpool in 1944. He was then billeted with families through the Home Counties and the Midlands before being sent to RAF Driffield as part of RAAF Squadron No. 462. In the Autumn of 1944, he flew 36 bombing missions over Nazi-occupied Europe, in support of the Allied invasion of the Low Countries and western Germany. In December, his squadron was redeployed to 100 Group at RAF Foulsham from which they flew missions engaged in electronic warfare until the end of the war. He was demobilised later that year and returned to Australia late 1945.

My grandfather's service file helped me build a timeline of where he was, and when, during the Second World War. This chronology was useful but there was much I still did not know. To write with justice about my grandfather's wartime experience would inevitably mean addressing, at least indirectly, what came after: his personal struggles with alcoholism, depression and (according to my grandmother) undiagnosed PTSD. While he was not alone in coming home scarred by the war, talking about depression and mental illness in its aftermath was very much a subject swept under the carpet in 'respectable' society. World War Two veterans were stoic heroes who had won a just war and maintained a stiff upper lip throughout. They were expected to perform this tragic myth of keeping calm and carrying on, in their post-military civilian lives. Like many other veterans, my grandfather used alcohol to self-medicate. His addiction almost destroyed him.

We are still not used to discussing the mental and emotional scars the Second World War left on the men who fought it. We rarely read about the personal, post-war struggles of that conflict's veterans outside a tightly defined field of experience—those of POWs in Japanese camps, for example, or surviving veterans of the D-Day landings (see Vento 2011). This contrasts starkly with narratives of shellshock, broken bodies and damaged minds are part of the cultural conversation around the legacy of the First World War. Meanwhile, in countries like Australia and the USA, we have grown accustomed to associating PTSD—first diagnosed in the 1970s and popularised through the 1980s—with veterans of the Vietnam War and other modern conflicts. However, when I share this with colleagues, family and friends, many are prompted to tell me about the experiences—of awkward silences, mental illness, addiction and sometimes violence—of their own families in the aftermath of war. While it has become socially and culturally acceptable to speak of the psychological damage wrought on veterans of the First World War and later conflicts, like the Falklands, Afghanistan and Iraq, exploring the emotional toll of the Second World War on the men who served and survived remains a taboo subject, in popular and media discourse as well as academia.

In my grandmother's telling of the story about her husband, it was England where my Hank learned how to drink. His days in Bomber Command were endured with an uncanny cocktail of emotions, of long stretches of boredom and restlessness punctuated by shorter, adrenaline-charged moments—when flying over enemy territory—of sudden excitement, panic and stress. Coming down from such 'highs' was tough. He began to fill his days with alcohol. Almost half a century later, while her husband was in rehab, my grandmother took up his fight with the Australian army. She argued, before a board of brigadiers and other senior brass, that my grandfather's problems with alcohol addiction and depression were a consequence of his military service. In effect, they were injuries that he had sustained during the war. In what was one of the first such cases of its time, she persuaded the army to grant my grandfather his war pension early, on health grounds. She stayed with him through the early years of his recovery, and they rebuilt their marriage and their lives together.

## REUNION

I learned about my grandfather's reunion with his aircrew from the family of Dutch Holland, his bomb aimer. In 1975, Bomber Command veterans came together in York, England, to make the 30th Anniversary of the end of the war. Like thousands of other airmen and their families, from all over the Commonwealth and former British Empire, my grandfather wanted to attend. With my grandmother, he embarked on the long journey, by air, from Adelaide to London. Both his navigator and radio operator—also with their spouses—joined them, their journeys starting in Sydney and Melbourne respectively. Arriving in the UK, though, they did not head directly to York. They took a detour to the historic market town of Warwick, where Dutch now lived. There, they were met by the three other Englishmen—from Derbyshire, Kent and Sheffield—who formed my grandfather's crew.

Hank had been sober for over half a decade when he and his crewmates met up for the first time in thirty years for their own private reunion. They spent a week together, travelling from Warwick to Gloucestershire then Norfolk and Yorkshire, touring their old airfields before finally joining the Bomber Command's 30th Anniversary celebrations in York. Some of these bases had fallen out of service but others were still in use, either by the RAF or the USAF during the Cold War. When they went to bases that were still in operation, they were welcomed as war heroes. Having kept the crew's logbook after the war ended, Dutch poignantly memorialised this tour with a final entry: 'Last Op.' Indeed, my grandfather's crew would never reunite again. Dutch had recently been diagnosed with terminal cancer. He died later that year.

That entry in Dutch's logbook and my grandfather's reunion with his aircrew inspired me. I imagined 'Last Op' would be about the lives of the men and their families as they meshed with national mythologies about WW2 as well as post-war social history. Through this rich intersection of war, biography and his history, I hoped to use the reunion as an ethnographic-historical 'site' for exploring how they negotiated the traumatic legacy of war. I saw potential to revisit the airfields they had called home during 1944–45 and experimenting across literary genres including the autobiographical novel, family memoir, ethnography and post-military history. One of the unpredictable qualities of engaging creatively with life writing—which can be experienced in equal measure as both danger and opportunity—is that the journey you begin may not lead you to the destination for which you planned. Why was I drawn to my grandfather's story? I did not yet have an answer to this question, one which I was yet to realise needed answering. As Philip Gerard has observed:

> Memoir . . . is not a pleasant stroll down memory lane, a kind of highlight reel of your life's best or worst moments. At its most powerful, it is driven by the heartfelt desire to come to a reckoning about some matter that disturbs you, keep you up at night, baffles you. You want to get to the bottom of it (2017: 83).

In short, the story I planned to write was not that which demanded to be told. My 'book'—as I imagined it—had other ideas.

## THE BOOK IS THE BOSS

When talking about writing narrative—whether in genres of fiction or non-fiction—we tend to envision the story as a fully formed thing, pre-existing in the writer's imagination. The role of the author is to sit down and put words to paper—quite literally, to write it down. As I started to tackle 'Last Op' in earnest, I discovered that this was not a helpful way to think about my own creative practice. I suspect this is probably true of writers everywhere, but it still came as a revelation to me.

I began by writing out great screeds of contextual information, about who my grandparents were, where they lived, my grandfather's wartime service history: dates, places, occupations and more. I gleaned raw data from my grandfather's army service file and put the information down on the page, this time in fully formed sentences. I also started describing the main events that I thought would be important to the story I planned to tell.

Much of this early work did not make it into the final 'cut' of 'Last Op.' The reason was obvious: it did not make for engaging reading. I was getting bogged down in the detail and the story was not able to breathe. But this was an important first step in my writing. There was comfort to be found in the recording of facts. It gave a sense of authenticity to the shape of the narrative I was attempting to discern through my writing. Recalling Michael Billig's earlier criticisms of sociological writing, I felt like I was on the right track. I was describing, after all, real people doing things in real places, at times that really happened.

However, small sections of that early writing did survive into the final manuscript; the book I originally envisaged inhabits the second and third chapters, entitled 'Last Op' and 'Dutch's Logbook' respectively. Much of what I was putting down, however, looked like preamble to me. Like a runner preparing for a 100-metre sprint, this was the warm-up before the race. It was only after a couple of thousand words or so had been committed to paper that I started to discern the spectral threads of the story that was beginning to emerge from the text. Then, I would write a couple of lines that would capture the essence of the tension on which I could then see my chapter being built. At this juncture, I would stop writing, take those sentences out and move them to the start, reorganising the material I had written to get a feel for how I might focus each chapter so that the narrative would more strongly propel forward.

What I often realised was that the chapter I was writing had a very different narrative purpose—of subject and theme, for instance, but often in terms of whom the central character would be—than I expected. Inspiration, for how to proceed, can be found in surprising, eclectic places. It was only after I re-watched the canonical Danny Boyle 'zombie' film *28 Days Later* that I realised one chapter I was writing would be stronger if I culled some imagery in which I had, until then, been considerably invested emotionally. In a DVD extra 'Pure Rage'—a documentary on the making of the film—Boyle described how he always cuts his favourite shot from a film. When asked why, he replied 'sheer bloody-mindedness.' What I think he really meant is that you should never let your favourite image get in the way of the story. I found this insight psychologically liberating. Immediately, the text flowed more freely, and the underlying story started to reveal itself more clearly.

This reshaped how I approached the rest of 'Last Op.' From all the chapters, important revelations and plot points were cut in service to the main story. I was ruthless in my editing. For instance, in the third chapter, 'Dutch's Logbook,' I removed a lengthy discussion of Keith, my grandfather's co-pilot and navigator, whose sexuality (he was gay)—like my grandfather's alcoholism—remained an unspoken fact of our family's extended network of honorary kin. Of course, such material will likely prove valuable and demand revisiting in future writing. For now, though, they did not belong in the narrative that 'Last Op' was becoming.

I also realised that the larger story arc of 'Last Op' was better served by less description, not more. I started to strip away long sections of description throughout the piece. This included descriptive passages of the landscapes to which the airfields belonged that my grandfather called home during the war. Those I decided to keep were now judicious choices, such as a section describing the tunnelling of vision that came with the onset of dusk at RAF Driffield, an abandoned airfield. Now unencumbered by superfluous prose, I started to feel that the narrative had room to breathe. I therefore turned my attention to building scenes—the conversation with my grandmother when she told me about her husband's alcoholism, my meeting with Dutch Holland's grandson—in order to show rather than tell. The story began to take on life.

I was reminded of JM Coetzee's suggestion that 'the secret of the word, story' is that it is 'a storing-place of memories (1986: 59). In his novel *Foe* (1986)—about the distortions of memory and narrative after a woman and a slave are rescued from a desert island in the South Atlantic and seek to sell their story to an esteemed writer—he writes that the storyteller 'must divine which episodes of his history hold promise of fullness, and tease from them their hidden meanings, braiding these together as one braids a rope':

> Teasing and braiding can, like any craft, be learned. But as to determining which episodes hold promise (as oysters hold pearls), it is not without justice that this art is called divining. Here the writer can of himself effect nothing: he must wait on the grace of illumination (Coetzee 1986, p88-89).

Cutting back on passages of unnecessary description, removing redundant narrative strands and stripping the story down to its main elements: I was beginning to find my way, teasing and braiding different episodes from both the lives of my grandparents and, of course, my own. 'Divination' captures that quality of discernment, what haunts your writing starts to take on visible form. Harnessing the simplicity of language and the evocativeness of the well-chosen metaphor were two qualities I wanted to bring to my writing.

Although my confidence was beginning to grow, there were still gaps in my story, things I didn't know from my grandparents' past. I struggled with this, debating the extent to which it would be acceptable to fictionalise certain parts of their story to plug those narrative gaps. Reluctant to do so, I decided that, wherever possible, I must stick to a factual account of what I knew. However, Lisa Jardine provided me with some reassurance on this question, of how to nail down what is authentic and 'true' in the historical account:

> Sometimes it takes something other than perfect fidelity to sharpen our senses, to focus our attention sympathetically, in order to give us emotional access to the past. Silence comes between the historian and the truth he or she looks to the sources to reveal. Thank goodness for the creative imagination of fiction writers, who can reconnect us with the historical feelings, as well as the facts (Jardine 2014).

Taking strength from this insight, I returned to other texts including examples of fictional works written in the style of memoir as well as the autobiographical novel (see Chee's excellent book of essays, 2018). This gave me both inspiration and licence, to include one- or two-sentence snapshots of scenes—all the detail contained within some of the memories that I can recall. Then there were impressions, feelings and thoughts that are truthful in that I remember feeling and thinking them but remain harder to situate within a linear narrative. Again, I found inspiration in surprising places. For instance, Tim Winton's *Land's Edge: A Coastal Memoir* proved helpful and inspiring. Divided into five chapters that read more like short essays, which organise the author's thinking about his relationship with the coast, the book did not progress as a chronological narrative but nonetheless followed a logical and compelling story arc.

Fully liberated and relishing experimentation in my creative writing, I also sought to craft longer scenes. I took my cues from two books, here. The first is *Angela's Ashes* by Frank McCourt, in which he describes the banter between Delia, Jimmy and other drinkers at a public bar (2015: 15-16). The scene is told as a dialogue between the characters. As a reconstruction of events, it comes across almost entirely as fiction. The second, though—which left a stronger impression on me—is a scene from Maxine Hong Kingston's *The Woman Warrior,* which mixes mythical elements with sections of dialogue involving members of her family (1989: 19-23). This guided me through the writing of the seminal conversation in which my grandmother tells me about my grandfather's alcoholism, a scene in which I mixed dialogue with my own imagined 'memories.'

Finally, one other book proved a major source of inspiration: Amy Liptrott's award-winning memoir of addiction and recovery, *The Outrun.* In later sections of her book, where she describes excursions to go watch birds in Orkney, or walk the shoreline of different islands, she inserts disarming memories from her drinking days—usually no more than a sentence or two—in the middle of beautiful writing about nature or history. Such moments serve to jar and interrupt the main flow of the narrative but accurately mimic the ways in which snapshots of memory intrude on our conscious thoughts. That her book should prove so influential on my MFA should not have surprised me. 'The book is the boss,' said the horror novelist Stephen King in a 2006 interview in *The Paris Review*, attributing the original quote to the twentieth century science fiction writer Alfred Bester—and 'Last Op' was not finished with me yet.

## WRITING AND RECOVERY

I mentioned earlier that my writing had been interrupted several times and underwent some false starts. My own mental health had been deteriorating over several years and, in May 2019, I suffered a crisis. Coincidentally occurring roughly fifty years after my grandfather's breakdown, I was briefly hospitalised before undergoing treatment for anxiety, depression and suicidal ideation. I also started attending Alcoholics Anonymous.

I did not want to write about my own experience of alcoholism. However, given my interest in my grandfather and the traumatic legacy the war had left on him, I began to wonder if I would have to address it head on. Alcoholism is a common theme in literature. We are all familiar, for instance, with that most tired and overused of stereotypes in crime fiction: the alcoholic detective, who drinks to forget. Many writers were also notorious alcoholics (cf. Laing 2014). More interesting to me, though, was the presence of that lesser spotted literary character: the recovering alcoholic.

During the first weeks of my recovery, I found myself returning to the books of my childhood. Reading was no straightforward matter. I found it difficult to focus, to retain information, and it often felt not so much a chore but physically exhausting. I worried that I had permanently lost the cognitive function to concentrate and absorb the words and sentences before me. This raised another question, about which I grew anxious: if I could not read anymore, would I be able to write again?

As a teenager, my favourite author had been Stephen King and I read his semi-autobiographical *On Writing: A Memoir of the Craft* almost a decade ago. I was drinking back then and remember reading much of the book while at the pub. I decided to have a fresh look at it. Just as I did as a young teenager, I found comfort in the ease of King's storytelling: a small victory itself. It was a relief to be swept along by his prose. But it was those sections where King writes about his own fears of being unable to write again—following his recovery from alcoholism—that really gave me strength:

> At the worst of it I no longer wanted to drink and no longer wanted to be sober, either. I felt evicted from life. At the start of the road back I just tried to believe the people who said that things would get better if I gave them time to do so. And I never stopped writing. Some of the stuff that came out was tentative and flat, but at least it was there. I buried those unhappy, lacklustre pages in the bottom drawer of my desk and got on to the next project. Little by little I found the beat again, and after that I found the joy again. I came back to my family with gratitude, and back to my work with relief . . . (King 2000: 110–111)

King's metaphor—of feeling evicted on life—spoke to my experiences of alcoholism. Looking back at my efforts to investigate the story of my grandfather's wartime experiences and his subsequent history of alcoholism and mental illness, I wondered whether my own creative practice was performing the twin functions of addressing my own struggles with alcohol and depression and giving shape to my recovery. It was true that when I eventually opened my laptop and began writing again—a process, as outlined above, of reorganising text, ruthlessly cutting what was redundant or superfluous, pruning back and focusing 'Last Op' to the story it was demanding to be—I had started to find the narrative beats. The insight I drew from Stephen King's direct, sometimes painfully honest account of his own history of alcohol addiction, is that while writing did not make him sober, it was an important step in his recovery. It was, amongst other things, a roadmap back to living.

## ON TRAUMA AND MILITARY CULTURE

The story that had haunted my original proposal—one that I did not originally intend to write—was now gaining stark form and taking solid shape. It was becoming easier to harness the various threads and to take control of the narrative voice. What did 'Last Op' really want to be about? An answer to that question had now offered itself. Although I was initially reluctant to grasp it, re-reading Amy Liptrott, Stephen King and others helped give me licence to finally do so.

A couple of months into my recovery, my mother had observed that I had begun to interrogate my own relationship with alcohol when I started writing about the personal story of my grandfather, his wartime service and the impact of his alcoholism on subsequent generations of my family. That interrogation would eventually lead me to ask whether I had, in a sense, inherited his illness: alcoholism. While it was not immediately obvious that this was where my writing was taking me, I credit the ghost in my creative imagination with guiding me to this question. I realised that—and to fully embrace my efforts to understand my grandfather's illness—I would have to put my own experience of alcoholism at the heart of 'Last Op.' It seemed that my interest in my grandfather was not so much a story I could tell at arm's length. Rather, I needed to put my own personal struggles in direct dialogue with his. Only when I accepted this did the links between different sections of the narrative become very clear and obvious. The story, from then on, wrote itself.

Throughout my writing, I thought time and again of the cultural theorist Mark Fisher's development of the concept of 'hauntology' (see Fisher 2014 and 2016), a term first coined by Jacques Derrida but which the French philosopher never really nailed down himself. Without becoming embroiled in how Fisher explains the application of this term to a wider socio-cultural moment—a theoretical backdrop that I did not find as helpful for reflecting on my creative practice—I was nevertheless drawn to his elaboration on hauntology:

> Haunting, then, can be construed as a failed mourning. It is about refusing to give up the ghost or—and this can sometimes amount to the same thing—the refusal of the ghost to give up on us (Fisher 2014: 22).

Inspired by Fisher – who committed suicide in 2017— after a lifetime of struggle with depression and mental illness, about which he has written in relation to hauntology—I imagined 'Last Op' as an exploration of failed mourning. In doing so, my thinking about my creative practice developed further: if 'Last Op' was about ghosts that I had not yet given up myself, it was just as true that they had not given up on me either. In this sense, my writing was about reclaiming what has been lost, and this speaks to what Fisher described as hauntology in an important way, albeit one that is particular to myself and my family.

As much as haunting is about failed mourning, it is also about lost futures. Fisher argues that when a society is haunted, in a cultural moment like that brought on by late capitalism and neoliberalism, it feels a sense of loss for a future once promised but now taken away. I suggest this can be felt personally, in relation to trauma and addiction. Did my grandfather mourn a lost future when he returned from the war in 1945? I cannot answer that, but when I was lost in the throes of alcoholism, I thought I had no future—a common despair you hear in the 'shares' of AA members all the time. Writing 'Last Op' was therefore not just an exercise in me exorcising old ghosts. It was also a process of organising my memories, 'storing' them (to riff off Coetzee again) as part of a forward narrative full of prospective promise. In this way, my writing ends on a note of optimism. This is the most surprising revelation to me, the least I would have expected when I began exploring the legacy of wartime trauma on my grandfather and his family.

I have sometimes troubled over the ethics of my efforts to empathetically embrace my grandfather's illness. I have little direct experience of military institutions—limited to a short stint of officer training in the Adelaide University Regiment in the early 1990s—and have never experienced war. Is it really fair for me to use my own struggles with mental illness and alcohol misuse to imagine myself into his shoes? I worry I am putting words into the mouth of a man who died almost two decades ago and cannot speak for himself. Having no way of testing the veracity of my writing about these issues against his personal testimony, I still have doubts. But I do think there is value in engaging creatively with these issues, in the absence of the hard facts of knowing what has come before. I do not think it is a stretch to speculate that such illnesses leave a mark on families and subsequent generations, to whom a trace memory of trauma may be handed down. Creative practice can open possibilities for deepening understanding of these challenging issues. It can also be experienced as unsettling, threatening even, exposing yourself emotionally. However, I think that there is justice here. I want to remember my grandfather not as a hero but rather a man, warts and all, capable of bravery and love but also sensitive and vulnerable. After the guns fell silent over European battlefields, he carried a troubled legacy into middle age and beyond. That legacy—of psychological trauma, alcoholism and addiction—remains, for so many, the unremembered story of World War Two. For me, that my grandfather overcame his addiction and rebuilt his life, with my grandmother's support, is at least as heroic as anything he did during the war.

# 10

# Stories Outside the Wire

*Rebecca Steel*

## LIFE BEHIND THE WIRE: A PLACE FOR CREATIVITY?

Growing up and trying to make sense of the world as a child living in a military environment presents challenges. In a world shaped by rules and regulations, it is common for service children to have adverse childhood experiences impacting on their health and well-being. The occupational demands of military life that are common across services mean that many military families are affected by high levels of mobility and frequent family separations. For service children, the experiences that go along with military life have a major influence on shaping their childhoods and family lives. For example, frequent moves and family separations have been shown to result in a high risk of emotional, behavioural, and attainment issues among children in military families (McCulloch and Hall 2018). The demands placed upon the serving person in military families mean that adopting a child-centred approach[1] is very difficult, and so as a result, the voices of service children within academic research are seldom heard. As civilians growing up in a military environment, military life presents tensions for service children and their family; the military always comes first. The expectation of personnel to respond to the needs of their vocation above the needs of the family means parental absence from events in their children's lives—such as starting school, birthdays, Christmas, parents' evenings, graduation, and hospital appointments—is the norm. It is likely, even expected, that service personnel will experience both a physical and emotional distance from their families due to the nature of their job.

This chapter considers the value of arts-based research methods for exploring these kinds of issues with military children, by drawing on our fictional storytelling project with service families, *Stories Outside the Wire*. Over the

**Figure 10.1 Stories outside the wire.**

space of a year, this arts-based participatory research project, funded by the Armed Forces Covenant Local Grants Fund, worked with military families (service children and spouses) to produce creative resources that could be used in the home, social, or educational settings to help service families with transition. An objective identified by participants was to create a tangible output in the form of a storybook that not only focussed on life in the military, but also included their collective lived experience of the military culture and community. The book is written for parents from military families to read to primary school–aged children as they move onto base, but it is also suitable for non-military children. It forms an information, advice, and guidance resource and includes signposting resources for new families as they move into the area. Copies are given to new children enrolling at the primary school on base, and the children read the book and then play the game as part of an icebreaker activity. The book itself has been shared throughout the Army Welfare service as a template that can be created in different areas. The project also featured as a case study in the *Service Children's Progression Alliance, Listening to Learn Report* (2018). Whilst the story is fictional, many of the places featured in the book are military bases in the UK and abroad, as the participants wanted to reflect the housing on base and familiar places. In addition to the books, the service children designed a board game based on what they perceive can go wrong and how and where they can access support to overcome challenges. The board game is a giant version where the young people are the pieces and physically move around the game themselves, discussing the issues where they land on the board and looking at how these scenarios apply to their lives.

Whilst the use of arts-based methods in *Stories Outside the Wire* was in part about finding participatory, community-led ways of providing support resources for military families, it also provides an example of how creativity and imagination can be mobilised in the generation of alternative knowledge about the military and military culture. We wanted to provide service children in Lancashire with the freedom to discuss the conflicting cultures of military life on the *inside* and civilian life on the *outside*. Based on the notion that stories are central to our means of communicating with ourselves and one another (Bruner 2002; Siegel 2015), the project's aim was to understand

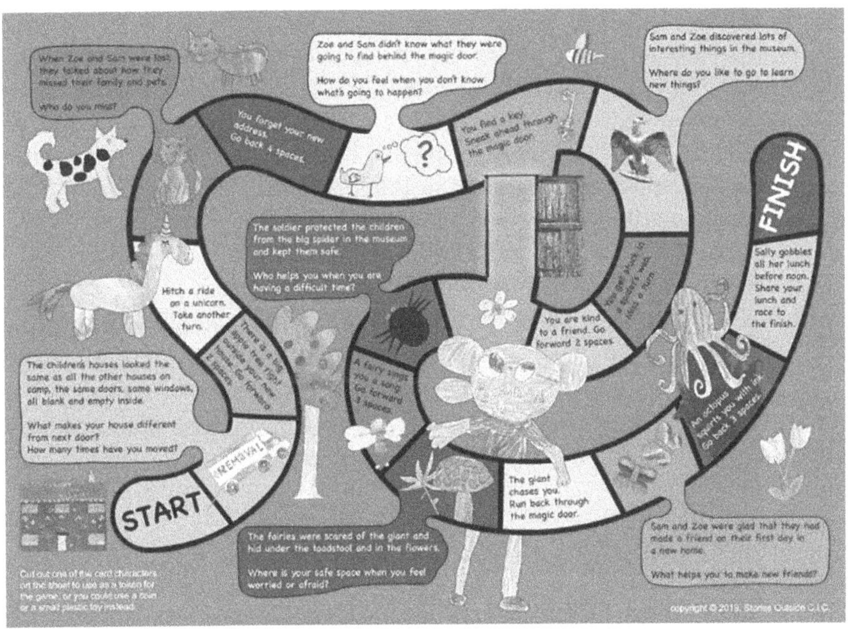


**Figure 10.2 The board game.**

children's perspectives of growing up as a service child and the challenges this presents from the perspective of service children and their family. Crucially, however, we also wanted to give a sense of agency to service children. This is a group of people who are very much affected by military life, but they are rarely given the opportunity to narrate their experiences or give an account of their lives in military families. Furthermore, service children have thus far not been considered within critical military studies scholarship to be political subjects with the capacity to tell us something interesting and valuable about the military as an institution and a way of life. *Stories Outside the Wire*, therefore, represents an alternative way of "knowing" the military.

For me, "creativity" provides an alternative way of thinking in an authoritarian environment of military culture. In this chapter, I argue that creative methods offer us the tools for rethinking both *how we tell* and *who tells* counter-narratives about military life. I explore through the power of creativity how service children were able to mobilise their imagination and find new ways to talk about aspects of their life-worlds that are otherwise difficult to articulate. Developing arts-based methods in our research design allowed us to make the focus of the study both relevant and accessible to participants, while the finished product provided an emotional and imaginative insight into the perspectives and lived experiences of this group. The co-creation of stories and illustrations in this project gave participants a route to freedom of expression and the ability to represent aspects of their lives by concentrating solely on the act of creating. *Stories Outside the Wire* provides us as researchers with an example of how we can engage service children in conversations around military culture and military life and empower them to create and speak using their own voice. The contribution of hearing from service children in the military community aims to challenge the dominant narrative of the establishment, which is the institutional voice of the military often reiterated through serving personnel. Through engaging service children in creative production, a fresh set of eyes are viewing life in service, telling their story and experiences from young people's perspectives of growing up in the military. By providing participants, the service children engaged in the research, with the opportunity to tell it like it is for them, the arguments presented in this chapter aim to restore the balance and freedom of speech in creating a level playing field for service children whose voices are regularly lost in the noise of the military.

## ABOUT *STORIES OUTSIDE THE WIRE*

The idea for the *Stories Outside the Wire* project had arisen from participant feedback on an arts-based research project we had delivered a few months earlier, carried out with the spouses and children from the same military community. The earlier project resulted in an exhibition in the Lancashire Infantry Museum, which placed the focus upon the families rather than the serving person. The visual displays produced for this exhibition included historical objects with stories from military families of the past and artwork produced by the participants fulfilling those same roles today. The displays included positive and negative accounts of life during time of service within the military family unit, emphasising the contrasting cultures of military and civilian life. The artwork for the exhibition aimed to centre the importance of family life and make links back to domestic life through objects that regularly form a part of home. It is not uncommon to find a gas mask or other forms of military kit in service persons' houses. The displays, created of tiles, drums, or medals, aimed to reflect this and explore their military connotations as objects often received by the serving person in acknowledgment of *their* service. When examining the pre-existing archives in the museum, it became evident that military history is so often told from the perspective of the service person, usually a white male of senior rank. As a challenge to these dominant ways of narrating and knowing within military history, the curator worked with military spouses in this project to find historical evidence of the role spouses had played in the regiment's history. We re-examined the contents of the museum with the aim of finding evidence of what families contributed to military history, starting with the present displays. The findings revealed that spouses had taken on key roles in the military community, particularly during times of need such as pandemics or conflict, as educators and nurses. Our exhibition focussed on telling these hidden histories and highlighting the importance of families and their contribution to the military in the past and through to the present featuring the participants of the project curating and participating in the exhibition.

Following the launch, the group reflected on the experience, as they had never been involved in a project that focussed on their role in the functioning of the military. Spouses often do not see themselves as having a role that is key to the military, despite their centrality in keeping the family together, supporting the service person, and bringing up children (sometimes whilst also working themselves), and all while existing in a constant state of transition and preparation for separation or relocation. An outcome from this initial project found military spouses acknowledging the integral role they play. Though this is not a role recognised in terms of pay, promotion, or medals, these spouses wanted to use their collective voice to "speak outwards" and highlight the labour that they provide for the military, as well as highlight (and therefore place equal value on) the things that they have achieved within their own lives, whether they be related to lone parenting, arranging a house move singlehandedly, studying for a degree or building a career.

Having seen their artwork and findings from the project exhibited alongside poignant regimental histories of white male, upper-class officers, the group of military families were proud of what they had achieved, and the stories they had told about their lives. The exhibition assigned military families with equal importance in the stories and histories of "*the military*" by displaying them together. This led one of the participants, a service child, to ask if they could produce their own book to tell their story of life in the military, and so the idea for *Stories Outside the Wire* was born. Knowledge about the military in the public domain is typically produced from official sources, such as the armed forces covenant, veterans or researchers working with the MoD or funding bodies with a particular interest in the military, such as the Forces in Mind Trust or the Armed Forces Covenant Fund Trust. There are many charities and networks established to promote and support the military community such as the Royal British Legion, SSAFA, Help for Heroes, and Forces Families Federations. All these methods of obtaining information about the military community generally focus upon the people in uniform and institution they serve. It is these "political subjects" who usually have the power and agency to speak about military life.

Within the project, through employing creative methods we are able to prioritise coproduction and offer a way of accessing new voices. Centring those service children and spouses who are not considered to be "political subjects" yet have something valuable or interesting to say about the military and their place within it. Through introducing these alternative narratives, we can gain an insight into how military families view themselves within the military. When we centre different voices in this way, the perspectives and lived experiences shared with us through creative practice, point to the broader issue of how the military impacts upon the social and cultural capital of service children and spouses. The military culture they know and live is very different to the serving person, who is the sole focus of the institution of which they are a part. The disparity that this institutional military power creates at the expense of the families, and their acceptance of it, creates new social structures and different ways of knowing military culture.

Our research methodology included interviews and focus groups, alongside a series of arts engagement sessions. These sessions were loosely designed around: "A Day in the Life of a Service Family," "Role Models," "Life on Base," and a few others. In these sessions, each participant was given a pack including a sketchbook, pens, and pencils, which participants could use to jot down any thoughts or drawings relevant to the topic. We regularly set participants off with arts materials and listened as the conversation flowed, while recording and later transcribing the discussions that emerged. The research included primary empirical data drawn from three groups of participants. These groups included: service children aged one to eighteen years-old, attending two separate youth clubs at two different military bases, and service children aged ten to eleven years-old attending primary school. A sample of thirty children in total contributed to the research and analysis, though a greater number of fifty were involved in the project. For many of the younger service children, this involved bringing painting sessions to toddler groups where they were able to get involved in the process of painting. In addition, we also interviewed spouses with caring responsibilities for service children and teaching staff.

Once we had gathered the "data," we provided a summary of the emergent themes to the creative writer who is also a military spouse. The writer compiled each storybook by matching the service children's illustrations and anecdotes to the plot. The production of each of the fictional storytelling books is based on an imaginative story featuring locations on camp and illustrations drawn and chosen by service children during the creative sessions. The moments where children illustrated and talked through their storyboards were instrumental to gathering ideas and generating formative themes. They provided emergent insights into how participants viewed themselves and their own lives, for example by examining the collective culture and identity of being "in the military" as well as the impact that this has, particularly in relation to deployment of parents and transition to civilian life or a different military base. The final product was something that provided not only support resources but an alternative way of thinking about military life, particularly transition and the impact upon service families. The project featured as a case study in the Service Children's Progression Alliance's Year of the Service Child Voice, Listening to Learn report[2] (2020).

## PARTICIPATORY ARTS INSIDE THE WIRE

Our aim in *Stories Outside the Wire* was to use participatory arts-methods to centre the voices of those members of the military community who are (usually) hidden and provide them with the means to speak outwards about military life. However, "speaking outwards" is not commonplace for service families. There is a level of secrecy and pride attached to service that extends to family life, and the expectations placed upon spouses who are required to support the service person to *do their duty*. Rachel Gribble *et al.* note that "[a]n additional, but under-researched, stressor for spouses is the relationship they have with the military as an institution. Military policies and procedures rely on personnel to be the conduit between the military and families, preventing spouses from feeling that they are fully participating in the military community" (2019, 3). Members of the armed forces face considerable restrictions on political freedoms that are taken for granted by most of the population. They are not permitted to join a trade union or political organisation, to speak to the public or media without permission or to stand for elected office (Armed Forces Act 2006). Furthermore, there is an expectation within military culture that service families similarly adhere to the rules and regulations of the military institution. This often creates an oppressive environment, where expressing views and opinions or providing insights into military life is feared to have repercussions on the service person and themselves. As a way of identifying barriers or issues commonplace in military culture, the creative methods employed gave participants their voice, so that they as individuals are both recognised and heard. Using art-based methods provides a platform for participants to "speak outwards" with the focus on the creative-method distracting the fact they are providing an insight into their thoughts and feeling and how they see themselves within the military community.

Military families are often part of a gated community and live behind the wire of a military camp, which is inaccessible to civilians. We sought to engage families in the creation of this new knowledge about the military through a multi-agency approach, working in trusted spaces across two military bases in Lancashire. This included the local primary school, community centres, military welfare services, and with the curator utilising space in Lancashire Infantry Museum. These were considered to be "safe" and neutral places, spaces where restrictions associated with living in a military camp are not enforced, and where participants could freely express themselves without fear of being reprimanded for speaking out or behaving in a certain way. My position as a military spouse, with service children of my own, gives me a presence within the community as an "insider" in the research. The team working on this project were familiar to the participants, which is important for gaining trust with hard-to-reach communities and when developing a shared understanding. The creative and participatory methods employed enabled us to be present in the community, as they prioritised coproduction and working closely with the participants. Families were able to engage actively in the process of inquiry, as researchers and participants collaborated in artmaking as a way of knowing (Leavy 2018). In the context of our participants, this meant that the service children and spouses were describing military life from their own perspectives, rather than those of the uniformed service. Using arts-based methods allowed us to take a holistic approach to the research process and explore the interconnections between epistemology, theory, and methods (Leavy 2020), particularly when it comes to understanding the impact of active service life on childhood and education. Through placing the voices of service children at the heart of the project, we were able to ensure that these voices were not only represented but *heard*, with their contributions manifested in tangible outputs that could be touched and felt.

As practitioners and researchers, we wanted participants to feel empowered to shape and inform the creative process. We began by appointing some of the more experienced and confident spouses with whom we had worked in our previous creative projects to leading roles where they encouraged and supported others in their participation. This ensured that military spouses were a part of the core team, having both ownership and creative license of the ideas generated. One member of this team noted that:

> Working with a group of professional women with their own spheres of expertise and a communal goal was a rewarding and enriching experience I won't soon forget. I can't articulate what it meant to be taken seriously again, by serious people. (Military Spouse 2018)

Barone and Eisner (2012) describe the importance of the role of artistry in social inquiry. In the context of this project, creativity provided a space for counter narratives to emerge from the inside, enabling emotional and imaginative engagement. Coproduction and co-creation in the project setting provided a method of working that recognises the complex relationships between people and organisations from different sectors, communities, and cultures. It emphasises a pluralistic model of the community based on interorganisational relationships, networks, collaborative partnerships, and other forms of multi-actor public action (Nabatchi *et al.* 2017). This approach allowed us to create a level playing field with the participants, giving each voice a sense of agency, equality, and worth as collaborators. This was particularly important given the focus of military life is often upon the service person rather than the family who are seldom heard.

The suitability of arts-based research and its participatory nature as valuing non-hierarchical relationships enabled participants to interact with the process as full and equal collaborators (Finley 2008). This approach offers flexibility and fluidity; there is no rigid set of rules or methods to follow, and artistic practices make way for spontaneity and emergences that were important to our work as a process of discovery. The united attitudes and values of the collective project team were driven by meeting the needs of a community, which can often be overlooked. We wanted *Stories Outside the Wire* to have impact and provide participants with the opportunity to be heard and speak outwards. This started with the "hidden" military community (children and spouses) feeling both listened to and valued. Introducing creativity to a life shaped by rules aimed to provide military families, particularly spouses and children, with an opportunity to convey how they feel, think, and experience the world around them. Our arts-based methods were employed as a way of blurring the boundaries between researcher/practitioners (Liamputtong *et al.* 2008), while also encouraging our creative practice to develop from the grassroots level up. Through these methods we were able to harness this community's collective voice, which enabled their thoughts and feelings to be heard, acknowledged, and taken seriously.

We wanted to create a level playing field with the service children involved in the sense that their ideas and stories were placed at the forefront of the project. Our participatory arts approach was informed by Bourdieu's notion of habitus and social constructs (1980 and 1986). Bourdieu sees power as culturally and symbolically created, and constantly re-legitimised through an interplay of agency and structure. The main way this happens is through what he calls "habitus," or socialised norms and tendencies that guide behaviour and thinking (Bourdieu 1980). In *Stories Outside the Wire*, we were able to place the emphasis on the *doing*, *the creating*, which allowed us access into the critical consciousness of the participants without them feeling under the spotlight. It also allowed us to be fully inclusive of the whole community, with babies and toddlers sat in their nappies armed with paint and brushes and the freedom to "create" whilst their mums had an adult conversation and a hot drink. Families involved were able to use the community spaces as they were intended, with familiar faces from the community such as the youth workers and adults acting in support roles. Integration was a really important factor for us, and the creative approach of arts-based research allowed us to not only be inclusive, but a part of the regular activity schedule designed by the welfare team on base.

It is important to mention my position here in more depth. In addition to being a researcher, I am a military spouse with three service children of my own. Whilst I do not belong to the same military service as the participants, there's a shared understanding and unspoken agreement fostered through lived experience of being a military spouse. But my position presents a particular tension in the context of this project. As qualitative researchers, our identities are inevitably mixed into our methodological approaches (Woodcock 2016); as a military spouse with service children, the judgment I apply when interpreting data and identifying emergent themes may not be the same judgment another researcher without my lived experience of military culture would apply. But at the same time, because the participants were aware of my lived experience it is arguable that they had a greater level of trust placed in me during the research process thus allowing me a deeper insight into their lives as a result. Crucially, my "insider" position enabled me to probe more deeply into things that were represented in creative ways, for example some of the fears the children expressed around parental separation and return as well as children being or feeling "lost" that may not have been clear to "outsiders" leading the research.

Our creative sessions provided a safe space for these discussions to take place. Findings from the data we collected in sessions allowed us to explore each participants perceptions of the barriers they face, which differed according to which group they belonged to; for children, discussions focused upon themselves, their families' employment, and identity, whereas for spouses (all of whom were female), discussions focussed on the broader implications of military life, primarily their children and husbands and lastly themselves. One spouse told us:

> Being an army spouse meant putting my career in second place to my husband's, and when my first run at motherhood resulted in multiples, I felt like I was waving goodbye to any chance at pursuing my own ambition, talent, or identity. (Military Spouse 2018)

Emergent theme analysis was viewed through the social constructivist lenses of Bourdieu (1980; 1986) and Wenger (1992; 1999; 2002) and related to identity and capital already acknowledged as important by the military community in which the research is taking place, for example service families feeling overlooked and unimportant in the context of military life. As Wenger explains, communities of practice develop through the existence of a common set of experiences, problems, and perspectives (Wenger 2002). In applying the framework of communities of practice to the analysis of data, we were able to identify key thematic areas where service children required support. We were able to organise the data into the following categories[3] Friends and family; Home and moving; Being scared and mental health "feeling safe"; Learning and school; Identity. This data was useful in gaining an insight into how service children and spouses viewed themselves, the military, and their place within it. The data allowed us to understand the impact of the service persons role on participants as an individual and family unit, the findings ranged from understanding the impact of absent parenting to participants concerns about death and separation. The arts-based methods provided us with a trusted space to explore the deeper meaning of what the participants were telling us through examining the creative outputs produced. The impact of the military environment permeated all aspects of the participants' lives and there was a particular focus on how institutional elements of military life, for example living on base, adhering to rules, following processes, can impact upon the human rights and freedoms of the families. Participants described the impact of military life as introducing limitations to their freedom of speech but also their freedom to move, in applying this to human rights the limitations of the military environment on families impacted greatly on their capacity to make their own decisions and to have a respect for their private and family lives, their homes and correspondence.

*Stories Outside the Wire* emphasised the importance of working creatively in a structured and controlled environment. Through the introduction of participatory arts-based methods into this world, we were able to build trust through listening and being present, giving families a sense of agency in a community where they lack recognition, and ensuring that their voices are heard.

## TELLING OUR STORY, FACT, OR FICTION?

Nind (2011) suggests that narrative and life-story work help us to value participants as expert witnesses in the active telling and retelling of their own experiences. But when considering the communication of ideas from young people whose voices are seldom heard, the journey from author to audience has particular significance (Satchwell 2019).

In *Stories Outside the Wire*, the service children worked together to decide what was important and what they wanted the story and illustrations to convey about them to the outside world. They did this through the act of fictionalising; for example, things that they found frightening about the camp and its surroundings took on metaphorical shape as a big giant with three eyes in the forest and an oversized spider in the museum. In contrast, there were friendly octopuses and sea creatures that lived in the ocean near the Cyprus base where many participants had recently been posted prior to arrival in Lancashire, and the uniformed services were represented in the stories as protecting the children from the scary things they encountered. Memories from shared lived experiences featured heavily, such as exploring with friends and family. For many of the participants, being in control of both the decisions and a piece of work was a new concept and experience. During the creative sessions we encouraged participants to share their thoughts and feelings, and this often resulted in the group downing crayons and paint brushes and taking a trip outdoors to collectively explore some of the places that featured in the illustrations being created. On one occasion, a service child found an old lock and keyhole in one of the old Grade II listed buildings on one of the military bases next to the community centre where the session was being held and took the group outside to see it. The group then made up imaginary stories about what is behind the "magic door," and this was a significant part of the process as everyone had different ideas. Through physically exploring places, we were able to understand thoughts and feelings sometimes stemming from difficult experiences that impacted on the children present.

The use of fairy-tale figures and pantomime villains as captured by the children's imaginations and creativity allowed us to discuss their lived experiences and how the characters created relate to key events in their lives. For us, fiction and imagination became ways of "giving voice" and agency to our participants. It gave service children the language to express their fears, thoughts, and feelings through fiction and storytelling, and helped us create the space for open discussion of topics like life and death, fear and safety, separation and anxiety, all of which are ever-present in military life.

Often the importance of the illustration or story being shared was who or what was missing from the picture; separation is a common theme in military families. The children would provide two versions of their family life one where the service person is present and one where they are deployed. Many times, it was the service person, usually the father figure in the family on active service leaving the rest of the family behind. Changing family dynamics can often mean service children have increased responsibility for siblings and household tasks and extended family members are often seen by service children as role models and support, for example:

> My Grandad, he helps me with everything. He loves his cups of tea and teaches me loads of things, even how to hammer nails in. I'm glad to have Grandad there when Dad isn't. (Military Child D 2018)

Moving between bases also clearly disrupted the children's educational experiences; one of the primary school pupils had moved fourteen times, and there wasn't anyone within the rest of the class who hadn't moved at least three times. It was clear from their experiences that transition, and mobility had an impact upon learning and school life:

> We get here to camp doing car journeys from Southport every day. Dad's still working here, and my mum is posted to Northern Ireland. My brother started a different secondary school in Southport, he was at one here, but someone smashed his face in, I want to go to the same school as him after here, but I don't know if I can get in yet. It takes me three hours to get home. (Military Child A 2018)

As part of the creative activities, we asked service children to illustrate short storyboards containing things that were important to them, what constituted home, this ranged from pets, belongings, and family members. Through listening to the information participants shared with us about their lives as service children, we were able to gain an insight into their thoughts and feelings. These were, again, often communicated through what they told us was missing:

> "Because of how often they're away some of the adults have been going away for like six months. My dad has been to Kenya, Afghan, USA, Italy, and Canada. It makes you feel sad and lonely. You actually feel lonely without your father" (Military Child B 2018).

Another participant told us, in contrast:

> For me it is the opposite way around, it's my mum that's away not dad, she's in the army. At one-point mum was going away, she's a medic, and she was worrying about what happens to me if she dies. I heard her, she was speaking on the phone and didn't know I was listening. (Military Child C 2018)

For our participants, transforming their experiences into fiction became an intricate and revealing process, which highlighted the meanings that could emerge through interaction between qualitative data and creative interpretation. During creative sessions, participants were focussed on making, drawing, thinking, and talking; this was a valuable process where the truth of everyone involved metamorphoses into a relatable story to military families. We could argue data loses "truth" when it becomes fictionalised, in this process of making illustrations and a story we found a collective truth emerges; one that all military families can relate to and understand. The book provides access to the military, what it is like to grow up and live in a community that is inaccessible to most.

The creative process of compiling the final book added further layers of interpretation about life from the perspectives of service children. When the group discussed the story, they drew on their interpretation of military life and imaginative storytelling to combat some of the challenges this life presents. This creative process provided a unique and critical insight into how they view the military community, ranging from how they viewed the purpose of military, the collective responsibility, and the roles of the serving person and their family members. An example of discussion topics around roles and responsibilities focuses heavily on single parenting, where older siblings were often seen by younger brothers and sisters in a parental role, stepping up to take on the responsibilities of the parent on deployment. This in turn often created a temporary instability in the family, when roles were expected to revert to normal on the return of the service person into the family unit.

Due to the amount of valuable qualitative data from the creative process of making the book, and the fact that when the participants had been physically moving around places they had discussed meanings and themes in more depth, we came up with the idea of a game. Participants in the project wanted to design this game using themes and fictional characters from the book, that were loosely based around all their collective experiences of military life. The idea to use the game as a resource and method of initiating play, as an icebreaker for service children new to the area, came directly from the service children. The game has been designed as a giant version where the service children physically take steps to move themselves around a life-sized board, using a giant dice to take turns and talk about each stage and what it means to them and "their journey" into military life. This offered a way for the children to bring their ideas to life and actively participate in the journey through being able to physically move around the game. The added value of this within the critical military research was accessibility, giving total ownership to the children playing the game and providing them with a space to discuss their lived experiences. This wasn't through a structured methodology such as survey or interview, which is arguably an alien concept to children. We were co-creating and learning together through the experience of creative play, in which is a natural environment for children to participate. This creative process enabled us to generate new data and insights into how service children view growing up in the military, how it impacts on them, how they view the world, their education, their families, their friends, and their hopes for the future.

## THE END IS OFTEN THE BEGINNING: DRAWING CONCLUSIONS

Participants in the *Stories Outside the Wire* project identified the greatest sacrifice of military life as being the experience of parental absence from the family unit. In the cases of some participants, both parents served so it was rare that the family unit were together. Within this theme, participants spoke of the absent parent including: anxiety for their safety, missing for key events such as birthdays or holidays, childcare, limited activities with single parent, mental health, day of departure, returning from deployment, and upsetting routines, dealing with situations made tougher by coping with absence and lack of an adult to help, and a change in family structure meaning siblings had to step up and provide support, which then shifted the family dynamics. The *Living in Our Shoes* report (2020) stresses that the quality of the child's home and family environment, as well as the quality of the relationship between the child and each parent, are crucial factors that influence child development. In addition, more than 70 percent of UK Service families stated that living separately from personnel as the result of unaccompanied postings has harmed the serving person's relationship with their family (Army Families Federation 2016).

The insights from our research shifted the focus of existing research away from adults and onto service children. We structured the research environment so that it was led by creative art-making and game playing, from developing this accessibility in a trusted space we were able to enter into how the service children thought and felt about lived experiences and future situations. We shifted the narrative onto them rather than the uniformed service person.

The structure of a controlled military environment often means that there is a reluctance among military communities to share their lived experiences. In *Stories Outside the Wire*, freedom of expression was central to the methods applied. As discussed earlier in this chapter, speaking out about the tensions of military life can cause family members to possess a fear of repercussions upon the service person and themselves. The value of creative methods in this scenario, as described in Leavy's evaluation criteria of fictional storytelling "resonance" figures highly as equating with both "validity" and "trustworthiness" (2015, 79).

The notion of resonance in this project directly relates to the participant and readers sense of "feeling with" or "feeling affinity with" the story being told and the narrator telling it. Where there is a sense of a harmonious connection, where the group comes together or isolates all relate to the resonance which may change during the creative activity of artmaking, storytelling, or game playing.

For us, it was important that this sense of resonance featured within the participants and this was indicated by the creative methods they chose to tell their story. Participants might have identified resonance with what is being said and how the story is being told. In this context, we can only draw conclusions from what service children tell us; but we can't know what they are *not* telling us.

*Stories Outside the Wire* provided us with the opportunity to further develop our research relationship with this specific military community, but also, crucially, helped us to tell counter-narratives about military life. Prioritising the voices of service children and spouses through adopting a participatory approach to learning about military life allowed us to hear from the families. For us, the co-creation of stories, illustrations, the book, and a life-sized board game led to the coproduction of new meanings about the realities of life in a military family. The creative process of making the story and illustrations was a constant process of translation and interpretation, producing the drawings, discussing their meanings and where they fit into the story. The richness of the qualitative data, findings, and outputs stemmed from adopting an inclusive participatory approach where the subjects of the research have ownership and control. Conrad and Campbell said of participatory research that in the best examples, "participants are involved in the research process from beginning to end. Together they set the research agenda, pose questions for inquiry, participate in the collection and analysis of 'data,' and decide the outcomes of the process, how the research will be used" (2008, 248). This is precisely the ethos demonstrated in *Stories Outside the Wire*.

The creative approach was fundamentally about the act of coproduction and collaborative creation. The power of arts-based research in the military community setting is its flexible method for education, community development and to a certain degree activism with service children as a marginalised group (Liamputtong *et al.* 2008).

In critical military research, adopting a flexible methodology represents an example of how fiction, metaphor, and imaginative storytelling can tell us something useful and interesting about growing up in the military. The process of fictionalising stories with participants highlighted how new knowledge can emerge in the space between qualitative data generation and creative interpretation. Prioritising messiness and experimentation in an unstructured space provided the participants with freedom as they placed trust in the process of creation. Metaphor and imagination gave service children a familiar voice they could use to articulate different ideas, without the constraint that often goes along with life in a controlled military environment. In practice, this meant that service children created unicorns, giants, lions, fairies, and octopuses, mythical and majestic creatures that offered ways of talking about experiences that were hard to put into words. McNiff (2018) describes these as the interdependent elements of subjective and objective reality; this is the art speaking for itself. Providing participants with an environment for enquiry that appreciates the ability of the arts to inform and inspire through expression. It is here within the interpretations of illustrations and fictional tales that arts-based research reveals its worth. Arts-based methods provided the military community with the opportunity to speak outward about military culture from the perspective of service children, a group whose voices are seldom heard and who live in a gated community behind the wire that "not a lot of people understand." In our research, this world emerged in a new way, as somewhere with the same houses as there is in military housing, lots of soldiers in uniform, a glittery unicorn, and the odd giant.

## REPORTS

Armed Forces Covenant (2012–2021). https://www.armedforcescovenant.gov.uk/.

Army Families Federation. 2016. AFF Big Survey 2016: The Future of Military Housing. Andover, Army Families Federation. Families Federation factsheet: armed forces information. Available at publishing.service.gov.uk.

Child Rights International Network. 2019. Conscription by Poverty, Depravation and Army Recruitment in the UK. Available at https://static1.squarespace.com/static/5afadb22e17ba3eddf90c02f/t/5d5bbf83278b3100018306a4/1566293898095/UK_recruitment_report_final.pdf.

Children's Commissioner. 2018. Kin and Country: Growing up as an Armed Forces Child. Available at https://www.fionabruce.org.uk/sites/www.fionabruce.org.uk/files/2018-06/KIN-AND-COUNTRY-Growing-up-as-an-Armed-Forces-child.pdf.

Department for Education. 2013. Service children in state school handbook. Available at https://www.gov.uk/government/publications/service-children-in-state-schools-handbook.

Ministry of Defence. 2021. JSP 752: Tri-Service Regulations for Expenses and Allowances. Available at https://assets.publishing.service.gov.uk/government/uploads/system/uploads/attachment_data/file/950387/20210101-JSP_752_v45_Jan_21.pdf.

Ministry of Defence. 2020. What you need to know about the Future Accommodation Model. Available at https://www.gov.uk/government/publications/future-accommodation-model-what-you-need-to-know/what-you-need-to-know-about-fam.

Ministry of Defence. 2020. Living in our Shoes: Understanding the Needs of the Armed Forces. Available at https://assets.publishing.service.gov.uk/government/uploads/system/uploads/attachment_data/file/895236/Living_in_our_shoes_Full_Report__1__embargoed_30_June.pdf.

Naval Families Federation. 2019. The effect of non-operational family separations on family functioning and wellbeing among Royal Navy/Royal Marine families. Available at https://nff.org.uk/wp-content/uploads/2019/02/Non-Operational-Separations.pdf.

# 11

# Autoethnographic Creativity

## *Re-remembering Military Service*

*Hannah West*

For me, researching how we understand war through women's stories is personal. I have had to explore my own military service and rethink how I understand my relationship with military power. Creativity has opened a space for me to reflect on my own "encounter" with the military and find my critical voice. Through a collaboratively produced music video, a short documentary film and a series of short poetic[1] documentary films, I have explored gendered experiences of military service and "front line combat" to challenge how we think about war and what it means to be a combatant. In this chapter, I will use these projects to argue that creative endeavours became a tool for sharing experiences, empowering reflexivity and ultimately helped me to situate myself as a researcher in the field of critical military studies. Although nerve-racking to expose one's personal story through this work, as these creative avenues became increasingly integral to my research process, interaction with other veterans gave me confidence to find my critical voice and weave it into my research. The co-constitution of knowledge with other female veterans in re-remembering military service as a woman has, at times, been shocking to revisit, revealing a gendered culture I couldn't see fully when serving.

The passage of time alone does not bring "critical distance." I didn't leave the military on a trajectory to critical feminist scholarship. I didn't plan to use "creative methods," and it wasn't written into my research design. It didn't even cross my mind until I was on maternity leave when I spotted an advert for the university film festival and said to my husband, "we could have a go at that"! And yet, I now put it down to being "creative" that my research (and I) has affected a transformation from an effectiveness-oriented enquiry of mainstream military studies to a critical feminist questioning of military power.

As a former Naval Air Engineer, I embarked on academic study as a quest to understand, and, to some extent, to justify, my participation in war: looking for what I felt had been the missing academic rigour to retrospectively underwrite the gendered policies I had been involved in. Through creative endeavours, a space was opened amongst fellow ex-servicemen and women for thinking anew about our military pasts, triggering memories, empowering participants, and helping me to find my critical voice. "Creativity" or being "creative" in my research is about "creating something from elements that already exist by putting them together in a new way" (Kara 2015, 11), and producing a new space for thinking differently. Where this book explores the critical space that being "creative" can open in military research, this chapter will explore the critical space that being "creative" can open in *military researchers*. In so doing, it will ask how finding a critical voice through creativity can help the marginalised voices of the military community to be heard and to "speak outwards."

My research explores how knowledge production about war is gendered and controlled to deny women a legitimate voice to narrate their war stories. Engaging directly with servicewomen, I examine how this comes about through the discursive construction of women combatants and the landscape of war to hide, contain, or make acceptable women's war labour. This is a chapter about foregrounding the voices of these women (and some men in talking about their gendered experiences of military service) and how I found the confidence to bring my own voice into this conversation. By hearing my story through other's words, hearing the stories of other servicewomen in their voices and looking at them "backward and forward, inward and outward" (Ellis 1999, 673), it became clear to me that these voices are missing from the mainstream narratives of war. Thinking differently about war through experimenting creatively with the voices and stories of servicewomen has built my confidence in telling the story of my research—the confidence to recognise "the value of singular, unique, and irreducible human experience" (Bulmer and Jackson 2015, 26)—and being empowered to use that story to question military power. Reframing the "narrative voice" in ways that allow for the "silenced voices of others and the silenced parts of ourselves to speak themselves" (Ellis 1997, 134) opens up a space for public audiences to think differently about popular narratives of women and war, "generating an affective response" to the embodied experience of war (Bulmer and Jackson 2015, 26).

My first creative endeavour was a music video[2] produced in collaboration with my husband, Tim West, who provided directing, editing and musical input, basing the lyrics on our conversations exploring my experiences of serving in the military and the transition to civilian life. These were accompanied with visuals about the relationship between identity and uniform, including scenes capturing different aspects of my service and civilian life from aircraft maintenance to caring for my children. We were very conscious of the folk-tradition, going back to the 1700s, in music and performance of portraying women, such as Mary Ambree, who, by adopting the persona of soldiers or sailors on the "front line," crossed the well-defended barricade around military masculinity (Lang n.d.). The piece was also influenced by more recent explorations of the cultural dissonances of women in war, by writers and musicians, for example in the BBC TV series *Our Girl* (Grounds 2013), and in the song "Pretty Young Soldiers," a folk-inflected contemporary pop song recently released by veteran rock balladeer, Sting (2016). We chose to juxtapose folk music and military uniforms to challenge and disturb gendered notions of military service through reimagining the gender-defying female soldier of traditional folk music.

Building on our music video, I wanted to expand the conversation beyond my own story to include others' voices. The second project, a short documentary film,[3] also produced by Tim West, saw us host a community-based workshop involving approximately a dozen local veterans—a cross-section of ages, former ranks, and services. The workshop explored their gendered reflections on military service with participants sharing their perspectives in small groups prompted by stimulating questions to encourage reflection. We then identified particular topics, which emerged from these discussions as well as interesting dynamics between participants before recording paired conversations in a TV studio. Having captured nearly two hours of footage, this was then edited to a short documentary film.

Struck by the vivid stories of "front line" service shared by former servicewomen from the Northern Ireland Troubles, I decided to build on our earlier creative work, to share their voices with a public audience beyond my academic writing. This third project is ongoing, delayed by COVID-19 restrictions on live theatre. In 2019, we were awarded funding[4] to produce a short, devised-theatre piece to present at a "scratch" or "prototype" night held at several local theatres. This was to be based on the transcripts of the Northern Ireland veterans to explore women's experiences of "combat" with a view to upscaling this to a bigger production (subject to securing more funding). Thus far, we have produced a short poetic documentary film[5] using the testimonies of the veterans accompanied by time-lapse drawings, which with three further films—all in work at the time of writing—will now form part of the theatre piece.

Finally, beyond these specific projects, I have also experimented with my own voice through numerous smaller creative endeavours. I have written a number of poems, presented captioned photographic images and posters representing my work, as well as embracing free-writing as a technique for helping me recall and order my thoughts. Through testing different creative media for presenting my voice, I have found ways to make things as familiar as well-worn items of uniform become strange objects before me. As I have stepped back from my creations, whether that means re-reading the poems or standing in front of the images, I see them as something new and am able to ask myself what they tell me that I couldn't see before. The new perspective on the familiar artefacts of my military past that I found through this creative process has encouraged me to extend this critical voice to bigger questions of military power and knowledge production.

This chapter is structured to narrate the story of being "creative" in my research, starting with reflecting on how I worked with my own story and then collaborated with other voices, through to how this helped me find my critical voice. The first section, "my story, our words," explores how reflecting on my own story through producing a collaborative folk music video provided me with a space to think about my past experiences and my current positionality in new ways. The second section, "our voices," looks at working with others' stories, whether the reflections of veterans on their military service as gendered or the recorded voices of Northern Ireland veterans. The final section, "my voice," reflects on how being creative opened up a space for me to find my critical voice through autoethnographic writing. I conclude by considering how I use this critical voice to affect change by opening a public conversation, and what creativity can bring to both the veteran scholar and research projects working with the military community.

## MY STORY, OUR WORDS

There's many a ballad that's centuries old,
That tells of young maidens whose love makes them bold,
They travel the world dressed in soldiers' attire,
And then seek their menfolk through sea, storm and fire.
Their cries still have echoes—for I have been shown
We can tell a new tale set in times of our own,

I knew such a woman—no man she desired
She sought travel and freedom—for she had aspired
To be bold and be different—on the wide salt-green sea
She would seek her adventure, she said unto me.
She told me she'd never be sailing alone:
In the wake of strong women who'd once held their own.

They were dressed in their kit from their very first days
They had signed for the Service, and all its strange ways.
"My duty," she thought, "is to follow the rules,
To be strong, to survive, and to learn my trade's tools."
She told of her training in letters sent home,
In a smart sailor's trappings, could she hold her own?

She tried her new clothes and grew into their size,
She was young, among men trying hard to seem wise,
As they swaggered and bragged, sporting lace on their sleeves,
A light-headed girl would by none be believed.
She told me abruptly that she'd changed her tune
And an officer's voice meant that she'd hold her own.

Soon the world's wars turned sour, and she was put to the test,
To the sand and the mountains, she went with the rest,
She set to her work there with scrupulous care,
Unlike some men around her, doing more than her share,
She told me with pride her work was well known,
Next to women or men she said she'd hold her own.

She marched through the ranks, but before long she knew,
That a woman's true self couldn't ever shine through
In the rough and the tumble, she asked herself why—
She was far from herself, she could not live a lie
She told me she'd dreamed of a family home,
She thought now of children—would she hold her own?

The balance of life, with two burdens so great,
The tiniest babe, against the great deeds of state,
Was a promise now broken; the rules had worn thin
The adventures had soured, why should she fit in?
She told how her dutiful spirit had flown:
If she wanted a fair world, then she'd build her own.
(Tim West,[6] *She'll Hold Her Own*)

In reading one's own story and then hearing it sung as a ballad, I am at once distanced from this tale and yet know it as my own. There is a disembodiment, a stepping away, that enables a renewed perspective—a critical distance—on my experience. It brought into stark relief the gendered narrative of my military service, an embedded gendering, from my motivations for joining up, through my experiences whilst serving and then my decision to leave. Perhaps surprising to an outsider, but I did not see my military service as gendered when serving. If asked at the time I would have said that I was treated on merit as an engineer. It was only towards the end of my time in the military as I became a wife and thought about starting a family that I even started to think differently about this. So, whilst this song was not a single turning point, it was another in a series of reflexive moments during this research—moments when I took "account of the self in relation to other subjects and objects" (Eagleton-Pierce 2011, 1)—which helped me to see my service differently.

The narrative construct of the ballad gave the piece a timeless quality, one that added my story to the many stories of women's participation in war that have gone before, the now-forgotten stories. Music has been employed by those fighting and those writing about them, "as a comforting tonic, as a political statement, as a tool for remembrance, and as a general pastime" becoming a "genre of folk music" "throughout societies" (Bateson 2019, n.p.). The ballad, as a narrative poem set to music, became a traditional form of expression for the "powerless" to hand down a lyrical oral history, sometimes patriotic, sometimes in protest (Mullen 2015, 211). Our ballad was written in quatrain with a two-line refrain repeating the phrase "hold her own" to give the piece the quality of a fable by emphasising this message. Moving chronologically through my life, each four-line stanza describes a new example of holding my own with the refrain playing on the ambiguity of the phrase "hold your own" differently conjuring a sense of possessiveness, resilience, and protectiveness.

We decided to use military uniforms in the visuals for the music video, as my interviews with servicewomen and women veterans repeatedly returned to military uniform as central to their understanding of their military identity, and in particular, how it marked them out as different to their male colleagues. Military uniform also set up an uncomfortable juxtaposition with folk music and the pastoral scenes of beaches and countryside, which were interwoven with these militarised images. By creating this site where symbols of peacefulness, through the picturesque pastoral scene, constitute the backdrop and foregrounding military uniforms, the familiar is rendered "strange" by setting it in an unfamiliar context, "expos[ing] its contradictions" and doing valuable work as a critical tool for unlocking new ways of seeing the military (Basham and Bulmer 2017, 62). Filming the uniform shots was the first time I had put on my uniform in several years, and beyond the relief that I could still get into it, it again felt somehow strange but at the same time familiar to be putting it back on again. Being in uniform again allowed me to do things that the timings of my military service had not permitted, such as holding my children wearing my uniform in the video, something that had not happened for real as my last day in uniform was before they were born.

As an ex-military scholar researching the military, being "creative" has been about memory and reflection, about "the possibility and impossibility of making the familiar strange" (Kumsa *et al.* 2015, 429). Bulmer and Jackson have explored how the veteran experience is "known" in their paper entitled "You Do Not Live in My Skin," considering to what extent we can make the unfamiliar of war knowable (2015). I have had to find ways of questioning what I know about my own embodied experience and have done this through creating distance between me and my service and opening a space to question. The "out of body" reflection that comes from revisiting your own

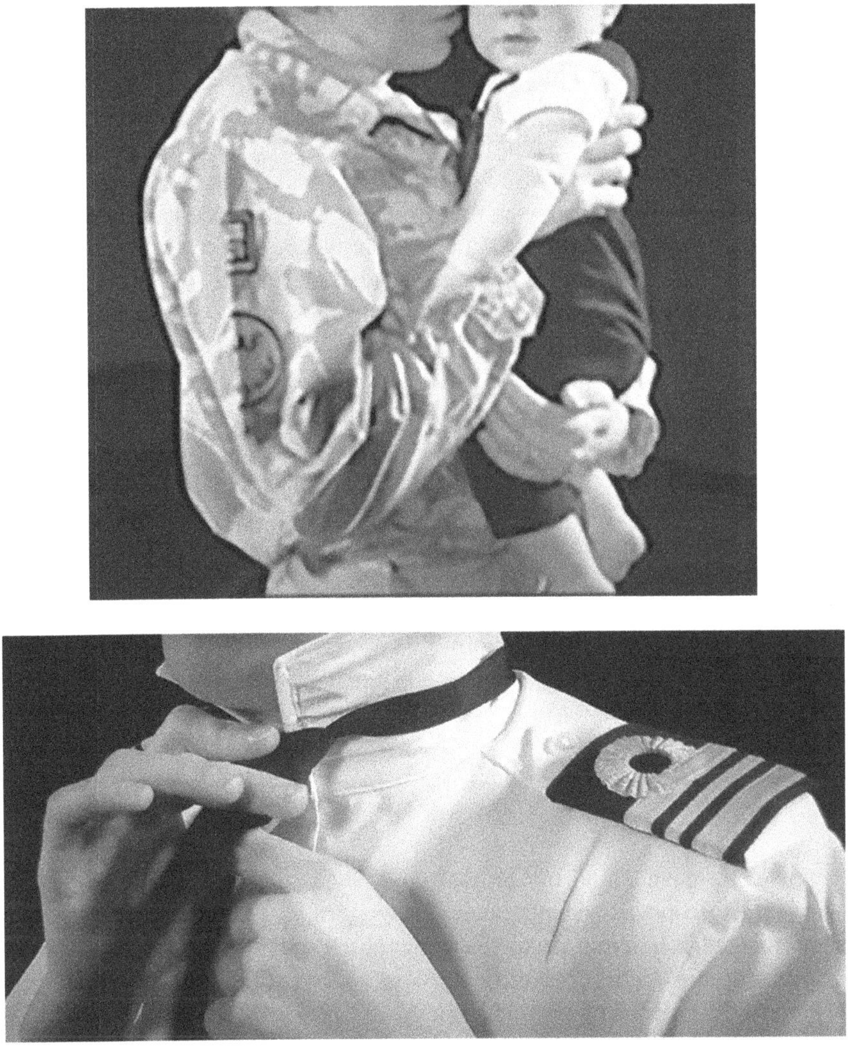

**Figure 11.1 Stills from the film *She'll Hold Her Own.***
*Source:* Reprinted with permission from Tim West.

narrative through a folk ballad written by someone else, was the start of a change in perspective, or as David Walker describes, a shift in my relationship with the military from one of "proximity to one of critical distance—or at least as critically distant as an ex-soldier-turned-researcher can possibly be" (2016, 256), raising a question I continue to grapple with.

There is a vulnerability to sharing one's story in this way. It is nerve-racking to stand up at seminars and conferences and make my personal story so visible, not least because I felt that the lyrics (which after all are my husband's words interpreting my experience) could so easily be misinterpreted. Phrases like "Unlike some men around her, doing more than her share" made me nervous that others would think I was trying to say that I was better than all the men. However, I negotiated this by acknowledging that this was my story, and I was not claiming it to be representative of everyone but wanted, instead, to start a conversation. I have used this video to create a space to try out what it meant to explore the tensions in my own story and to consequently challenge public audiences to question mainstream narratives of women and war.

I had decided to work on this music video because it sounded like a fun way to do something a bit different with my research. And as I moved on to the documentary film, I still saw this as a public engagement activity not least because it was paid for by public engagement funding, and I kept getting asked to speak about it in the context of public engagement and research impact. I thought of it as an outcome of my research, but gradually I started to realise that it was helping me to reflect on my own experiences and beginning to shape how I saw my research. I began to reframe my research questions in ways that were more political and feminist, empowering me to see my academic project as a critical encounter to destabilise military control over knowledge production. The evolution of my thinking on my military experience and military power was empowered by the space this creative work was making, which was in turn helping me to situate myself in the field of critical military studies.

## OUR VOICES

I would not have found my critical voice by solely reflecting on my own story in isolation. Reaching out to other former servicewomen has been instrumental in helping me to see things differently. Triggered by my early conversations with Sophy Antrobus (West and Antrobus 2023), I recognised what could be gained by bringing together a larger group of veterans. So, I set up a workshop with veterans—men and women across the rank and service spectrum—where we explored our gendered experiences of military service, informally sharing our pasts and recognising our common experiences. But this soon triggered "emotional recall" or "imagin[ing] being back in the scene emotionally and physically" to "remember other details" (Ellis 1999, 675), whereby we realised what we had forgotten, what we had normalised. I simultaneously had to reflect on the construction of memory and what was influencing "the choice of language, theme and emphasis" as experiences were being articulated to me (Dyvik 2016, 136). Natalya Vince's work describes how, in Algeria, "women who participated in the war almost forgot themselves" (2015, 4). And as I revisited my own memories, I remember the dawning realisation that I was shocked by some of what I had experienced but buried.

The co-constitution of knowledge with other former servicewomen, in remembering military service as a woman, revealed a gendered culture I couldn't see fully when serving (West and Antrobus 2023). I had either completely forgotten some behaviours or simply ignored them because they had become a normal and expected pattern of behaviour. I recalled having my bra strap undone by passing colleagues when at work for a laugh, having photos of my colleagues' genitals left on my camera if I didn't guard it closely on a night out, and being provided with lockable cages for drying our underwear at sea to prevent it being swiped by male sailors (West and Antrobus 2023). Not only this, but I would have found this funny—"banter"—at the time. These memories had paled into the distant past, overwritten by what seemed a positive career story. But revisiting them with other former servicewomen, increasingly comfortable in my skin as a feminist, has made me question how I perceived the organisational culture I was embedded in. Creating a non-judgemental creative space, away from the military, meant participants arrived enthusiastic to be part of a novel process of reflection, to share and contribute to creating something new from these memories, something to start a new public conversation.

Not all my interactions with former servicewomen have been shared moments of realisation and like-mindedness about our common experiences of oppression by a male institution. I felt real discomfort when some former servicewomen, veterans of Northern Ireland, described their military identity in ways that proudly recognised the chivalrous behaviours of male colleagues in protecting them. But I began to see that it was okay to acknowledge both generational and political differences with participants. Nonetheless, meeting with former servicewomen from Northern Ireland really influenced my thinking about servicewomen's enduring relationship with the "front line." I had a naïve expectation that they had been employed in traditional clerical roles. I was just not expecting quite such emotional testimonies of frontline service. One of my interviewees started in tears, such was the emotion of just sharing her story. And their voices and stories were so powerful, telling of such exposure to frontline combat whilst they were unarmed and wearing skirts. Their stories told of servicewomen's lives put at risk. These voices were so strong that I couldn't see them contained as quotations written down in a thesis or academic paper. Their voices needed to animate their stories of frontline combat and hence exploring creative means to do this. These words of Jean Elshtain capture this sensation:

> I found many voices clamouring for attention. Some shouted, others whispered; several wept. While some of these voices challenged certain of my own

> assumptions, I have not tried to shut them up. For there are sanctimonies to deconstruct, amnesias to lift, stories to remember. (1995, 164)

There is again a vulnerability in sharing our stories with each other. And yet, as Maya Eichler and Jessica Wiebe reflect, "making ourselves vulnerable through dialogue creates the opportunity for more intimate connections and for knowing ourselves by knowing others" and that creative methods help us through this discomfort (2019, 83). In my experience this comes about through creating an experimental, relaxed, and safe space, in which the creation of something new through our voices engenders an excitement about collectively being part of this co-constitution in some way, that we become more comfortable. As we articulate buried memories of gendered behaviours, practices, and harassment, we experience what Eichler and Weibe have called sharing the weight, unburdening ourselves of our pasts and bringing them into the light (2019, 88).

It was one thing hearing these stories and them challenging my thinking, my memories and my assumptions, but it was another thing moving to sharing these stories. Sharing the stories of others comes with an ethical responsibility. These films had a political message to convey, albeit indirectly through the poetic mode, to challenge public audiences to see the military experience as gendered and to recognise the longstanding yet invisible presence of women on the front line. Practically this meant cutting two hours of footage from the veteran workshop down to fifteen minutes. There was co-constitution of knowledge in that participants were bringing their own experiences, on the themes we suggested, to create an oral repository of memories. But whilst participants had control over what they wanted to share, they were not directly involved in the creation of the films. In curating the knowledge that was shared with us, we had to consider how we built an engaging narrative arc to connect different extracts and what themes we wanted to communicate. We decided to open with stories about alternative military masculinities and move on to the tension between servicewomen and military culture as a means of grouping together the different conversations we had recorded. Ultimately, it was our call how we edited the footage and decided what was in and what was out. Alexandra Hyde talks about how in the writing of poetry she was consciously creating a distance between her and the object she created, "a constructedness that happens at my hand" (2014). Editorial decision-making created something new from the words of our participants, something which in its relative brevity was more impactful, more powerful but which was also in itself a different thing, a new creation. For "no matter how we stage the text, we—the authors—are doing the staging" (Richardson 1992, 131).

As a researcher collaborating with creative practitioners, whether musicians, the artist, the director, I felt myself to be at the centre of an ethical, creative tension between the creatives and the participants. It wasn't an overt or intended tension on anyone's part; it was a tension I felt in myself about my responsibility to the participants. I didn't anticipate this, but it came out in a conversation with the director, my husband, that sounded like this:

> Me: I've heard back from the individual whose audio we want to work with. She's happy for us to go ahead.
>
> Director: Great, so I'll get that sent out to [the artist] and we'll get going.
>
> Me: Oh, hang on, I mean are you sure? So soon? Does she need it right away?
>
> Director: We have got consent, right?
>
> Me: Well, yes, but you know she was in tears in that interview, right from the start. It was a big deal for her to share her story. She has trusted me; I just don't want to let them down.

In recruiting participants, I contacted the regimental museums, and being able to share my background as a fellow servicewoman, I was connected with gatekeepers, through whom all other participants were identified. I am conscious that I had very privileged access to women veterans of the Ulster Defence Regiment and Royal Ulster Constabulary, the sort of access which other researchers remarked on with surprise. Former servicewomen were happy to talk to me, they frequently responded with their consent citing their trust in me and their enthusiasm for the project. After going through a second ethical clearance (beyond that required when I conducted the original interviews) to ask for permission to use their audio files for a creative piece, we were, on paper, ready to proceed. But as the conversation above shows, I reacted badly to this at first. I suddenly felt very responsible for the women, protective of them. I felt a reluctance to share their story with people I didn't know and hadn't built up trust with. I had felt the bond of former service build a relationship of trust with them during interviews and attributed to this their willingness to share with me their stories, their upset, their honesty, and openness. Whilst I hadn't served in Northern Ireland, we knew what it was like to be a woman serving in the military, we shared jokes about the uniform or behaviours we'd encountered, and we understood what it means to go out of a secure compound with a loaded weapon, not knowing what might happen. Added to this, I had served in Afghanistan alongside army colleagues whose patrolling experience was learnt on the streets of Northern Ireland, so I had picked up a basic appreciation of what it had been like through them too.

Through the stories we shared with each other in these interviews, they knew that I had experienced service life as a woman deployed to a conflict zone.

Whilst these veterans of the Northern Ireland Troubles had less involvement in the creative practice of this film, I was overwhelmed by their trust in me as I set out to them what we wanted to do and received universally strong support. Having their oral testimonies, we still needed a visual element to the film and settled on a veteran artist with whom we have worked to produce time-lapse drawings (consulting with the participants where we have needed guidance on the specifics of uniform detail) to accompany the audio. We have been deliberate in our decision-making for drawings to evolve with the servicewoman drawn either first or last to fit with the narrative of the film. Despite the enthusiasm of participants and knowing they had given their consent for us to include their voices in the film and they were to be anonymised, it still took me some time to reconcile my nervousness with my enthusiasm to foreground their story. I remind myself of their enthusiasm for the project as a much-needed opportunity for their stories to be heard and I came to see myself as facilitating their "speaking outwards." Miriam Cooke writes insightfully about "women at the front" and how "you can see them but until recently you could not speak them" and that "it is not enough for women to have been there; they have to write and interpret what it means to have been there" (1993, 177). Through creativity we have given voice to women's silence, expressing their stories through their testimonies (Lipton and McKinley 2017) striving towards a nascent "activist discourse [which] may become an agent of change beyond discourse" (Cooke 1993, 177). Giving voice to this creativity as an activist discourse, has seen me expanding the space I had created first for myself and then with fellow veterans, to engage new public audiences in this conversation about women's war labour. The films have been screened as part of the Bath Fringe Festival and Up Late at the Holburne Museum, and we aspire to taking the devised theatre piece to military museums. Producing accessible, short creative pieces opens this conversation in ways that allow audiences unfamiliar with the subject to ask questions and share opinions that are vital to the women participants who so want their voices heard.

Conversation with fellow veterans helped me to experiment and feel comfortable in my new position—initially just as ex-military but gradually as a critical scholar—becoming methodologically significant by creating a space to start sharing our memories of military service. It soon became a space where we realised what we had forgotten, gradually started to question these buried memories and finally became shocked by them, in realising what we had normalised (West and Antrobus 2023). The space we open is a space sometimes of comfort but often of discomfort, reflecting the "tension between our entanglement and disentanglement in webs of power relations" where nascent feminist critique challenges loyalty, pride, and comradery (Kumsa *et al.* 2015, 429; Hyde 2014). Not everyone with whom I revisited these memories saw the campaigns we had served in with the same critical lens, questioned a military culture that perhaps remained important to them now, or had the same political aspirations. I felt at times torn between loyalty to those I had trained and served with and yet sometimes found myself tentatively navigating their reluctance to engage with the more critical aspects of my research, particularly when talking to veterans across a generational divide. But I learnt to view their experiences in the context of the period they were serving in, acknowledging as one interviewee said that "each generation makes steps forward" (Bea Kingdon, WRAC veteran, NI-3, 2019).

## MY VOICE

I always knew my research was going to relate to my own experiences in the military. I have written about Female Engagement Teams when I had been heavily involved in the initial UK policy making on my return from Afghanistan. It was a given that I would draw on this experience. But I did not anticipate the study being as reflexive and leading to me weaving my own autoethnographic narrative and reflections through my doctoral thesis, inserting my own "'shadow narrative' to help us understand my place as teller" (McFadden 2011, 534). I started my research with no thoughts of creativity or creative methods and yet creative practice has fostered a space for me to find my critical voice. In so doing, I reframed my research from studying women's participation as combatants to an intervention into British Army attempts at exploring the limits of women's agency and the control rendered by gendered power over knowledge production. I do not think I would have had the confidence to navigate to a positionality whereby I saw my research as a critical feminist intervention as I do now without the critical voice I found through these creative spaces.

I was encouraged to try free-writing, and this was something I took up in earnest when on a maternity break from my studies. As a former naval engineer, not entirely at ease with extended writing of any form, I would not have felt bold enough to try something like that had I not already started to think about being creative with my research. I started to write about my childhood, my upbringing, my life experiences, and it became something I just needed to get down on paper. It is not something I have included in my academic writing, but I don't think I could have pursued my academic writing—often in the first person and incorporating a personal reflection—if I hadn't got this down on paper first. It was about acknowledging where I had come from to be where I am now and given it was a story about being at a girls' school, being a woman in the military, becoming a wife, becoming a mother, I needed to think about all of these things to understand what I was bringing with me to my research.

Having relaxed my writing style from my early literature reviews expressed as a former military engineer writing a military brief, notable for their absence of my voice, this free writing gave me the courage to write what I wanted to say. I found the confidence to weave my own personal reflection into the narrative of my writing, for example writing a literature review as a series of letters to my former self at different stages in my military career capturing the lengthy evolution of my understanding of the literature. This autoethnographic writing produced a "self-narrative that critique[d] the situatedness of self with others in social contexts" allowing me to position myself as active agent with narrative authority over many hegemonizing dominant cultural myths' (Spry 2001, 710–11).

Becoming an active agent through creativity in writing to re-remember my military past, I was able to reflect on my experience of Female Engagement Teams (FETs), the point of greatest intersection between my military service and my research. My confused and conflicted reflections on FETs had drawn me into my field of research, wanting to better understand and contextualise my experiences, and they became a turning point in my critical thinking. I had worked on coordinating female engagement efforts in the Provincial Reconstruction Team in Helmand during my deployment and became involved in UK FET policy on my return to the UK. Reading deeply critical reports of this policy felt personal at the time (Azerbaijani-Moghaddam 2014). Over time I came to see the findings of this report as sound, recognising our own efforts as tokenistic and piecemeal, such has been the critical turn in my own thinking. This change in perspective was gradual, and began to permeate my thinking about military power over knowledge production and its implications for women's war labour on a much bigger scale.

I have found autoethnography liberating in giving me the space and creativity to foreground my positionality to narrate my research, feeling "empowered when I began to uncover ideas that challenged my previous belief in my own situatedness" (Taber 2005, 298). Through autoethnography I have been able to learn from my insider-outsider perspective, "to throw light onto the dark recesses of the military interior" and "imagine more effective ways to hold powerful institutions to account" (Ware 2016, 240–41). My veteran identity was "driv[ing] the research from the outset" (Heggie 2003, 28), whilst simultaneously motivated by the "powerful desire to investigate sociologically my former life and to find out who I had been" (Hockey 2016, 208). Exploring my personal narrative of military service through autoethnography has paralleled my research intervention to "challeng[e] the construction of master narratives" (Spry 2001, 720) and question the "propositions implicit in master narratives or dominant discourses [which] are widely accepted as self-evident" (Muncey 2010, 31). I believe this approach brings an honesty to what is written, exposing the nuances of my own sometimes conflicted feelings on the various subjects to help the reader navigate the complexity. Autoethnographic writing has helped me to consider not just on my own military service, but its impact methodologically in reflecting on the way in which I interacted with interviewees and how I interpreted archival records given my background. I have become committed to exposing women's stories to undermine the tools of their exclusion and re-centering my own story alongside theirs as a means of making these voices heard and making them a part of a reconceptualization of war and military service.

## CONCLUSION

Researching how we understand "combat" and the "front line" through women's stories has been a personal encounter. Creative practice has become methodologically significant, helping me to find my critical voice and shaping my research into the feminist intervention it has become. Through engaging with the narrative ballad of my own story to conversations with veteran researchers I have been able to distance myself from my experience in creative ways that have helped to make the familiar strange, giving me the confidence to find my critical voice and situate my research in the field of critical military studies. The confidence I found through working on the films translated to my writing where autoethnography has brought a richness by weaving my narrative through my research. I have felt uncomfortable, I have felt vulnerable, but I have also felt supported and safe both to be challenged and to ask my own questions. I could not have found my voice on my own, I needed to explore and experiment through creativity and conversation with others.

And in turn, telling the stories of former servicewomen has been a reflexive and empowering experience for them given how long their voices have been marginalised. A creative output has the advantage of being accessible, allowing participants to engage more easily with its creation, feeling a sense of involvement in its development. Similarly, such creative endeavours allow research to transgress the boundaries of the academy and reach new public audiences.

Although these creative projects have been shared on social media individually and at various conferences and public arts events, I find my ambition for creativity in my research grows, and I reach out to wider audiences seeking to challenge popular narratives of women and war. In so doing, I continue to question how to harness "affective solidarity" (Hemmings 2012, 150) to engender change through co-creating these works with fellow veterans as a part of the critical feminist project.

It is well known that the transition from military service to becoming a veteran is a challenging one for many. Mainstream military studies lacks the critical veteran voice (Antrobus and West, 2022), and I would argue that a critical space can be opened through creativity. Beyond veteran scholars, this has application for engaging the military community in research too, where I have creativity brings a means of unlocking the familiar, helping to see it anew. This is fundamental to generating new insights into the military and questioning military power, a project at the heart of critical military studies.

# 12

# Bald Men Sharing a Comb

## *War Veteran Subjectivity in the Documentary Play Minefield*

*David Jackson*

In 1985, three years after the ending of the Falklands War (Guerra de las Malvinas), the Argentine writer Jorge Luis Borges said in an interview that he thought "the Falklands thing was a fight between two bald men over a comb" (Clarin 1983). To me, a former Royal Marine who experienced the war firsthand, the war was simply the result of two nations being thrown together by their individual political circumstances of the time. Regardless of the reasons behind the conflict, young men on both sides died and many returned home with life-changing injuries. It is something I have carried with me for the last 40 years. I am not alone in this; war changes you forever. As a veteran researcher, I bring to my writing, and to all my work, the messy entanglement of my subjectivity as a war veteran, academic, performer and a disabled person. My experience of the Falklands war has shaped all of those identities.

In what follows I explore my involvement in *Minefield /Campo Minado*, a piece of documentary theatre, which brings together veterans from opposing sides of the Falklands-Malvinas War. Through examining the creative modes of storytelling in *Minefield*, I argue that bearing witness to these stories through theatre can evoke a different, more empathetic understanding of war veteran subjectivity. At a broader level, in this chapter I engage directly with the messiness of my subjectivity and question what it might mean for military researchers to embrace their own multiplicity using creative methods.

## HOW IS THE CANVAS PAINTED? HOW IS THE STAGE SET?[1]

An experience of war undoubtedly changes veterans' and their families' lives forever, but the ways we represent such an experience have changed very little. Military research that specifically explores the lives of veterans and families is dominated by an overbearing prominence of research that objectifies veterans. Research from the early twentieth century talked of the impact of war on veterans in terms of insanity, lunacy, mental deficiency, shock, and neurosis (see for example Eder 1917; Adrian & Yealland 1917). This trend persisted throughout World War II, for example through exploration of the effectiveness of treatments for war neurosis (see Beccles 1942). In 1980, the term *PTSD* was formally recognised as a mental health disorder, which was a significant moment in the history of military and veteran's research. Since then, over twenty-eight thousand research papers have been indexed in The National Centre for Post-Traumatic Stress Disorder under the Department for Veterans' Affairs in the USA. Whilst this research has undoubtedly had an impact on the treatment of PTSD from combat, it nevertheless looks at veterans through a very narrow lens as objects to probe and poke. The dominance of research that objectifies veterans feeds into the historical and cultural stereotyping already seen enshrined within the mass media, art and now social media representations. As Bulmer and Jackson (2016, 2) write:

> Representations of injured veterans as heroes (Kelly 2013; Woodward, Winter, and Jenkings 2009), symbols of national pride (Ministry of Defence 2014), or victims deserving of our sympathy (Kirkup 2013) all fail to acknowledge the complex experiences of those living with the embodied effects of war. Mainstream academic and policy research routinely objectifies veterans as "problems to be solved." (Ashcroft 2014)

I can fully understand why those seeking an alternative narrative might fly the white flag of surrender in the face of, quite frankly, staggering figures on trauma and PTSD among veterans. So, too, can I understand why a counter-narrative might struggle when set against the huge body of work that identifies veterans as a "problem to be solved." However, I feel strongly that there has to be another way of representing unheard stories that do not fit comfortably within the dominant narratives surrounding post-military and post-war life. In 2000, I wrote the following in a journal entry: "As I gazed out of the window of the train, I realised I was tired. I was tired of hearing others speak for me. What do they know? What do they care? I realised that I had a voice and I could speak for myself" (Jackson 2000).

On reflection, I have realised that what set me out on my creative journey was an inability to find answers to existential questions of who I am and who I want to become as a war veteran, as a researcher, and as a human being. It has been a process of continuous reflection on my own experiences and how I might find a voice for them. Creativity became a central component of my research; my master's dissertation drew on song writing[2] and lyrical analysis as a way of exploring my embodied experience of war and its aftermath, and during my doctoral studies I experimented with multimodal and creative ways of reflecting on and representing my experience of returning to the Falkland Islands on the twenty-fifth anniversary pilgrimage. The creativity at the heart of my work became a form of emancipation from the cultural identity scripts that have governed my identity as a war veteran with a mental health disability.

In 2015, I was approached by a member of the production team for the documentary theatre play *Minefield/Campo Minado*, to be interviewed about my post–Falklands War life. I was then invited to attend an audition and meet the director, Lola Arias. After investigating the director's work, I saw so much in her way of working that resonated with me. I realised that through telling my story I might be able to give voice to other veterans who fought in the Falklands War and, more poignantly, pay homage to those who did not return. My stories that were eventually included within the play were first witnessed by the director, and then went through a process of negotiation between the production team and myself before I performed them. This process revealed the messiness of my life story as a performer, a disabled veteran damaged by the experience of war, and a researcher who reflects on and writes about the life stories of veterans and their families. *Minefield* became a vehicle through which I was able to confront my own entangled subjectivities, which ultimately was productive and enlightening for my thinking as a critical military studies researcher. It is not always helpful to think about our positionalities in very rigid terms, as "researcher," "veteran," "artist," or "performer"; we never just wear one "skin."

There has been an increased focus on creative interventions in veteran studies over the last few years, with recent examples exploring the therapeutic functions of humour in group art therapy with war veterans (Kopytin and Lebedev 2015), photo elicitation as a method for recovery from substance abuse (Sestito et al. 2017), and art therapy as a mental health resource for veterans with PTSD (Lobban and Murphy 2020). *Minefield*, in contrast, is not an example of how creativity can be used for recovery or for therapy, but instead how it can be used to tell a different kind of story about (and crucially, with) veterans. Furthermore, what both this chapter and *Minefield* itself offer is the kind of engagement with these stories that prioritises empathy. I argue that through multimodal forms of representation including text and spoken word, digital photography and video, music, lyrics, poetry, and others, *Minefield* evoked multi-layered acts of witnessing in which empathetic engagement was central.

For me, creativity is not just about "research methods," but also about being curious (Bulmer 2021) and engaging differently with the world. What creative methods offer is a more meaningful and evocative way of centring this curiosity in our work. In the case of my creative practice, this is about retelling and (re)presenting what it is like to live in the world as a veteran and member of a veteran's family. Creative research, as Sinding, Gray, and Nisker put it, "moves in, rearranges our understandings of ourselves and the world, and goes home with us in ways that traditional social science research representations rarely do" (2008, 462). In what follows, I do not advocate for my audiences to replicate *my* version of creativity within military research, and neither do I provide a how-to account of theatre-as-creative-method. Rather, my aim is to show and tell. From the beginning of this chapter, I have started to walk you through my creative journey. This journey continues through an exploration of war veteran subjectivity through the play Minefield/Campo Minado. As you read, I am asking you to walk alongside me.

## MINEFIELD/CAMPO MINADO

*Minefield/Campo Minado*[3] is a contemporary documentary theatre production that brings together veterans from opposing sides of the Falklands-Malvinas War, and focuses on our lives before, during, and after the conflict. The cast is made up of three Argentine veterans (Ruben Otero, Marcelo Vallejo, and Gabriel Sagastume), two former Royal Marines (Lou Armour and me) and a former Gurkha soldier (Sukrim Rai). The play lasts for one hour and forty-five minutes, and we inhabit the stage for all this time. It was performed at the Brighton Fringe in May 2016, followed by ten shows at the Royal Court Theatre in London as part of the London International Theatre Festival. To date, it has been performed 190 times in twenty countries and thirty-eight cities.

Our performance is the culmination of our collective stories. These were created through a process of collaboration when they were told and retold to Lola Arias,[4] the director, then edited and reedited into the final piece of theatre. This was a process that although necessary, "felt like a surgeon's knife removing a piece of my embodied self" (Jackson 2016). There is no backstage production crew on hand to facilitate compliance with the "norms" of theatre production, such as lighting and sound. We are the crew. On stage

**Figure 12.1 Minefield/Campo Minado stage set up.**

there is a white projection screen and props to the left and right including a drum kit, guitars, and amplifiers.

Everything that happens during the performance is visible and open to scrutiny, which during the early performances gave me "a feeling of being naked under the eyes of the other" (Jackson 2016). We change our outfits, prepare the props for upcoming scenes, and operate the digital cameras that project the artefacts of war such as old letters, photos, and remnants from the battlefield. Those same cameras project our images, giving the audience an opportunity to form a connection not only to our stories but with the emotions and feelings we carry. In addition, we support each other as co-stars in our co-performers' stories, we play music "in confrontational punk mode" (Taylor 2016), become satirists, drag artists, and comedians, and over the years acted as technical crew members by resolving microphone issues and other multimedia technical idiosyncrasies. It is a complex representation of the experiences of former enemies, who do not speak each other's languages, across a stage and for an international audience. *Minefield* plays with that audience, through juxtapositions of time, place, and scale, to present a fractured and provocative account of war. It transcends simplistic accounts of national heroes pitted against belligerent enemy others, even those who can subsequently reconcile at war's end. The play falls uneasily within the genre of documentary theatre but has been described as verbatim theatre, testimony theatre, or theatre of the real (Finburgh 2017) and autobiographical documentary theatre (Tiechert 2020), where the physical co-presence of bodies is foregrounded "as the very site of the documentary claim to truth" (Garce and Wasserman 2006). Lola Arias describes the play as a social experiment that functions as a time machine (Sosa 2017).

*Minefield* has generated much academic interest. For example, Maguire (2018) explores how the role of autobiographical body, narrative repetition, and formal reflexivity "demand, though ultimately confound, an empathetic connection between performer and audience" (Maguire 2016, 471), while Blejmar (2017) similarly considers how the autobiographical narratives foster empathy. Sosa (2017) reflects on how the "high risk, highly exposed public encounter" (179) changed perspectives about the war and those that took part in it. She suggests that it exposed both audience and performer to a common vulnerability beyond international boundaries. Tiechert (2020), who worked as a production assistant during the rehearsals, examines how drama therapy might provide additional theoretical understandings to conceptualise the play and its emotional aspects. Finburgh (2017) explores Jean-Luc Nancy's notion of "violence without violence," as set out in his essay "Image and Violence" (2003), and how *Minefield/Campo Minado* "disarticulated the spectacles of power, heroism and virtuosity that are often weaponized by leaders and by the dominant media for the purposes of fighting and winning wars" (163). Graham-Jones (2019) writes about the use of supertitles, their use throughout the play, and the consequences for the politics of translatability and untranslatability. Lastly, Perera (2019) explores how *Minefield/Campo Minado* challenges concepts of hegemonic masculinities where "the echoes of their own vulnerability, away from heroic bellicosity and proudly self-sufficient masculinities and violence" (95) are laid out. In contrast to this body of work, this chapter does not explore *Minefield* via the "detached" scholarly analysis of an outsider, but rather by centring the complexity of my own subjectivity, as at once a disabled veteran, performer/participant, artist, and researcher.

## SO I STOOD AT THE BAR WITH A WORLD WAR II SPITFIRE PILOT: THE ACT OF WITNESSING

*Minefield/Campo Minado* is a collection of personal accounts which were negotiated through a process of storytelling by the cast and the production team. An important part of this process was the act of witnessing. Witnessing is never a solitary act, and it implies a relationship between the performers themselves, and between the performers and the audience, that is characterised by obligation. In these relationships, we are all obligated to engage with alternative "truths" in a way that is vulnerable and open to change.

The act of witnessing between performers was always carried out in a relationship of empathetic understanding and mutual respect. Our first meeting in the rehearsal space was "stage-managed" by the production team; the Argentine performers arrived whilst Lou and I waited in a café for a call. Later,

I reflected in my diary about this first meeting: "What were they expecting? Another war? Another battle?" (Jackson 2016). My experience of meeting the "enemy" was no different to meeting other veterans who had been to war. We did not speak Spanish, and the Argentines did not speak English. But there was an unspoken connectedness, and I felt this very strongly. Gabriel (2021)[5] similarly described how *Minefield* helped him to overcome his prejudices about British soldiers and identify common ground:

> Finding that opposite, "the enemy," was a person very similar to me, with the same pains or fears and the same joys. (Questions for performers 2021)

The witnessing between performers during the rehearsal process and during the subsequent performances created an understanding of one another's experiences that was fluid and ever-changing. It is by listening and "hearing" these utterances that they "serve as a way to validate membership of some kind of community" (Rosen 1998, 60). We performed a kind of collaboration with one another by giving technical support as well as being part of each other's scenes, which, in turn, made each story *all our* stories.

The audience also take part in the act of witnessing. By witnessing the cast's stories, theatregoers are invited to look anew at the social and cultural processes that inform their way of knowing. By prioritising personal experience, the play offers freedom from the dominant discourses about war and its aftermath. For example, in the therapy scene where I perform my current profession as a psychologist and Marcelo is my client, he says:

> I mixed anti-depressants with alcohol and threw myself into the reservoir. I did not know how to swim. The veterans pulled me out of the water. . . . And now I'm a swimmer. (Arias 2017, 56)

In this scene, Marcelo unshackled himself through sport from the "mad, bad, and sad" stereotype that is dominant in veteran research, the medical model of "veteran recovery," and popular culture. After throwing himself in the water, he decided to learn to swim and went on to be a successful triathlete, competing in the Iron Man world championships. In that same scene I retell how my understanding of my mental health disability complemented my current work as a psychologist working with veterans and their families:

> I get really angry because more people had committed suicide than were actually killed during the war. . . . I currently work with Afghan, Iraq and Malvinas veterans. (Arias 2017, 57)

Scenes such as these have a powerful impact on audience members. Ann, whose husband fought in the war, said:

The play brought to life the horrors, the unexpected humour and the bonding that came from extreme circumstances and I really understood why despite everything, he would do it all again. I have a real insight into why he has PTSD and what a special man he is, even more than I already knew! (Questions for families 2021).

Kate reflected on the aftermath of war as an experience:

> After watching Minefield (Campo Minado) you realise how war can destroy everything in its path. Men and their families, how everyone on whatever side you are on, we are all the same human beings, and all suffer the same emotions (Questions for Audience 2021).

Grace, an Argentine audience member, said:

> I also experienced deep pain over the consequences of the war. To imagine that this actually happened and that these men represent the thousands of men who suffered was devastating. (Questions for Audience 2021)

From these extracts, we can see that the audience are invited into the world of the performers through the evocation of feeling, understanding, and reflection. Audiences come to the theatre as a meeting place of collaboration that can encourage connections and empathy, as well as emancipatory moments in which there are evocative and powerful insights into the lived experiences of others (Sparkes 2002). Sparkes goes on to say that this genre of performance tells, rouses, and disturbs by bringing to an audience's attention their own involvement in social processes about which they might not have been aware. *Minefield* gives audiences the opportunity to look inwardly so they can reflect on, understand, and connect with stories in their own lives. However, whether they are from within our circle, veterans, or "outsiders," no audience is a universal one bereft of their own resources, different tools, values, personal philosophies, and embodied experiences. All these factors play a role in the kinds of understanding that audiences take away. As a result, *Minefield* exemplifies how theatre can play with the multiple overlapping subjectivities of audience and cast as a way of developing multiple new critiques.

By witnessing our performances, war veterans in the audience were also given powerful new insights into their own experiences. Colin, a former Royal Marine who was diagnosed with PTSD following his involvement in the Falklands War, wrote:

> For me it gave me, quite simply, reconciliation and a better understanding of events. The beginning of your doctorate that resonated was of being a complete alien in civvie street. . . . Walking around in some parallel universe. . . . Since returning down south and then going to Argentina to see the play I have welled

> up a few times in those uncontrolled moments of emotional overload. However, it is not so much of a biggie this year as I understand it is okay to feel this way. It has only taken 39 of them. (Questions for veterans 2021)

John, a veteran who did not go to the Falklands but served in other conflicts, said:

> I think most Vets have seen death close up, whether, its civilian casualties of war or a friend dying by your side and those parts of the play that relived those moments were provoking and thought rendering. (Questions for veterans 2021)

Antonia, who was an Argentine conscript serving with Compañía A, Regimeiento 7 de Infantería, replied to the question "how did the play connect with your experiences of the war?" as follows:

> The connection was immediate because the work reflects stories that identified within me. The play took care of the details that almost no one had dealt with and finally confirmed that similar things happened on both sides. (Questions for veterans 2021)

Earlier in the chapter, I discussed the messy, entangled and incompleteness of my own subjectivity. From the extracts above, we can see that there is an equally messy and entangled process of coproduction and witnessing taking place in the performance, in which the audience are implicated. This messy entanglement is not just about an empathetic engagement with the performer's stories, but also about what happens when the audiences leave the shared space of the theatre. How do they continue to connect, in their own lives, with the stories they have witnessed? To what extent do they think differently? It is often in the period after leaving the performance space that new knowledge and understandings are created. This is the power of theatre.

A further component to this process of co-production and meaning-making is embodiment. The term *embodiment* is a complex one; however, it is generally accepted to be both an *existential condition* and a *process* in which meaning-making is taken into or upon the body (Csordas 1999), relating to our existence within culture and our existence as cultural bodies. Embodiment consists of everything we can be aware of, especially our own mental states, our bodies, our environments, our physical and social interactions. This is the level at which we speak of the "feel" of the experience (Lakoff and Johnson 1999, 103).

Our experiences of the Falklands-Malvinas War are distinctive to us. When we go on stage, we carry the spaces, interactions, and experiences of going to war within our bodies. The act of performance allows our embodied experiences to be present in that moment. Sometimes it is deliberate, and a way of "feeling" those experiences to tell them effectively, and sometimes they can appear suddenly from deep inside you triggered by a "moment" on stage. In one example, Lou discloses how the feelings of past experiences in his life were "remembered" through the rehearsal process: "During rehearsals some questions brought back memories of something in my past that I never told anyone about. I began to have sleepless nights, flashbacks. My mind would just go wandering off" (Arias 2017, 53). Similarly, in the therapy scene, Marcelo describes how the war was trapped in his body:

> It is not easy to get rid of that hatred. I couldn't listen to English music. I couldn't see English films. If my son spoke to me in English because he was taught at school, I'd chase him out of the house. (Arias 2017, 56)

As we perform the play and the audience witness our testimonies, fragments of our embodied experiences become shared and resonate in different ways between performers, as well as between the audience and the cast. The laughter from the audience creates a sense of community, while their silence during some of the evocative and emotional scenes communicates the shared feeling of intimacy and connection. When audience members leave the theatre with tears in their eyes, it is not only an altered understanding of war veterans' lives that they take with them, but an altered understanding of their own.

## MULTI MODAL REPRESENTATIONS: DEAR FLORENCIA, I FIND IT HARD TO TALK ABOUT THE LIVES WE LEAD HERE

*Minefield/Campo Minado* is a multimodal narrative that "allows discourses to be formulated in particular ways (ways which personify and dramatise discourses amongst other things)" (Kress and van Leeuwen 2001, 22). The play uses photography, audio, text, video, and visual imagery, as well as the artefacts of memory in the form of photographs, diary entries, letters, and old film. Put together as a whole, these fragments form different articulations and representations of our experiences that are often metaphorical or symbolic. The multimodality of the play and its impact on international audiences was commented on by Fara, the sound engineer. He said:

> Most of the people that have seen the play here in Argentina and in other parts of the world leave the theatre moved, most cried. They have told me that was a unique experience not only for the importance of the history told but also the importance to the technical way of telling this history. (Questions for Production team 2021)

The images used, for example, have many meanings depending on how they are presented within each scene; it is the audience's personal experience that informs the meaning they take on. On the one hand, images were used which reference historical and cultural aspects of the past and, as with other media used within the play, are a form of communication. However, images were also used to evoke personal memories. Photographs that are both artefacts of our storied lives and taken from magazines and newspapers were chosen for their ability to evoke memories within both the cast and audience, and as such work to narrow the distance between the performer and the audience. For example, this included a picture of Lou in an act of surrender being led out of Government House, Port Stanley, by the Argentine forces on April 2nd in 1982. He talks about this photograph in the play whilst pointing at it projected onto a large screen:

> As we are escorted outside, a photographer from Gente[6] stepped forward and took our picture. That picture travelled the world. . . . It was on the front page of *The Sun*, *The Times*, *The Daily Mail*. . . . And I felt ashamed. (Arias 2017, 16)

Most importantly, the images have been essential to capture what was hard to put into words; this is akin to what Ong (1982) calls "orality" (as cited in Weber 2008, 45). There is a picture of a letter sent by Gabriel to his wife during the conflict projected on to the screen as he describes the poignance and intimacy of that moment many years later. Through this image, we offer the audience an empathetic encounter with a private moment in the life of a young man at war.

There are also several video clips used in the play, which are both artefacts of our lives and projected video from the cameras on stage. This includes news footage from both countries; a video Marcelo made during a return to the islands in 2009; an excerpt from the documentary *The Falklands War: The Untold Story* (Yorkshire TV, 1987), in which Lou was interviewed when he was younger projected images of toy soldiers acting out Gabriel's story in the scene *Minefield*, as well as a globe being manipulated to give a sense of Sukrim's post–Falklands War life. The globe is projected onto the screen and turned by Ruben as Gabriel describes Sukrim's life after the war. It moves from country to country with description of what role he was performing in each place. Video helps to tell a different veteran's story, evoking a sensory experience that makes it possible for the audience to differently understand the embodied and emplaced nature of war veteran experience as told through *Minefield*.

Within the play, there are several pieces of music. These are "Zamba de mi Esperanza" (Morales 1964).[7] a well-known Argentine folk song sung by Marcelo; "Don't You Want Me Baby" by the Human League (Oakley

1981); "Get Back" by the Beatles (Lennon and McCartney 1969); a traditional Nepalese folk song called "Narou, Narou, Saili" (Dhruba n.d.) sung by Sukrim; "Yo Nepali Sir Uchli" (Pradhan n.d.), a national Nepalese song; "Marcha de las Malvinas" ("March of the Malvinas") (Obligado and Tieri 1939),[8] and "The War Song" (Conti and Armour 2016). Lola Arias uses music to represent our wider stories in a way which goes beyond the spoken text, as each song offers a unique insight into our embodied experiences (Bresler 2008). Compared to the spoken word, music has a heightened ability to invoke emotion, and therefore add depth and resonance to the stories told, whilst at the same time generating new symbolic and metaphorical meaning. Music is affectively powerful and encourages the audience to bring their own meaning and experiences to the story, which subsequently works to break down the barrier between the cast and the audience. The use of music is also political. At one point in the play, Argentine cast members sing "Marcha de las Malvinas," a song embedded in the Argentine culture. It maintains a strong political connection with the issue of sovereignty and provides a culturally and historically rooted sense of Argentina's claim to the Malvinas. Still today this song is taught in schools from the age of six. Elsewhere, we see the irony of "enemies" singing "Get Back" at each other with emphasis on the chorus, as I sing "Get Back" looking at the Argentines and they sing it back to me. The chorus of the song represents the claim and counterclaim regarding the sovereignty of the Falkland Islands, but it is told anew through the genre of pop music.

The piece of music that has had the most impact on audiences and the performers is "The War Song"[9] (lyrics quoted in Arias 2017, 6):

> Would you vote to go to war?
> Would you send your sons and daughters to war?
> What would you fight for: the queen? La Patria? Oil?
> Would you go to war?
> Would you? Would you? Would you?
> Have you ever been to war?
> Have you ever killed anybody?
> Have you watched men die?
> Have you? Have you? Have you?
> Have you ever been ignored by a government that sent you to war?
> Have you watched a friend commit suicide?
> Have you held a dying man in your arms?
> Have you? Have you? Have you?
> Have you ever seen a man on fire?
> Have you watched a guy drown in an icy sea?
> And have you ever visited a dead friend's grave with his mother?
> Have you?

> Have you ever been to war?
> Have you ever been to war?

During our first run of shows at the Royal Court, the BBC 4 *The Saturday Review* (BBC 2016) described this song as "a bewildering, punky number played just about adequately and alienating filled with rage." I remember writing to the BBC feedback programme asking whom they expected to come on stage, the Rolling Stones? I came to the conclusion they did not get it. It is a representation of that anger war veterans feel and have felt historically about their experiences and the inadequacy of societies to respond to these experiences. As Gabriel describes, after playing the song: "[s]ometimes I feel angry, sometimes I feel emotionally tired, sometimes I feel happy because I feel good about the show. Angry at everyone, my country and the war" (Questions for Performers 2021). Ruben writes that: "[t]he last song is the anger unleashed. It is to release everything we have inside" (Questions for Performers 2021).

When Colin, a veteran of the war and a member of the audience, was asked, "What about the play had most impact on you?" he replied:

> The final song, being emotionally invested in the words combined with the overall intensity brought on a flashback and subsequent panic attack. If I could have felt my legs, I would have taken myself away from the situation. I would have run out of the theatre. (Questions for Veterans 2021)

This final song, which ends the play, disrupts the empathetic relationship between audience and performers that had been previously established. The juxtaposition of connection and disconnection starkly and deliberately positions audiences as the "other." The lyrics shock the audience and force deeper and more honest reflection on the consequences of war for veterans on both sides of the conflict. In an interview for *The Observer* (2017), we all agree that the last song is a piece of supercharged catharsis that expresses our deepest frustrations. I described it as "the best stress-buster in the world. . . . The audience during that song represents both societies, British and Argentine. There are journalists who take it personally—suck it up, buttercup. It's a challenge about politicians and societies sending young men to war" (*Observer* 2017).

Through its use of multi modal representation and the prioritising of empathetic engagement, *Minefield* challenges dominant depictions of veterans. It illustrates how theatre, performance, and creative arts more broadly can help us wrestle with troublesome questions in military studies in a way that embraces feeling, emotion, and uncertainty. The immersive nature of the play enables an empathetic connection that blurs and sometimes breaks down the positionalities of audience/performer, veteran/non veteran, and us/other. Yet the final act presents a jarring and almost violent encounter with veterans' reality. In forcibly placing the audience in opposition to us through the final song, we reclaimed our collective identity of "veteran" and became united by our shared knowledge of war as hell (Lane 1974). Something that is missing from veteran research and wider cultural representations is a truthful engagement with veterans' anger, and with the fundamental problem of the violence of war. I have myself grappled with how to engage with and represent this violence and anger in my work. While there are no neat answers, working on *Minefield* has given me the space and opportunity to explore these questions through creative practice and performance. Something that critical military studies scholars might take away from this, therefore, is that creative modes of engagement can help us to wrestle with subjects that are by their very nature challenging, contentious, and multifaceted.

## FINAL SCENE: YOU DO NOT LIVE IN MY SKIN

*Minefield* has played to international audiences to much critical acclaim. It was cited as one of the top ten plays in London by the *Evening Standard* (2016). We have played over ninety shows in Buenos Aires, Argentina. Every show has been sold out and received standing ovations every night. I was very lucky to be chosen to perform in *Minefield*, and I am very proud of what six non-actors have achieved. It has been a privilege to speak to so many veterans and their families after the shows around the world including Korean war veterans from the United States and the UK; many Falklands-Malvinas veterans and families from Britain and Argentina; Iraq, and Afghanistan veterans; veterans from the Troubles in Northern Ireland; veterans from Ukraine who fought against the incursion of Russia on their borders; and the grandson of a Russian soldier who survived Stalingrad. I have held many of these proud men in my arms as they shed tears of their loss and memories from war. These reactions to bearing witness to our stories by veterans shows the emotional and affective power of *Minefield.*

I am troubled by conventional modes of representation around veterans and their families, which often objectify "the veteran" as a social problem. The government estimates there are 2.7 million veterans living within the UK (Office for Veterans Affairs 2020), yet, as mentioned earlier in the chapter, research focuses on a small minority of this community. What is needed to gain a more nuanced understanding of veterans and their families is for scholarship in this area to take a risk and move towards more engaging methods of research. Importantly it is not just about mobilising "creative methods," but rather finding new ways to prioritise coproduction, curiosity, and creative ways of knowing the world.

In this chapter, I have explored how *Minefield* contributes to societal understanding of veteran subjectivity (before, during, and after war) and how the use of creativity offers new and evocative ways to engage with veterans and their families. The play is made up of an amalgamation of thoughts, feelings, memories, sounds, and interactions that are felt, remembered, and embodied. These messy woven aspects of veterans' subjectivity are neglected within current research. *Minefield* poses questions about the representation of veterans as one-dimensional subjects and offers opportunities to examine the cultural production and reproduction of veteran identities and experiences. For example, its use of music can "allow for interpretation of the visible and invisible and the tangible and intangible" (Bresler 2008, 227) and presents a tableau of sounds that draws the audience into a different way of hearing, seeing, and feeling. The multiple sensory forms of representation give audiences permission to enter empathetically into the act of witnessing and "invites the cultivation of multiple forms of listening" (Speedy 2005, 289). Indeed, during the performance our stories emerge from our living bodies as they interact with the space, the audience, and the cast. *Minefield* therefore plays with the status of veterans in cultural representations as "objects" of pity, scrutiny, and analysis, by putting the veteran subject *on stage.* In this way, veterans become both the *performers* and the *performance*; indeed, the play illustrates how the two cannot be separated. Furthermore, *Minefield* illustrates how new meaning and understanding about veteran lives and experience can be created at the intersection between cast and audience, and for me personally between my entangled identities of veteran, researcher, and performer.

*Minefield* provides an example of what the "deliteralisation of knowledge" (Eisner 2008, 5) through film, photography, music, lyrics, and poetry can offer us in military research. Neilsen (2008) suggests that the characteristics of this type of inquiry embrace "liminality, ineffability, metaphorical thinking, embodied understanding, personal evocations, domestic and local understanding and an embrace of the eros of language" (94). I argue that creative ways of knowing offer us more ethical possibilities for engagement with military communities, in that they can prioritise feeling, experience, as well as the freedom and agency of military subjects, in ways that other methodological approaches cannot. In this chapter, I have not presented *Minefield* as an example of theatre-as-method at work. Instead, I have shown how the use of creative and innovative methods can give voice to unheard narratives in military research.

The responsibility to speak truth is one that I bear myself; however, I do not take it on wearing only one "skin." I am a military studies researcher, but I am also a war veteran who has a mental health disability, and I cannot cast these skins off. I come with a messy, fractured incompleteness. I am work in progress. At a more personal level, then, creativity allows me to embrace these entanglements, my own messiness and incompleteness, and bring this to my research in a meaningful way. This is something that we could all do more of, as critical military studies researchers. As academics, we are "trained" to think critically, but there appears to be no room for being critical of oneself, or acknowledging our own messiness, incompleteness, and fallibility. What are the prejudices, biases, and assumptions we bring to our work? What stories do we really want to tell, and what are our motivations for telling them? How much are we influenced by the politics of research institutions and academic publishing? Are we prepared to take risks?

For me, an important question relates to how we as researchers represent the violence of war and the anger that is felt by veterans and their families. Despite cultural and political efforts to make war and its violent impacts on people (in this case, veterans) palatable, the inherent violence of it will always be an insurmountable issue. Researchers need to move away from a model that attributes veteran anger to their being mad, bad, or sad, and towards one that more honestly and openly confronts complexity and uncertainty. I strongly believe as a veteran that scholars of veteran studies have an ethical responsibility to find new ways of speaking, listening, and seeing that prioritise empathetic engagement with unheard and silenced stories. As Speedy (2008) tells us, "'the truth' is a slippery and multi-storied customer and few of us know what is deemed to be good and what is deemed to be the 'telos' or ethical substance of other people's lives, except those with insider knowledges" (50). *Minefield* is a risky text with the potential for harm; it is a story of hesitation, a journey into the unknown, and we can never anticipate how our audience will respond. But in the moment that we walk onto the stage, the audience and cast become welded together as part of the same story. There is an ethical responsibility to come to this encounter with vulnerability, openness to changing your mind. You can craft your own meanings, and there is great power in that.

While I use *Minefield/Campo Minado* as an example of "creative methods at work," I want to end the chapter by highlighting that the ethical responsibilities that go along with acts of witnessing do not only apply to "staged" performance. This chapter is itself a part of my performance as "veteran," and in reading this you have become a witness. This performance may raise questions, perhaps uncomfortable ones, about sending young men to war and how the aftermath of that experience impacts the veteran, their families, and the wider community, but it is fundamentally about giving voice. A voice that is sometimes very difficult to set free.

As we pass the fortieth anniversary year of the Falklands/Malvinas War, the *Minefield/Campo Minado* journey is still not complete. In 1982, on my return home from war, I realised I had lost a part of me. My life in the Royal Marines was not about exercises with blank ammunition anymore: "I had lost my innocence" (Jackson 2000). I had changed forever. *Minefield* has become a part of my journey to find the essence of who I am:

> I have stood on stage in Argentina fighting back the tears. As I waited in line, I thought about my country's government's hand in this. The death of a young man fighting for his country. I felt the eyes of the sold-out audience staring into my very soul. Suddenly, I held in my arms an Argentine mother who had lost her son during the war. Tears flowed down my face as I felt I was fragilely holding all mothers who have lost sons and daughters from war. How can I put into words what happened last night? How does one represent those emotions I felt? Are there any words and are they sufficient to tell this story? (Jackson 2018)

When words alone fail, creativity may help us get closer.
Epilogue: The lights go off.

# Notes

## PREFACE

1. Women Warriors was a collaborative participatory theatre project between Workie Ticket Theatre CIC, me, and nine women veterans in the North East of England, which ran for ten months between January and October 2019. The aim of the project was to shed a light on the often-untold experiences of women during and following military service, by creating a piece of theatre based on their real stories.

## INTRODUCTION

1. "Creative" in the sense that they find new ways of using established approaches or develop creative practices as methods in themselves.

## CHAPTER 1

We would like to thank Flight Lieutenant Richard Weeks and Wing Commander Alun Walton (RAF Fylingdales) and Kevin Booth (English Heritage) for their support and assistance with the work underpinning this chapter. Our thanks to Fylingdales Archive for permission to reproduce the images from their collection.

1. See, for example, Jonathan McDowell's *Jonathan's Space Report* (https://planet4589.org/index.html (accessed 26th March 2021) or the Union of Concerned Scientists' *UCS Satellite Database* (https://www.ucsusa.org/resources/satellite-database (accessed 26th March 2021), plus a plethora of commercial satellite monitoring companies.

2. The archive website is at https://fylingdalesarchive.org.uk/ (accessed 26th March 2021).

3. Michael Mulvihill, Leverhulme artist in residence, School of Geography, Politics and Sociology, Newcastle University, UK. Leverhulme grant reference AIR-2014–028, 2014–15.

4. *Turning Fylingdales Inside Out: making practice visible at the UK's Ballistic Missile Early Warning and Space Monitoring Station.* Rachel Woodward, Chloë Barker, Neil Jenkings, and Michael Mulvihill, AHRC grant reference AH/S013067/1, 2020–23.

5. The UK's Whole Force concept, evident in defence policy documentation from the early 2010s and explicitly positioning defence as reliant on armed forces, private sector contractors, the volunteer Reserve, echoes practices dating back over fifty years at RAF Fylingdales.

6. A noumenon is a thing in itself, as distinct from a phenomenon that is knowable through the senses.

7. Detailed archive documents are available at https://www.norad.mil/About-NORAD/NORAD-History/ (accessed 25th March 2021).

8. Engineering and Technology history Wiki, "Oral-History: Hal Walker" (2019) *IEEE History Centre.* 829 https://ethw.org/Oral-History:Hal_Walker (accessed 8th April 2021).

9. Available at https://www.norad.mil/About-NORAD/NORAD-History/ (accessed 25th March 2021).

10. J.K. Gerhart (1962) 'Ballistic Missile and Space Weapons Detection Systems.' In *North America Air Defense Command and Continential Air Defense Command: Historical Summary July–December 1962.* Colorado: NORAD HQ, 35. Documents available at https://www.norad.mil/About-NORAD/NORAD-History/ (accessed 25th March 2021).

11. RCA Heritage Program (2015) Interview with Ed Nossen. *RCA Oral History Transcripts.* 11. https://rdw.rowan.edu/rca_histories/11 (accessed 8th April 2021).

12. See also in this volume: Michael Mulvihill *All things bright and beautiful the lord bomb made them all: More than human creativity and the cyborg geology of nuclear weapon design.*

13. https://www.listennotes.com/podcasts/skylab-3-living-and-working-in-space-H49fJw3x-Yh/. (accessed 16th April 2021).

14. Representations of land as unproductive, unused space is a long-standing justification strategy for otherwise unpopular military land uses; see, for example, Valerie Kuletz's (1998) examination of rationales for nuclear testing in the southwest United States on lands productively occupied by indigenous Americans for thousands of years before their designation by white settlers as "desert."

15. https://nsquare.org/.

16. https://rusi.org/projects/uk-project-nuclear-issues.

## CHAPTER 2

1. https://dronecenter.bard.edu/files/2019/10/CSD-Drone-Databook-Web.pdf.

2. https://www.navy.mil/Press-Office/Testimony/display-testimony/Article/2433784/senate-armed-services-subcommittee-on-readiness-and-management-support-holds-he/.

3. https://uwaterloo.ca/centre-peace-advancement/grebel-gallery/about.

4. Budget restraints for the exhibition precluded my work with a larger pool of participants.
5. Pseudonyms have been used to preserve privacy.
6. I use the terms *drone* and *UAV* (Unmanned Aerial Vehicle) interchangeably.
7. http://www.dronesurvivalguide.org/.

## CHAPTER 3

1. The research benefited from the support of a Royal Geographical Society (with IBG) Small Grant and the Jasmin Leila Award 2017.
2. Provision of an airborne force (1940–1941), Air Ministry and Ministry of Defence: Flying Training Command and Technical Training Command: Registered Files and Reports, AIR 32/2. The National Archives (TNA), London.
3. Past Present and Future of RAF (1938–1945), Marshal Sir John Slessor: Papers, AIR 75/112. TNA.
4. Royal Air Force Station Operations Record Book (1940–1944), Ringway, AIR 29/512. TNA.
5. World War II: ERP21, aircraft production and training programmes (1940–1942), Division within AIR AIR75/22. TNA.
6. Work of Airborne Forces Experimental Establishment (1940–1945), Airborne Forces Experimental Establishment, AVIA 44/536. TNA.
7. ARMY (Code B, 88): Parachute troops: training (1942–1943), Air Ministry and Ministry of Defence: Registered Files, Air 2/7575. TNA.
8. ARMY (Code B, 88): Parachute troops: training (1943–1945), Air Ministry and Ministry of Defence: Registered Files, AIR 2/7576. TNA.
9. Parachute Training School Ringway, previously Parachute Training Squadron, (1940–1947), Air Ministry and Ministry of Defence: Operational Records Book, AIR 29/520. TNA.
10. Central Landing Establishment: parachute training (1941–1942), Air Ministry: Army Co-operation Command: Registered Files, AIR 39/84. TNA.
11. Letters\Files in Box 52, (1939–1957), Rudolf Laban Archive, L/E/52/11. University of Surrey Archives & Special Collections (UoS), Guildford; Letters\Files in Box 51, (1937–1958), Rudolf Laban Archive, L/E/51/70. UoS.
12. Industrial Rhythms, (1940s–1950s), Rudolf Laban Archive, L/E/76/8. UoS.
13. Ibid; Industrial Rhythms, (1940s–1950s), Rudolf Laban Archive, L/E/76/6. UoS.
14. Lecture Notes on Various Subjects, (1930s–1950s), Rudolf Laban Archive, L/E/33/52. UoS.
15. Ibid.
16. Industrial Rhythms\Files in Box 65, (1940s-1950s), Rudolf Laban Archive, L/E/65/67. UoS.
17. Industrial Rhythms (1940s–1950s), L/E/76/8.
18. Ibid.
19. Ibid.
20. Letters\Files in Box 51.

21. Ibid.
22. Industrial Rhythms\Air Ministry\Correspondence, manuscripts and notes (1942–1954), Rudolf Laban Archive Papers, L/E/74/1. UoS.
23. Ibid.
24. Ibid.
25. Industrial Rhythm\Interview with Chief Air Marshal Sir J.S (1946), Rudolf Laban Archive, L/E/65/68. UoS.
26. Industrial Rhythms\Air Ministry\Correspondence, manuscripts and notes (1942–1954).
27. Industrial Rhythms (1940s–1950s), L/E/76/8.
28. Lecture Notes on Various Subjects (1930s–1950s).
29. Lecture Notes on Various Subjects (1930s–1950s).
30. Industrial Rhythms\Air Ministry\Correspondence, manuscripts and notes (1942–1954).
31. Ibid.
32. Ibid.
33. Lecture Notes on Various Subjects\Files in Box 33 (1930s–1950s), Rudolf Laban Archives L/E/33/49. UoS.
34. Industrial Rhythms\Air Ministry\Correspondence, manuscripts, and notes (1942–1954).
35. Ibid.
36. Ibid.
37. Central Landing Establishment: parachute training (1941–1942), Air Ministry: Army Co-operation Command: Registered files, AIR 39/84. TNA.
38. Industrial Rhythms\Air Ministry\Correspondence, manuscripts, and notes (1942–1954).
39. Ibid.
40. ARMY (Code B, 88): Parachute troops: training (1940–1945), Air Ministry and Ministry of Defence: Registered Files, AIR 2/7577. TNA.
41. Industrial Rhythms\Air Ministry\Correspondence, manuscripts, and notes (1942–1954).
42. Ibid.
43. Ibid.
44. Ibid.
45. Ibid.
46. Ibid.
47. Ibid.
48. Ibid.
49. Ibid.
50. Ibid.
51. Ibid.
52. Ibid.
53. Ibid.
54. Ibid.
55. Ibid.

56. Industrial Rhythm\Interview with Chief Air Marshal Sir J.S.
57. Ibid.

## CHAPTER 4

Thanks to Chloë Barker, Alison Williams, Rachel Woodward, and Alice Cree for their input and encouragement developing this chapter.

1. The title of this chapter refers to an adaption of the hymn "All Things Bright and Beautiful" for the film *Beneath the Planet of the Apes* (1970) by composer Leonard Rosenman. The scene depicts a race of humans who have descended from survivors of a nuclear war singing to a leftover weapon, which they have dedicated as their God.
2. For geology of Southwest New Mexico, see http://www.nmnaturalhistory.org/volcanoes/valles-caldera-jemez-volcanic-field (accessed 25 May 2021).
3. Oppenheimer spoke this phrase in the television documentary *The Decision to Drop the Bomb* (1965). A clip of the interview can be viewed at https://www.atomicarchive.com/media/videos/oppenheimer.html (accessed 25 May 2021).
4. With the exception of Lesley Poling-Kempes *Ghost Ranch,* who gives an account of the impact of the bomb on the Ghost Ranch—see chapter 4 and reference list for this chapter. Sascha T Scott also pieces together a little documentation in which Georgia O'Keeffe refers to the bomb, also see reference section of this chapter.
5. For discussion for new materialist approaches to geopolitics, see J. Dittmer (2017), *Diplomatic Material: Affect, Assemblage, and Foreign Policy*, Durham: Duke University Press, and M. DeLanda (1991), *War in the Age of Intelligent Machines*, New York: Zone Books.
6. My art practice exploring the influence of nuclear weapons on our phenomenological sense of the everyday lead me to becoming an academic researcher see https://www.vane.org.uk/artists/michael-mulvihill (accessed 26 May 2021).
7. For overview of Art for Art's sake see https://www.theartstory.org/definition/art-for-art/ (accessed 26 May 2021).
8. A similar warhead to the US W76 is used by the United Kingdom on their Trident Continuous At-Sea Deterrent. The warhead is known as Holbrook and built by the Atomic Weapons Establishment. See //www.defensenews.com/global/europe/2020/02/25/britain-confirms-new-nuclear-warhead-project-after-us-officials-spill-the-beans/ (accessed 27 May 2021).
9. For wooden heatshields on spacecraft, see http://www.astronautix.com/f/fsw.html (accessed 28 May 2021).
10. The original decision to use lava glaze was based on the names of the primaries and secondary nuclear components of the UK ET.317 warhead known as Jenny Reggie Cleo and Tony. They evoked 1970s suburban life as depicted by television sitcoms such as "Terry and June" or "George and Mildred." This observation chimed with a comment that the UK Trident submarine base at Faslane was stuck in a Polaris heyday. Lava glaze was a popular ceramic look for the period and conceptual offer away of collapsing domestic space with nuclear military, see Mulvihill 2019. For lava glaze, see https://ceramicartsnetwork.org/daily/ceramic-glaze-recipes/mid-range

-glaze-recipes/marilees-lava-glaze-cone-6-oxidation-or-reduction/ (accessed 27 May 2021).

11. For design specifications of W76, see http://www.nuclearweaponarchive.org/Usa/Weapons/W76.html (accessed 26 May 2021).

12. For modification to W76 and strategic implications, see https://thebulletin.org/2017/03/how-us-nuclear-force-modernization-is-undermining-strategic-stability-the-burst-height-compensating-super-fuze/ (accessed 26 May 2021).

13. For debate and controversy of the W76-2 warhead, see Vipin Narang https://warontherocks.com/2018/02/discrimination-problem-putting-low-yield-nuclear-weapons-submarines-dangerous/ (accessed 28 May 2021) and https://inkstickmedia.com/after-the-apocalypse-us-nuclear-policy/ (accessed 28 May 2021).

14. For cost analysis of US nuclear weapons, see https://www.nti.org/analysis/articles/costs-us-nuclear-weapons/ (accessed 26 May 2021).

15. Since the late nineteenth century, Taos had attracted Modern Artists, particularly those from New York City, who were drawn by the brilliant open space and artistic culture of the Taos Pueblo. For historical overview, see https://taos.org/what-to-do/arts-culture/taos-history/art-history/ (accessed 27 May 2021).

16. Fauve and Fauvism refer to the term *wild beast* coined by art critic Louis Vauxcelles on seeing the work of Henri Matisse and and André Derain. It seemed to resonate with Emilio Segré description of the landscape and the Oppenheimers' collection of Fauvist paintings. For more on Fauvism, see https://www.tate.org.uk/art/art-terms/f/fauvism (accessed 27 May 2021).

17. Oppenheimer stated he had two loves, physics and New Mexico, that became entwined at Los Alamos (Smith and Weiner 1980, 10).

18. For account of Georgia O'Keeffe desert practice, see https://www.c-span.org/video/?310650-1/life-artwork-georgia-okeeffe (accessed 14 July 2021).

19. The Atomic Heritage Foundation argue that this collecting activity may have contributed to an exoticisation of the Pueblo who adapted the production of their ceramics to meet the desire of individual collectors at LANL and National Museums.

20. Few accounts remain of the Pueblo experience of working on the Manhattan Project, although Los Alamos recruited considerable numbers from the local Pueblo population to build the bomb, and many, like Popovi Da, had a significant role in the weapon's success. For Native American experience of the Manhattan Project, see https://www.atomicheritage.org/history/native-americans-and-manhattan-project (accessed 28 May 2021); also see Lacie Heeley's article on disproportionate effect nuclear weapon industry on communities, https://www.pri.org/stories/2018-01-30/make-and-maintain-americas-nukes-some-communities-pay-price (accessed 28 May 2021).

21. The William Robert Johnson online archive provides a nuclear attack scenario on the section of the Rio Grande valley in Texas, see http://www.johnstonsarchive.net/nuclear/nukergv.html (accessed 26 May 2021) and http://www.johnstonsarchive.net/nuclear/nuclearwar1.html (accessed 26 May 2021).

22. For Georgia O'Keeffe's fallout shelter, see https://www.prweb.com/releases/2013/6/prweb10793480.htm (accessed 27 May 2021) and https://www.washingtonpost.com/lifestyle/travel/a-pilgrimage-to-the-stark-desert-landscape-that-inspired-painter

-georgia-okeeffe/2019/11/14/c6702bf2-0564-11ea-b17d-8b867891d39d_story.html (accessed 27 May 2021).

23. To stress Trinity had profound health implications for those downwind of the explosion who are still campaigning for recognition more than seventy-five years after the test, see https://www.atomicheritage.org/history/tularosa-basin-downwinders (accessed 27 May 2021) and https://www.trinitydownwinders.com/ (accessed 27 May 2021), and for a broader account of the human cost of nuclear weapon tests, see https://www.icanw.org/nuclear_tests (accessed 27 May 2021) and my own work on about nuclear test veterans in *A British Guide to the End of the World* https://www.bbc.co.uk/programmes/m000b1gn (accessed 27 May 2021).

24. Discussion as a part of a preamble to futures workshop by N-Square and the School of International Futures hosted by United Kingdom Projects on Nuclear Issues at their annual conference 8–10 June 2021.

25. See https://nsquare.org/2019/12/20/greater-than/ (accessed 15 July 2021).

## CHAPTER 5

1. I would like to express my thanks to the British International Studies Association for the Early Career Research Grant (XCBI01), which supported this research.

2. This notion of process comes in for particular emphasis by Combat Paper, with the "About" page of its website emboldening and capitalising it: "Rag hand paper-making is a **PROCESS** in which plant based fibers used in textiles are repurposed for paper" (Combat Paper n.d., original emphasis).

## CHAPTER 6

1. TNA, HO186/14: Committee of Imperial Defence Report 1516-B, dated 9 February 1939, 3.

2. TNA, HO191/3: *Camouflage of vital factories and key points, 1939–1945*, MoHS, Section 6, 14.

3. TNA, HO186/1987: *Memorandum*, R.V. Darwin, to T.R. Cave-Browne-Cave, dated 11 November 1943.

4. TNA, HO191/31: *R.E.N. 525: The Viewing Room of the Research and Experiments Department of the Ministry of Home Security at Leamington Spa*, T.A. Littlefield, dated 26 June 1945.

5. TNA, HO191/3: *Camouflage of Vital Factories and Key Points*, MoHS, Section 4, 13.

6. TNA, AIR2/3437: *Camouflage*, L.M. Glasson, c. December 1938.

7. TNA, HO191/31: *R.E.N. 525: The Viewing Room of the Research and Experiments Department of the Ministry of Home Security at Leamington Spa*, T.A. Littlefield, dated 26 June 1945.

## CHAPTER 7

The authors are grateful to the participants of the "Conflict & Intimacy" project for being so brave, generous, and imaginative in the sharing of their stories. Thank you also to Rachel Woodward for providing helpful comments and revisions on this chapter.

1. This research is funded by the Economic and Social Research Council (ESRC), grant reference ES/T008334/1. The research is in collaboration with Workie Ticket Theatre CIC, a Tyneside-based feminist theatre company with a commitment to creating real positive social impact through theatre.

2. By "military institutions," we do not just refer to the MoD, but also the myriad organisations, funders, charities, and representatives who act and make decisions in service of the military and militaristic values (see Caddick forthcoming).

3. Shared through conversation between the authors and Helen-Marie Tuiwaiwai, author and director of *InValid Voices* performed at Army@TheFringe, 2018.

4. The theatre workshops for this project were facilitated by Lindsay Nicholson.

5. The writing workshops for this project were facilitated by JoJo Kirtley (Workie Ticket Theatre CIC).

6. *Magnolia Walls* is written by JoJo Kirtley with Alice Cree, produced by Workie Ticket Theatre CIC, and directed by Corinne Kilvington (with assistance from Charlotte Ryder), dramaturgy by Helen-Marie O'Malley (Tuiwaiwai).

7. The Economic and Social Research Council is part of UK Research and Innovation (UKRI), which is a "non-departmental public body sponsored by the Department for Business, Energy and Industrial Strategy (BEIS)," so whilst it is independent of the MoD, it is ultimately funded by the British government and arguably by an economy that funds the MoD also (https://www.ukri.org/about-us/who-we-are/).

## CHAPTER 8

1. This research was funded by the Academy of Finland.

2. Hast & Cast: Ei Niin Pelottava Asia, 2019, Sook Records. YouTube link: https://www.youtube.com/watch?v=kDNG6dB54J8. Spotify link: https://open.spotify.com/album/58dajcR2caGOM7iSVONANM.

## CHAPTER 10

Without the contributions of the following partners in this project, none of what you have just read would have been possible. In accordance with coproduction in its truest sense, heartfelt thanks go to Sarah Hicks Art, Army Welfare NW, Lancashire Infantry Museum, Weeton Primary School, the College for Military Veterans and Emergency Services at the University of Central Lancashire, and most importantly, the military families who trusted us with their stories.

The ethics for this research were in accordance with the guidance given by The British Educational Research Association (BERA 2011) and the requirements of the University of Central Lancashire Ethics Committee. Permissions to gather data in the public interest, and consent from participants involved, was obtained from parents and data-sharing agreements with the school and community centre established ahead of delivery. We also ensured any data gathered was confidential and feedback from participants anonymous, with the opportunity for participants to withdraw from the process or receive support with any topics of conversation which could be emotive.

1. See https://www.fionabruce.org.uk/sites/www.fionabruce.org.uk/files/2018-06/KIN-AND-COUNTRY-Growing-up-as-an-Armed-Forces-child.pdf.

2. https://www.scipalliance.org/assets/files/Listening-to-learn-FINAL-ONLINE-2020_05_14.pdf.

3. These categories were not too dissimilar to the MoD Army transition sheet 6 (HARDFACTS), a guide used to support military personnel transition to civilian life. HARDFACTS forms a checklist for aspects of service personnel's lives including, Health; Accommodation; Relocation; Drugs; Alcohol and Stress, Finance and Benefits, Attitude, Thinking, Behaviour and Welfare; Children and Family; Training, Education and Employment and Supporting Agencies. Transition to civilian life | The British Army (mod.uk).

## CHAPTER 11

The research and writing of this chapter was supported by an ESRC Doctoral Studentship (Student number 159400979), the University of Bath Public Engagement Progression Fund (£2500 for the devised theatre), the South West Doctoral Training Programme's Student-Led Collaboration Fund (£3000 for the Northern Ireland veteran films), the South West Doctoral Training Programme's Impact Fund (£780 for the veteran workshop and documentary film), and the University of Bath's Public Engagement Seed Fund (£488 for the music video).

The author thanks Tim West for his super creative input and support, Simon Wharf for his amazing audio-visual technical support, and Jordan Holland for her artistic flair. The author is indebted to Sophy Antrobus for our valuable conversations, my wonderful workshop participants, and the Northern Ireland veterans, whose words form part of our latest films.

1. Poetic documentaries "draw on the historical world for their raw material but transform this material in distinctive ways," seeing "the historical world anew" through "mood, tone and affect," opening up "the possibility of alternative forms of knowledge" (Nichols 2017, 102–05).

2. https://hannah-west.org/hannah-west/creativeprojects/shell-hold-her-own/.

3. https://hannah-west.org/hannah-west/creativeprojects/uniformly-served/.

4. The author gratefully acknowledges the Southwest Doctoral Training Programme's Student-Led Collaboration Fund for funding this project.

5. https://www.youtube.com/watch?v=-DldkCo9UTY.

6. Reprinted with permission from Tim West.

## CHAPTER 12

1. This chapter is framed and written in a way that prioritises the creative and autoethnographic voice, using lines from my journals and the play to title the chapter's "Acts."

2. The first song that I had written was called "Were You There Do You Care?" (Jackson, 1998).

3. The trailer for the play can be found at https://vimeo.com/229739383. Further excerpts of the play filmed at the Edingburgh Theatre festival can be found at https://www.bbc.co.uk/events/ewxxj5/acts/ac4wbp.

4. For more information see https://lolaarias.com/.

5. The names of the cast of the *Minefield* are used as they are already within the public domain. However, the names of other participants in the interviewing process have been changed.

6. *Gente* (*Gente y la actualidad*) is the most popular Argentinian gossip magazine, which came into much criticism for supporting the National Reorganisation Process (Military Junta) between 1976 and 1983.

7. Originally written by Mendoza Luis Profili in the 1950s and published under the pseudonym Luis H. Morales in 1964, it is the most popular song in Argentine folk music and one of the thirteen most popular songs in popular music in Argentina.

8. The "Marcha de las Malvinas" (in English: March of the Malvinas) is a patriotic anthem of Argentina. It is sung in demonstrations to assert Argentinian sovereignty claims over the Falkland Islands and taught in schools from the age of six.

9. In 2019, during the third tour of Argentina, the cast went into the studio and recorded the "War Song." I then used photographs and video to symbolically represent the lyrical content contained within the song. It is available at: https://www.youtube.com/watch?v=3oTNykHXwmA.

# Bibliography


Adey, P. 2008. Aeromobilities: Geographies, subjects and vision. *Geography Compass,* 2(5), 1318–36.

Adey, P. 2010. *Aerial life: Spaces, mobilities, affects*. Oxford: Wiley-Blackwell

Adey, Peter.,Whitehead, M., Williams, A.J. 2011. Air-target: Distance, reach and the politics of verticality. *Theory, Culture and Society*, 28 (7–8): 173–87.

Adrian, E. D. & Yealland, L. R. 1917. The treatment of some common war neuroses. *The Lancet*. Vol. 192, 867–72.

Åhäll, L. 2019. Feeling everyday IR: Embodied, affective, militarising movement as choreography of war. *Cooperation and Conflict,* 54(2) 149–66.

Ahmed, S. 2006. *Queer Phenomenology: Orientations, Objects, Others*. Durham: Duke University Press Books.

Alexis-Martin, B. 2018 Geographies of nuclear warfare: future spaces, zones and technologies. In R. Woodward (ed.) *A Research Agenda for Military Geography*. London: Edward Elgar.

Anderson, J., Adey P., and Bevan P.. 2010. "Positioning place: polylogic approaches to research methodology." *Qualitative Research* 10 (5): 589–604.

Antony, A. 2017. Minefield: Two sides of the Falkland's war—On stage. *The Observer*. 12th November 2017.

Antrobus, S. & West, H. 2022. 'This is all very academic': Critical Thinking in Professional Military Education. *RUSI Journa*l, 167(3), 78-86. https://doi.org/10.1080/03071847.2022.2112521.

Arias, L. 2017. *Minefield. A play by Lola Arias*. London: Oberon Books

Arndt, O., von Rappard, M., Schönenbach, J., and Wee, C. (*Eds.*) 2009. *Embedded Art: art in the name of security*. Argobooks: Berlin.

Art therapy with war veterans. *Art Therapy: Journal of American Art Therapy Association*

Ashcroft, M. 2014. The Veterans' Transition Review, Biteback Publishing: London.

Ashmore, P., Craggs, R., and Neate, H. 2012. Working-with: Talking and sorting in personal archives. *Journal of Historical Geography.* 38(1). 81–89.

Azarbaijani-Moghaddam, S. 2014. Seeking out their afghan sisters: Female engagement teams in Afghanistan (CMI Working Papers No. WP 2014:1). Bergen.

Bailey, A.R., Brace, C and Harvey D.C. 2009. Three geographers in an archive: Positions, predilections and passing comment on transient lives. *Transactions of the Institute of British Geographers,* 34(2), 254–69.

Banks, M. 2001 *Visual Methods in Social Research.* Sage: London.

Barad, K. 2003. Posthumanist performativity: Toward an understanding of how matter comes to matter. *Signs*, 28(3): 801–31.

Barnes, T. 2008. Geography's underworld: The military–industrial complex, mathematical modelling and the quantitative revolution. *Geoforum* 39, 3–16.

Basham, V. M., & Bulmer, S. 2017. Critical military studies as method: An approach to studying gender and the military. In R Woodward and C Duncanson (*eds.*), *The Palgrave International Handbook of Gender and the Military*, 59–71. https://doi.org/10.1057/978-1-137-51677-0.

Basham, V. M., & Catignani, S. 2018. War is where the hearth is: Gendered labor and the everyday reproduction of the geopolitical in the army reserves. *International Feminist Journal of Politics*, 20(2), 153–71. https://doi.org/10.1080/14616742.2018.1442736.

Basham, V.M. 2016. Gender, race, militarism and remembrance: The everyday geopolitics of the poppy. *Gender, Place & Culture*, 23(6), 883–96.

Basham, V.M. and Bulmer, S., 2017. Critical military studies as method: An approach to studying gender and the military. In C. Duncanson & R. Woodward (*Eds.*). *The Palgrave International Handbook of Gender and the Military* (59–71). London: Palgrave Macmillan.

Basham, V.M., Belkin, A. and Gifkins, J. 2015. What is critical military studies? *Critical Military Studies*, 1(1), 1–2.

Basl. K. 2020. This is not a military uniform: An essay about combat paper and me, *Prometheus Dreaming*, 2(4). https://www.prometheusdreaming.com/this-is-not-a-military-uniform.

Bateson, C. V. 2019. Music and war. In *Military History*. Oxford: Oxford University Press. https://doi.org/10.1093/obo/9780199791279–0188.

BBC, 2016. Saturday Review. 4 June 2016.

Bea Kingdon, WRAC veteran, NI-3, 2019, Interviewed by Hannah West, 5 February.

Beccle, H. C. 1942. The nature and treatment of some war psychoses. *Medical Press*. Vol. 208, 136–39.

Behrens, R.R. 2002. False colors: Art, design and modern camouflage. Dysart, Iowa: Bobolink.

Bell, C. 2018. Celebrity power and powers of war: The rise of the COINdinistas in American popular media. *Critical Military Studies*, 4(3), 244–63.

Ben-Ari E, Levy Y. 2014. Getting access to the field: Insider/outsider perspectives. In J. Soeters, P.M. Shields, and S. Rietjens (*eds.*), *Routledge Handbook of Research Methods in Military Studies*. London: Routledge, 9–18.

Berg, B.L. 2008. Visual Ethnography. SAGE *Encyclopedia of Qualitative Research Methods*. Thousand Oaks CA: SAGE Publications. 935–38.

Berndtsson, J. and Kinsey, C (*Eds.*). 2016. *The Routledge Research Companion to Security Outsourcing*. London: Routledge.

Bharucha, R. 2014. *Terror and Performance*. Routledge: Oxon.

Bhattacharyya, G. 2018. *Racial Capitalism: Questions of Reproduction and Survival*. London: Rowman & Littlefield.

Bilal, W. n.d. *168.01*. https://wafaabilal.com/168h01s/.

Bilal, W. n.d.b. *Conflict Exchange*. https://wafaabilal.com/cx/.

Billig, M. 2013. *Learn to Write Badly: How to Succeed in the Social Sciences*. Cambridge: Cambridge University Press.

Black, I.S. 2010. Analysing historical and archive sources. In *Key Methods in Geography. 2nd ed*, In N. Clifford., S. French., and G. Valentine (eds.), 466–84. London: Sage.

Bleiker, R. 2009. *Aesthetics and World Politics*. Basingstoke and New York: Palgrave Macmillan.

Blejmar, J. 2017. Autofictions of postwar: Empathy in Lola Arias' Minefield/Campo Minado. *Latin America Theatre Review*. Vol. 50(2), 5-25.

Bloomberg, R. 2015. Dancing to a Tune: The drone as political and historical assemblage. *Culture Magazine* 16:1–24. Accessed April 27, 2021. https://culturemachine.net/vol-16-drone-cultures/dancing-to-a-tune/.

Boal, A. 2019. *Theatre of the Oppressed*. London: Pluto Press.

Borgdorff, H., Peters, P., and Pinch, T. 2019. *Dialogues Between Artistic Research and Science and Technology Studies*. London: Routledge.

Borgdorff, H. 2011. The production of knowledge in artistic research. In M. Biggs and H. Karlsson (Eds.). *The Routledge Companion to Research in the Arts*. London: Routledge, 44–63.

Bos, D. 2018. Answering the call of duty: Everyday encounters with the popular geopolitics of military-themed videogames. *Political Geography*, 63, 54–64.

Bos, D. 2021. Popular geopolitics 'beyond the screen': Bringing modern warfare to the city. *Environment and Planning C: Politics and Space*, 39(1), 94–113.

Bourdieu, P. 1977 *Outline of a Theory of Practice*. Cambridge: Cambridge University Press.

Bourdieu, P. 1990. *The Logic of Practice*, R. Nice (trans.). Cambridge, Polity.

Bourdieu, P. 1994. *In Other Words: Essays Towards a Reflexive Sociology*, M. Adamson, (trans). Cambridge: Polity.

Bousquet, A. 2018. *The Eye of War: Military Perception from the Telescope to the Drone*. Minneapolis: Univ. of Minnesota Press.

Boyle, D. 2003. *28 Days Later*. UK: DNA Films.

Bradley, H. 1999. The seductions of the archives: Voices lost and found. *History of the Human Sciences* 12 (2): 107–22.

Braidotti, R. 2012. 'Interview with Rosi Braidotti,' by Rick Dolphijn and Iris van der Tuin in R. Dolphijn and I. Van der Tuin (eds.), New Materialism: Interviews and Cartographies. Ann Arbor: Open Humanities Press, 19–37.

Braidotti, R. 2011. *Nomadic Theory: The Portable Rosi Braidotti*. New York: Columbia University Press.

Breed, A. 2014. *Performing the Nation: Genocide, Justice, Reconciliation*. Chicago: The University of Chicago Press.

Bresler, L. 2008. The music lesson. In G. Knowles & A. Cole. (*Eds.*). *Handbook of the Arts in Qualitative Research: Perspectives, Methodologies, Examples and Issues*. Thousand Oaks, CA: Sage.

Brickell, K. 2015. Towards intimate geographies of peace? Local reconciliation of domestic violence in Cambodia. *Transactions of the Institute of British Geographers,* 40(3) 321–33.

Broadhurst, S. 1999. *Liminal acts: A critical overview of contemporary performance and theory*. London: Cassell.

Brooker, P. 2019–2020. Sky Lab 3: Living and Working in Space. https://open.spotify.com/show/6n4XL8KH1atmkwclbr9CWy.

Browne, S. 2015. *Dark Matters: On the Surveillance of Blackness*. Durham, NC: Duke Univ. Press.

Bruner J. 2002. *Making Stories: Law, Literature, Life*. Cambridge, MA: Harvard University Press.

Buckingham, D. 2009. Creative visual methods in media research: Possibilities, problems and proposals. *Media, Culture and Society*, 31(4), 633–52.

Bulmer, S. & Jackson, D. 2016. "You do not live in my skin": Embodiment, voice, and the veteran. *Critical Military Studies*. Vol. 2, No. 1 & 2, 25–40.

Bulmer, S. 2021. Research conversation, 19th July 2021

Burton, A (*ed.*). 2005. *Archives stories: Facts, fictions and the writing of history*. Durham: Duke University.

Butler, J. 2011. *Bodies That Matter: On the Discursive Limits of Sex*. London and New York: Routledge.

Butler, J. 2004. *Undoing Gender*. Abingdon: Routledge.

Caddick, N. forthcoming. *The Cultural Politics of Veterans' Narratives*. Edinburgh: Edinburgh University Press.

Carter, S. and McCormack, D. 2014. Affectivity and geopolitical images. In J. Dittmer,and Sharp. J. (*Eds.*) *Geopolitics: An Introductory Reader*, 319–23. London: Routledge.

Carter, S., Kirby, P., and Woodyer, T. 2017. Ludic or playful geopolitics. In M.C. Benwell and P. Hopkins (eds.), Children, Young People and Critical Geopolitics, 61-73. London: Routledge.

Cassidy, D.C. 2005. *J. Robert Oppenheimer and the American Century*. New York: Pi Press.

Catignani, S., and Basham, V. M. 2021. The gendered politics of researching military policy in the age of the knowledge economy. *Review of International Studies* 4, 211–30. https://doi.org/10.1017/S0260210521000036.

Cave-Browne-Cave, Thomas R. 1945. Camouflage for the protection of civil factories and its application to peace-time purposes. *Journal of the Royal Society of Arts* 93 (4690), 260–75.

Charrett, C. 2020. The wheel that lost its chair Or how they came to bomb Palestine. *Critical Studies on Security*. Advanced online publication. https://doi.org/10.1080/21624887.2020.1824444.

Chee, A. 2018. *How to Write an Autobiographical Novel*. London, UK: Bloomsbury.

Clifford, J., and Marcus, G. (*Eds.*) 1986. *Writing Culture: The Poetics and Politics of Ethnography*. San Francisco, CA: University of California Press.

Closs-Stephens, A. 2016. The affective atmospheres of nationalism. *Cultural Geographies* 23, 181–98.

Coetzee, J. 1986. *Foe*. London, UK: Penguin.

Cohen, S. (*Ed.*) 2004. *International encyclopaedia of dance*. Oxford: Oxford University Press.

Combat Paper. n.d. About Combat Paper, Workshops & Process. Available at https://www.combatpaper.org/about.

Conrad, D. and G. Campbell., 2008. "Participatory Research—An Empowering Methodology with Marginalised Populations." *Knowing Differently: Arts-Based and Collaborative Research Methods. Hauppauge, NY:* Nova Science Publishers.

Conti and Armour. 2016. "The War Song." In L. Arias. *Minefield. A play by Lola Arias*. London. Oberon Books, 64–65.

Cooke, M. 1993. Wo-Man, Retelling the War Myth. In M. Cooke & A. Woollacott (Eds.), *Gendering War Talk* (177–204). Princeton: Princeton University Press.

Cosgrove, D., and Fox, W. 2010. *Photography and Flight*. London: Reaktion.

Coward, M. 2006. Against anthropocentrism: The destruction of the built environment as a distinct form of political violence. *Review of International Studies* 32(3), 419–37.

Cowen, Deborah. 2014. *The Deadly Life of Logistics: Mapping Violence in Global Trade*. Minneapolis: Univ. of Minnesota Press.

Cox, C. 2018. *Sonic Flux: Sound, Art and Metaphysics.* Chicago: University of Chicago Press.

Cree, A. 2020a. 'People want to see tears': Military heroes and the 'Constant Penelope' of the UK's Military Wives choir. *Gender, Place and Culture*, 27(2) 218–38. https://doi.org/10.1080/0966369X.2019.1615414.

Cree, A. 2020b. Sovereign Wives? An emotional politics of precarity and resistance in the UK's Military Wives Choir. *International Political Sociology*, 14 (3), 304–22. https://doi.org/10.1093/ips/olaa013.

Cree, A. and Caddick, N., 2020. Unconquerable heroes: Invictus, redemption, and the cultural politics of narrative. *Journal of War & Culture Studies*, 13 (3), 258–78.

Cree, A., 2019. Encountering the 'lively' in military theatre. In R. Woodward (*ed.*) *A Research Agenda for Military Geographies, 162-173.*. Cheltenham: Edward Elgar.

Croft, C. 2015. *Dancers as diplomats: American choreography in cultural exchange*. Oxford: Oxford University Press.

Csordas, T. J. 1999. Embodiment and cultural phenomenology. In G. Weiss and H. F. Haber. (*Eds.*). *Perspectives on Embodiment: The Intersections of Nature and Culture*. New York: Routledge.

Cusick, S. 2006. Music as torture, music as weapon. In Bull, M., Back, L. and Howes, D. (*Eds.*) *The Auditory Culture Reader*, 379–91. London: Bloomsbury Publishing. cuts-to-benefits.html.

Dalton, J. 2020. Model making as a research method. *Studies in the Education of Adults* 52, 52(1), 35-48.

Dandeker, C., Wessely, S., Iversen, A. and Ross, J. 2006. What's in a Name? Defining and Caring for "Veterans": *The United Kingdom in International Perspective, Armed Forces and Society* 32, 2: 161–77, Central Office of Information.

Daulatzai, A. and S. Ghumkor. 2021. Damage Control: The Unbearable Whiteness of Drone Work. *Jadaliyya*, March 16, 2021. Accessed April 23, 2021. https://www.jadaliyya.com/Details/42483/Damage-Control-the-Unbearable-Whiteness-of-Drone-Work.

Dauphinee, E. 2016. Narrative engagement and the creative practices of international relations. In Amoureux J.L. and Steele B.J. (*eds.*). *Reflexivity and International Relations: Positionality, Critique and Practice, 44-60.* Oxon: Routledge.

De Pedro, K., Astor, R., Benbenishty, R., Estrada, J., Smith, G. and Esqueda, M. 2011. The children of military service members: challenges, supports, and future educational research, *Review of Educational Research*, 81 (4), 566–618.

DeLanda, M. 2016. *Assemblage theory*. Edinburgh: Edinburgh University Press.

DeLanda, M. 2000. *A thousand years of nonlinear history*. New York: Swerve Editions.

Deleuze, G. and Guattari, F. 2000. *Anti-Oedipus: Capitalism and Schizophrenia.* Translated by Robert Hurley, Mark Seem and Helen R Lane. Minneapolis: University of Minnesota Press.

Deleuze, G. and Guattari, F. 2013. *A Thousand Plateaus.* Translation Brian Massumi, London: Bloomsbury, 2013.

DeSilvey, C. 2007. Salvage memory: Constellating material histories on a hardscrabble homestead. *Cultural Geographies, 14(3), 401-24.*

Dhruba, K. n.d. Narou, Narou, Saili. Radio Nepal Song Library. Kathmandu.

Ditmars, H. 2019. Veterans and artists draw creative profit out of war. *The Art Newspaper*, 8 May. https://www.theartnewspaper.com/2019/05/08/veterans-and-artists-draw-creative-profit-out-of-war.

Dittmer, J. and Gray, N. 2010. Popular geopolitics 2.0: Towards new methodologies of the everyday. *Geography Compass* 4(11), 1664–77. doi:10.1386/ jwcs.2.2.211_1.

Dowling, R., Lloyd, K. and Suchet-Pearson, S. 2017. Qualitative methods II: "More-than-human" methodologies and/in praxis. *Progress in Human Geography* 41(6), 823–31.

Dwyer, C., and Davies, G. 2010. Qualitative methods II: Animating archives, artful interventions and online environments. Progress in human geography, 34(1), 88-97.

Dyvik, S. L. 2016. 'Valhalla rising': Gender, embodiment and experience in military memoirs. *Security Dialogue*, 47 (2), 133–50. https://doi.org/10.1177/0967010615615730.

Dyvik, S.L. and Welland, J. 2018. War ink: Sense-making and curating war through military tattoos. *International Political Sociology*, 12 (4), 346–61.

Dörr, E. 2007. *Rudolf Laban: The dancer of the crystal*. Plymouth: Scarecrow Press.

Eastern Eye. 2020. *Army and The Arts: How the Military Unites Communities*. Retrieved from https://www.easterneye.biz/army-and-the-arts-how-the-military-unites-communities/.

Eder, M.D. 1917. *War-shock, the Psycho-neuroses in War Psychology and Treatment*. Oxford: Heinemann.

Edkins, J. 2013. Novel writing in international relations: Openings for a creative practice. *Security Dialogue*, 44 (4), 281–97.

Edwards, B., and Gilbert, D. 2008. "Pizzadilly!": The re-imagining of Piccadilly Circus 1957-1972. *Planning Perspectives*, 23(4), 455-78.

Eichler, M., & Wiebe, J. L. 2019. The art of discomfort: Engaging in dialogue on war. *Critical Military Studies*, 5 (1), 83–88. https://doi.org/10.1080/23337486.2018.1432753.

Eisner, E. 2008. Art and knowledge. In G. Knowles and A. Cole. (*Eds.*). *Handbook of the Arts in Qualitative Research: Perspectives, Methodologies, Examples and Issues*. Thousand Oaks, CA: Sage.

Ellis, C. 1997. Evocative autography: Writing emotionally about our lives' In William G. Tierney and Yvonna Lincoln, (Eds.). *Representation and the Text: Re-Framing the Narrative Voice*. Albany: State University of New York Press, 115–39.

Ellis, C. 1999. Heartful autoethnography. *Qualitative Health Research*, 9 (5), 669–83. Retrieved from http://journals.sagepub.com.ezproxy1.bath.ac.uk/doi/pdf/10.1177/104973299129122153.

Elshtain, J. B. 1995. *Women and War*. Chicago: University of Chicago Press.

Enloe, C. 1988. *Maneuvers: The International Politics of Militarizing Women's Lives*. Berkeley: University of California Press.

Enloe, C. 2015. The recruiter and the sceptic: A critical feminist approach to military studies, *Critical Military Studies*, 1(1), 3-10.

Farish, M. 2016. Reflections on research in military archives. InA. Williams, N. Jenkings, M. Rech, and R. Woodward (Eds.). 21-29. London: Routledge.

Faux, W. 2020. *How the Army is Using the Arts to Ask Tough Questions*. Herald Scotland. Retrieved from https://www.heraldscotland.com/news/18606305.agenda-army-using-arts-ask-tough-questions/.

Female First. 2020. *The Art of Making a Modern Soldier*. Retrieved from https://www.femalefirst.co.uk/features/the-art-of-making-a-modern-soldier-1252826.html.

Fenge, L.A. 2009 "Professional doctorates—A better route for researching professionals?," *Social Work Education*, 28 (2):, 165-76, , Routledge, London.

Feynman, R.P. 1992. *Surely You're Joking Mr Feynman: Adventures of a Curious Character*. London: Vintage.

Finburgh, C. 2017. Violence without Violence: Spectacle, War and Lola Arias's Minefield/Campo Minado. *Theatre Research International, 42 (2), 163-78.*

Finley, S. 2008. Arts-based research. In J.G. Knowles and A.L. Cole (eds.) Handbook of the Arts in Qualitative Research: Perspectives, Methodologies, Examples, and Issues, 71-81. Thousand Oaks: Sage.

Fisher, J. 2003. On Drawing. In C. de Zegher and A. Newman (eds.) Stages of Drawing: Gesture and Act. London and New York: Tate Publishing and the Drawing Centre.

Fisher, M. 2014. *Ghosts of My Life: Writings on Depression, Hauntology and Lost Futures*. Alresford, UK: Zero Books.

Fisher, M. 2016. *The Weird and the Eerie*. London, UK: Repeater Books.

Forsyth, I. 2017. *Second World War British Military Camouflage: Designing Deception*. New York: Bloomsbury Publishing.

Forsyth, I. 2016. Biography and the military archive. In A. Williams., K.N. Jenkings., M. Rech., and R.Woodward (eds.) The Routledge Companion to Military Research Methods, 44-57. London: Routledge.

Foucault, M. 1977. *Discipline and Punishment: The Birth of the Prison.* Penguin: London.

Foucault, M. 2011. Society must be defended, 17 March 1976. In I. Szeman and T. Kaposy (*Eds.*). *Cultural Theory: An Anthology*. Malden, MA: Wiley-Blackwell.

Franz, N. 2017. Targeted killing and pattern-of-life analysis: Weaponised Media. Media, *Culture & Society,* 39 (1),111–21.

Fregonese, S. 2017. Affective atmospheres, urban geopolitics and conflict (de) escalation in Beirut. *Political Geography,* 61, 1–10.

Gagen, E., Lorimer, H., and Vasudevan, A (eds.). 2007. Practising the Archive: Reflections on methods and practice in historical geography. London: Historical Geography Research Group.

Gallagher, K. 2020. *Killer Optics. Ploughshares Special Report*, Accessed May 7, 2020. https://ploughshares.ca/pl_publications/killer-optics-exports-of-wescam-sensors-to-turkey/.

Gallagher, C. 2004. Teaching about political violence: A primer on representation. Journal of Geography in Higher Education, 28(2), 301-15.

Gange, D. 2017. Retracing Trevelyan? Historical practice and the archive of the feet. *Studies in Ecocriticism,* 21 (3), 246–61.

Gerard, P. 2017. *The Art of Creative Research: A Field Guide for Writers*. Chicago: University of Chicago Press.

Gibson, C. 2006. Decolonising the production of geographical knowledges? Reflections on research with indigenous musicians. *Geografiska Annaler*, 88 (3), 277–84.

Goffman, A. 2015. *On the Run: Fugitive Life in an American City*. London, UK: Picador.

Gorman A. 2021. *Doctor Space Junk vs The Universe: Archaeology and the Future*. Cambridge: MIT Press.

Graham Jones, J. 2019. The translational politics of surtitling: Lola Arias's Campo Minado/Minefield. In *Lola Arias: Re-enacting life*. Aberysth. Performance Research Books.

Graham, S. 2010. *Cities Under Siege: The New Military Urbanism*. Verso: London.

Grasseni, C. 2004. Video and ethnographic knowledge: Skilled vision in the practice of breeding. In A.I. Alfonso., L. Kurti., and Pink S (eds.) Working Images: Visual Research and Representation in Ethnography, 12-27. London: Routledge.

Grayson, K. 2016. *Cultural Politics of Targeted Killing: On Drones, Counter-insurgency, and Violence*. Oxon: Routledge.

Greene, D. 2015. Drone Vision. Surveillance and society, 13 (2), 233-49.

Gregory, D. 2010. War and peace. *Transactions of the Institute of British Geographers*, 35, 154–86.

Gregory, D. 2011. The everywhere war. *The Geographical Journal*, 177(3), 238–50.

Gregory, D. 2012. From a view to a kill: Drones and late modern war. *Theory, Culture & Society,* 28(7–8), 188–215.

Gregory, D. 2013. *Theory of the Drone 3: Killing Grounds*. Accessed May 6, 2021. https://geographicalimaginations.com/2013/07/29/theory-of-the-drone-3-killing-grounds/.

Gregory, B. 2021. *A History of the Artists Rifles*, 1859–1947. Barnsley: Pen & Sword.

Grewal, I. 2017. The technopolitics of visuality in postcolony and empire, 343–66. In L. Parks, and C. Kaplan (*eds.*). 2017. *Life in the Age of Drone Warfare*. Durham, NC: Duke Univ. Press.

Gribble, R., Goodwin, L., Orma, S., Fear, N.T. 2019. 'Happy wife, happy soldier: How the relationship between military spouses and the military institution influences spouse well-being: In R. Moelker., M. Andrew., and N. Rones (eds.) *The Politics of Military Families: State, Work Organizations, and the Rise of the Negotiation Household*. London: Routledge.

Grosz, E. 2008. *Chaos, Territory, Art: Deleuze and the Framing of the Earth*. Columbia University Press.

Grounds, T. 2013. *Our Girl. UK: British Broadcasting Corporation*. Retrieved from https://www.bbc.co.uk/programmes/p0260ych.

Gupta, A., and Ferguson, J. 1997a. *Culture, Power, Place: Explorations in Critical Anthropology*. Durham, NC: Duke University Press.

Gupta, A., and Ferguson, J. 1997b. *Anthropological Locations: Boundaries and Grounds of a Field Science*. San Francisco, CA: University of California Press.

Haines, G. 2019. The Artists Rifles: A history of the Regiment. Art UK. Retrieved from https://artuk.org/discover/stories/the-artists-rifles-a-history-of-the-regiment#:~:text=The%20Artists%20Rifles%20regiment%20was,was%20located%20at%20Burlington%20House.

Hall, S. 2001. Constituting an Archive. Third Text 49, winter 1999–2000. https://www.tandfonline.com/doi/pdf/10.1080/09528820108576903.

Hanska, J. 2015. Tohtoriupseeri—Kriittinen tutkija vai selvitysmies? Tieteellisyyden ja upseeriuden yhdistäminen puolustusvoimien tutkimuskentän pyörteissä. In A. Nokkala., J. Hanksa., and M. Häyry (eds.) Akateemisuus ja upseerius: Tieteen, tutkimuksen ja johtamisen ristivetoa puolustushallinnossa,, 39–66. Maanpuolustuskorkeakoulu.

Haraway, D. 1991 Cyborg manifesto: Science, technology, and socialist-feminism in the late twentieth century." In *Simians, Cyborgs and Women: The Reinvention of Nature*, 149–81. New York: Routledge.

Harper, R.H.R. and Randall D.W. 1992. Rogues in the Air: An Ethnomethodology of 'Conflict' in Socially Organised Airspace. Technical Report EPC-1992–109 http://citeseerx.ist.psu.edu/viewdoc/download?doi=10.1.1.70.5630&rep=rep1&type=pdf.

Hast, S. 2019. Autopsy of a militarized body: Introducing the short documentary *Nothing too Bad, Critical Military Studies*, 5(1), 89–93.

Hast, S., and Bagheri Nesami, M. 2021. Falling like a Monster, *Research Catalogue*, 2021 (15), https://doi.org/10.22501/ruu.889932.

Hast, S. 2018. Sounds of War: Aesthetics, Emotions and Chechnya. Vol. 2018. Bristol: E-International Relations. www.e-ir.info.

Hast, S. 2020a. Synching the martial body: Poetic encounters with Finnish cadets.' *Critical Military Studies*, December 1–24. https://doi.org/10.1080/23337486.2020.1861738.

Hast, Susanna. 2020b. Walking with soldiers: How I Ssopped worrying and learned to love cadets. *Journal for Artistic Research, Research Catalogue*, no. 21. https://doi.org/10.22501/jar.700528.

Hawkins, H. 2013. *For Creative Geographies: Geography, Visual Arts and the Making of Worlds*. New York: Routledge.

Hawkins, H. 2015. Creative geographic methods: Knowing, representing, intervening. On composing place and page. *Cultural Geographies*, 22 (2), 247–68.

Hawkins, H. 2019. Geography's creative (re) turn: Toward a critical framework. *Progress in Human Geography*, 43(6), 963–84.

Hedström, J. 2019. Militarization in five vignettes, *Critical Military Studies*, 5 (2), 189–90.

Heggie, J. K. F. 2003. Uniform Identity? Lesbians and the Negotiation of Gender & Sexuality in the British Army Since 1950. PhD thesis, University of York.

Hemmings, C. 2012. Affective solidarity: Feminist reflexivity and political transformation. *Feminist Theory*, 13(2), 147–61. https://doi.org/10.1177/1464700112442643.

Hewitt, K. 1983. Place annihilation: Area bombing and the fate of urban places. *Annals of the Association of American Geographers,* 73 (2), 257–84.

Higate, P., & Cameron, A. 2006. Reflexivity and researching the military. *Armed Forces & Society*, 32(2), 219–33. https://doi.org/10.1177/0095327X05278171.

Hitchins, H. & Mountford, F. 2016. Evening Standard.

Hochberg, G.Z. 2015. *Visual Occupations: Violence and Visibility in a Conflict Zone*. Durham, NC: Duke Univ. Press.

Hockey, J. 2016. The aesthetic of being in the field: Participant observation with infantry. In A. J. Williams, K. N. Jenkings, M. F. Rech, & R. Woodward (Eds.), *The Routledge Companion to Military Research Methods*. Abingdon: Routledge.

Holvikivi, A. 2019. Gender experts and critical friends: Research in relations of proximity. *European Journal of Politics and Gender*, 2(1), 131–47. https://doi.org/10.1332/251510819x15471289106068.

hooks, b. 1995. *Art on My Mind: Visual Politics*. New York: New Press.

Horlock, M. 2018. *Joseph Gray's Camouflage: A memoir of Art, Love and Deception*. Unbound: London.

Horn, D. 2010. 'Boots and bed sheets: constructing the military support system in a time of war.' In L Sjoberg L and S Via (*eds.*) *Gender, War, and Militarism, 57–68* Santa Barbara, CA: Praeger Security International.

Horst, H., and Hjorth, L. 2014. Visualising Ethnography: Ethnography's Role in Art and Visual Cultures. *Visual Studies,* 29(2),125–27.

Horvath, A., Thomassen, B., and Wydra, H. (*Eds.*) 2015. *Breaking boundaries: Varieties of Liminality.* Oxford: Berghan.

Howell, A. 2018. Forget 'Militarization': Race, Disability and the 'Martial Politics' of the Police and of the University."*International Feminist Journal of Politics,* 20 (2), 117–36. https://doi.org/10.1080/14616742.2018.1447310.

Hudson, M. 2020. *On Blackamoor: History, Memory, Nature of the North York Moors*. Saltburn: Te Me No Press.

Hyde A. 2016. The present tense of Afghanistan: Accounting for space, time and gender in processes of militarisation. *Gender, Place & Culture*. 23(6): 857–68.

Hyde, A. 2014. Omissions and admissions: Poetic writing, feminist ethnography and empathetic violence. *Journal of Narrative Politics*, 1(1), 24–40.

Imperial War Museum, nd. 'West End or Western Front.' Retrieved from https://www.iwm.org.uk/history/west-end-or-western-front.

Ingram, A. 2019. *Geopolitics and the Event: Rethinking Britain's Iraq War through Art*. Oxford: John Wiley & Sons.

Irigaray, L. 2004. "To Paint the Invisible" Translated by Helen Fielding. *Continental Philosophy Review*, 37, 389–405, available at doi: 10.1007/s11007-005-5755-9 (accessed May 27 2021).

Jackson, D. 1998 Were you there do you care? Unpublished.

Jackson, D. 2000. Masters Research Diary. Unpublished.

Jackson, D. 2016. Rehearsal Journal. Unpublished.

Jackson, D. 2018. Minefield Journal. Unpublished.

James, T. 2002. Pure Rage: The Making of '28 Days Later.' UK: Picture Production Company.

Jardine, L. 2014. A point of view: When historical fiction is more truthful than historical fact. http://www.bbc.co.uk/news/magazine-29060077 [Accessed 7 September 2020].

Jarvis, L. and Robinson, N. 2019. War, time, and military videogames: Heterogeneities and critical potential. *Critical Military Studies*, 7(2), 192–211.

Jones, M.E. 2011. *The Muse Is Music: Jazz Poetry from the Harlem Renaissance to Spoken Word*. University of Illinois Press.

Jones, M. 2012. Combat Paper Project. *The Book Art Blog*, May 16. http://thebookartblog.blogspot.com/2012/05/combat-paper-project.html.

Kapadia, R.E. 2019. *Insurgent Aesthetics: Security and the Queer Life of the Forever War*. Durham: Duke University Press.

Kaplan, C. 2006. Mobility and war: The cosmic view of US 'air power.' *Environment and Planning A*, 38, 395–407.

Kaplan, C. 2018. *Aerial Aftermaths: Wartime from Above*. Durham, NC: Duke Univ. Press.

Kara, H. 2015. *Creative Research Methods in the Social Sciences: A Practical Guide* (1st ed.). Bristol: Policy Press.

Karina, L. and Kant, M. 2003. *Hitler's Dancers: German Modern Dance and the Third Reich*. Oxford: Berghahn Books.

Kelly, J. 2013. Popular culture, sport and the 'hero'-fication of British militarism. *Sociology*, 47(4), 722–38.

King, S. 2000. *On Writing: A Memoir of the Craft*. London, UK: Hodder and Stoughton.

King, S. 2006. *The Art of Fiction*. https://www.theparisreview.org/interviews/5653/the-art-of-fiction-no-189-stephen-king [Accessed 20 September 2020].

Kingston, M.H. 1989. *The Woman Warrior: Memoirs of a Girlhood Among Ghosts*. New York, NY: Vintage International Edition.

Kirkup, J. 2013. Wounded veterans are spared cuts to benefits. *The Telegraph*, February 14.

Kirtley, J. & Cree, A. 2022. *Magnolia Walls*. Directed by Corinne Kilvington, by Workie Ticket Theatre, 24–25 June. Northern Stage, Newcastle Upon Tyne.

Kopytin, A. & Lebedev, A. 2015. Humour, self-attitude, emotions and cognitions in group. Journal of the American Art Therapy Association, 30 (1), 20-29.

Kosminsky, P. 1987. The Falklands War. The Untold Story. Leeds. Yorkshire Television.

Kress, G. & van Leeuwen, T. 2001. Multimodal Discourse: The Modes and Media of Contemporary Communication. London: Hodder Education.

Kuletz, V. 1998. *The Tainted Desert: Environmental and Social Ruin in the American West.* New York: Routledge.

Kumsa, M. K., Chambon, A., Yan, M. C., and Maiter, S. 2015. Catching the shimmers of the social: from the limits of reflexivity to methodological creativity. *Qualitative Research*, 15(4), 419–36. https://doi.org/10.1177/1468794114538897.

La Capital. 2012. Borges y la Guerra de Malvinas. https:// www.lacapital.com.ar/politica/borges-y-la-guerra-malvinas-n381346.html/amp.

Laing, O. 2014. *The Trip to Echo Spring: On Writers and Drinking*. London, UK: Picador.

Lakoff, G. & Johnson, M. 1999. *Philosophy in the Flesh: The Embodied Mind and Its Challenge to Western Thought.* New York: Basic Books.

Lambeth, B. 1999. Air power, space power and geography. In Gray, C., and Sloan, G. (*Eds.*) 2014 *Geopolitics, Geography and Strategy*, 63-82. Oxon: Abingdon.

Lane, M. 1974. *War Is Hell! Williams T. Sherman's Personal Narrative of His March through Georgia*. Philadelphia. The Beehive Press.

Lang, A. n.d.. *Mary Ambree.* Retrieved from https://poetandpoem.com/Andrew-Lang/Mary-Ambree.

Larkin, M. Flowers, P, Smith, J. 2009 *Interpretative Phenomenological Analysis: Theory, Method and Research*, SAGE, London.

Le Corbusier, 1987 [1934]. Aircraft. London: Trefoil.

Leavy, P. 2009. *Method Meets Art: Arts-Based Research Practice*. New York: Guilford Publications.

Leavy, P. 2018. Handbook of Arts-Based Research. New York and London.

Leavy, P. 2020. "Method Meets Art. Third Edition: Arts-Based Research Practice," Guildford Publications.

Lennon and McCartney, 1969. "Get Back." Taken from *Let It Be* by The Beatles. London. Apple Records.

Lewis, D., Modirzade, N., and Blum, G. 2017. The Pentagon's New Algorithmic-Warfare Team. Lawfare. June 26, 2017. Accessed May 6, 2021. https://www.lawfareblog.com/pentagons-new-algorithmic-warfare-team.

Liamputtong, P., Rumbold, J., Aldridge, D., Alexander, L., Allen, J., and Bagley, C. 2008. *Knowing Differently: Arts-Based and Collaborative Research Methods*. Hauppauge, NY: Nova Science Publishers.

Lipton, B., & Mackinlay, E. 2017. *We Only Talk Feminist Here.* 61–84. https://doi.org/10.1007/978-3-319-40078-5.

Liptrott, Amy. 2016. *The Outrun.* UK: Canongate Books.

Lobban, J. & Murphy, D. 2020. Understanding the role of art therapy can take in treating veterans with chronic post-traumatic stress disorder. *The Arts in Psychotherapy.* Vol: 62. 37–44.

Lorde, A. 2017. *Your Silence Will Not Protect You.* London: Silver Press.

Lorimer, H. 2003. Telling small stories: spaces of knowledge and the practice of geography. *Transactions of the Institute of British Geographers.* 28(2), 197–217.

Lynes, B.B. Poling-Kempes. L and Turner T.W. 2005. *Georgia O'Keeffe and New Mexico: A Sense of Place.* Princeton: Princeton University Press.

MacKenzie, M., Gregory, T., Shah, N., Barkawi, T., Haastrup, T., Eichler, M., Wegner, N. and Howell, A., 2019. Can we really "forget" militarization? A conversation on Alison Howell's martial politics. International Feminist Journal of Politics, 21(5), .816-836.

Maddrell, A. 2008. "The Map Girls: British women geographers' war work, shifting gender boundaries and reflections on the history of geography." *Transactions of the Institute of British Geographers*, 33(1), 127-48.

Maguire, G. 2018. Screening the past: Reflexivity, repetition and the spectator in Lola Arias' Minefield/Campo Minado 2016. *Bulletin of Latin American Research*, 38(4), 471-86.

Manning, E. 2016. *The Minor Gesture.* Durham: Duke Univerity Press.

Brady, S., and Mantoan, L. 2017. *Performance in a Militarized Culture.* Routledge & CRC Press. https://www.routledge.com/Performance-in-a-Militarized-Culture/Brady-Mantoan/p/book/9781138740808.

Marcus, G., and Fischer, M. 2014 [1986]. *Anthropology as Cultural Critique: An Experimental Moment in the Human Sciences (Second Edition).* Chicago, IL: University of Chicago Press.

Martin, G. and Steuter, E. 2010. *Pop Culture Goes to War: Enlisting and Resisting Militarism in the War on Terror.* Plymouth: Lexington.

Maslow, A. H., 1943. A theory of human motivation, *Psychological Review*, 50, 370 – 396.

Mason, O. 2021. Moving across the field: Researcher mobilities and immobilities during international fieldwork. In M. Ajebon., A. Diego., C. Kwong (eds.) Navigating the Field, 13-24. Springer.

Matless, D. 1990. Definitions of England, 1928-1989: Preservation, modernism, and the nature of the nation. Built Environment, 16(3), 179-91.

Matless, D. 1998. *Landscape and Englishness.* London: Reaktion.

Mbembe, A. 2003. Necropolitics. *Public Culture* 15(1), 11–40.

Mbembe, A. 2016. *Necropolitics.* Durham, NC: Duke Univ. Press.

McConnell, F. 2017. Liminal geopolitics: The subjectivity and spatiality of diplomacy at the margins. *Transactions of the Institute of British Geographers,* 42(1), 139–52.

McConnell, F., Moreau, T., and Dittmer, J. 2012. Mimicking state diplomacy: The legitimizing strategies of unofficial diplomacies. *Geoforum,* 43, 804–14.

McCourt, F. 2005. *Angela's Ashes.* St Ives, Great Britain: Harper Perennial.

McCulloch, J., and Hall, M., 2018. The Education of Children from Military Families: Identity and Agency. *Educational Futures*, 9 (2)

McFadden, M. H. 2011. Borders, boundaries, and the necessity of reflexivity: International women activists, Rosika Schwimmer (1877–1948), and the shadow narrative. *Women's History Review*, 20(4), 533–42. https://doi.org/10.1080/09612025.2011.599606.

McNeill, William H. 1995. *Keeping Together in Time: Dance and Drill in Human History*. Cambridge, Mass.: Harvard University Press.

McNiff, S. 2018. Arts-Based Research, Jessica Kingsley Publishers.

McSorley, K. 2014. Towards an embodied sociology of war. *The Sociological Review*, 62, 107–28.

Menter, I., Elliott, D., Hulme, M., Lewin, J., and Lowden, K. 2011. *A Guide to Practitioner Research in Education*. London: Sage.

Michel, A.H. 2019. *Eyes in the Sky: The Secret Rise of Gorgon Stare and How it Will Watch Us All*. NY: Houghton Mifflin Harcourt.

Mikkola, H. 2021. Personal communication, 17 March 2021.

Millar, K.M., and Tidy, J. 2017. Combat as a moving target: Masculinities, the heroic soldier myth, and normative martial violence. Critical Military Studies, 3(2), 142-60. https://doi.org/10.1080/23337486.2017.1302556.

Mills, C. Wright. 2000 [1959]. *The Sociological Imagination [Fortieth Anniversary Edition]*. Oxford: Oxford University Press.

Mills, L. 2023. Facing Torture through art and the afterlives of war: Behind the mask. In Cox, R., Donnelly, F. & Lang Jr., AF (*Eds.*), *Contesting Torture: Interdisciplinary Perspectives*, 139–64.

Mills, L. (forthcoming). Un/masking in/securities: Trauma, the grotesque and military healing arts programmes. *Critical Studies on Security*.

Mills, S. 2013. Cultural historical geographies of the archive: Fragments, objects and ghosts. Geography Compass, 7(10), 701-13.

Mindrup, M. 2019. *The architectural model: Histories of the miniature and the prototype, the exemplar and the muse*. Cambridge, MA: MIT Press.

Ministry of Defence. 2014. Invictus Games team honoured at Pride of Britain Awards, October 7. https://www.gov.uk/government/news/invictus-games-team-honoured-at-pride-of-britain-awards.

Mirzoeff, N. 2011. *The Right to Look: A Counterhistory of Visuality*. Durham, NC: Duke Univ. Press.

Moilanen, A. 2014. 'Suomalaisjoukkojen saldo Afganistanissa: 65 henkeä uhkaavaa tilannetta.' Yle uutiset, 17.12 https://yle.fi/uutiset/3-7692429 Accessed 4 March 2020.

Moore, C., and Shepherd, L. 2010. Aesthetics and international relations: Towards a global politics. *Global Society*, 24, 299–309.

Morales, L. 1964, *Zamba de mi Esperanza*. New York. CBS.

Mould, O. 2018. *Against Creativity*. London: Verso.

Mullen, J. 2015. *The Show Must Go On! Popular Song in Britain During the First World War*. Farnham: Ashgate.

Mulvihill, M. 2019. The Four-Minute Warning Drawing Machine: Revealing the Assemblages of Nuclear Deterrence. PhD diss, Newcastle University.

Mulvihill, M. 2021. Purple haze: The psychedelic sound of nuclear deterrence. Inkstick, 1st February 2021, https://inkstickmedia.com/purple-haze-the-psychedelic-sound-of-nuclear-deterrence/ (accessed 26th March 2021).

Muncey, T. 2010. *Creating Autoethnographies*. London: SAGE Publications Ltd.

Mäkinen, J. 2019. 'Ollako Vai Eikö Olla: Sotilas Ja Kansalainen Yhteiskunnallisissa Suhteissaan.' Tiede Ja Ase, 76, 126-46.

Nabatchi, N., Sancino, A., Sicilia, M. 2017. *Varieties of Participation in Public Services: The Who, When, and What of Coproduction*. Harvard: Harvard University Press.

Nancy, J. 2003 Image and violence. In, *The Ground of the Image*. J. Nancy (ed.) The Ground of the Image (trans. J. Fort), 15-26. Fordham, NY. Fordham University Press.

Naylor, S. 2006. Nationalizing provincial weather: Meteorology in nineteenth-century Cornwall. *British Journal for the History of Science* 39(3), 407–33.

Neilsen, L. 2008. Lyric inquiry. In G. Knowles & A. Cole. (*Eds.*). *Handbook of the Arts in Qualitative Research: Perspectives, Methodologies, Examples and Issues*. Thousand Oaks, CA: Sage.

Newlands, E. 2014. *Civilians Into Soldiers: War, the Body and British Army Recruits, 1939–45.* Oxford University Press.

Nichols, B. 2017. *Introduction to Documentary (Third).* Bloomington: Indiana University Press.

Nind, N., 2011 Participatory data analysis: a step too far? *Qualitative Research,* 11(4), 349–63.

NSquare. 2019. *Greater Than: Nuclear Threat Professionals Reimagine Their Field.* New York: NSquare.

Nye J. 2008. Public diplomacy and soft power. *The Annals of the American Academy of Political and Social Science,* 616(1), 94–109.

Oakley, P. 1981. "Don't You Want Me Baby." Taken from *Dare* by The Human League. A and M records.

Obligado & Tieri, 1939, Marcha de las Malvinas (March of the Malvinas). *Poetic Musical Competition.* Buenos Aries.

Obradovic, L. 2017. Quantitative approaches to researching gender and militaries. In C. Duncanson and R.Woodward (*eds.*) *The Palgrave International Handbook of Gender and the Military, 73-87.* London: Palgrave Macmillan.

Office for Veterans Affairs. 2021. https://commonslibrary.parliament.uk/research-briefings/cb7693/#:~:text=The%20MOD%20estimated%20that%20in,veterans%20residing%20in%20Great%20Britain.

Ong, W. J. 1982. *Orality and Literacy. The Technologizing of the Word.* London: Routledge.

O'Neill, M. and Roberts, B. 2020. *Walking Methods: Research on the Move*. London: Routledge.

Paglen, T. 2009. *Blank Spots on the Map: The Dark Geographies of the Pentagon's Secret World.* London: Dutton.

Pain, R. 2015. Intimate war. *Political Geography*, 44, 64–73. https://doi.org/10.1016/j.polgeo.2014.09.011.

Parker, I. 1993. *Complete Collector's Guide to the Rollei TLR*. Jersey: Hove Photo Books.

Parks, L., and Kaplan, C (eds.). 2017. *Life in the Age of Drone Warfare*. Durham, NC: Duke Univ. Press.

PBS Newshour. 2012. Veterans Shred Uniforms to Create 'Combat Paper' Artwork, May 1. https://www.youtube.com/watch?v=xb3K-Sd4cPA.

Pearson, A.W. 2002. Allied military modelling during World War II. Cartography and Geographic Information Science, 29(3), 227-41.

Pelias, R.J. 2004. *A Methodology of the Heart: Evoking Academic and Daily Life*. Walnut Creek, CA: Alta Mira Press.

Perera, V. 2019. Event and masculinities in the art of Lola Arias. *Latin American Theatre Review. 53(1), 79-100.*

Pink Floyd. 1983. The Final Cut: Requiem for a Post War Dream, Pink Floyd Music Ltd, Harvest.

Pinkerton, A., and Benwell, M. 2014. Rethinking popular geopolitics in the Falklands/Malvinas sovereignty dispute: Creative diplomacy and citizen statecraft. *Political Geography,* 38, 12–22.

Poling-Kempes, L. 2005. *Ghost Ranch*. Tuscon: The University of Arizona Press.

Pomarède, J. 2018. Normalizing violence through front-line stories: The case of American Sniper. *Critical Military Studies*, 4(1), 52–71

Poole, D. 2005. An excess of description: Ethnography, eace, and visual technologies. Annual Review of Anthropology, 34, 159-79.

Pradhan, (Date unknown) Yo Nepali Sir Uchli.

Pratt, G., and Johnston, C. 2014. Filipina domestic workers, violent insecurity, testimonial theatre and transnational ambivalence. *Area, 46*(4), 358–60.

Price-Styles, A. 2015. MC origins: Rap and spoken word poetry.' In J.A. Williams (ed.) The Cambridge Companion to Hip-Hop, 11-21. Cambridge: Cambridge University Press. https://books.google.fi/books/about/The_Cambridge_Companion_to_Hip_Hop.html?id=Ha0PBgAAQBAJ&redir_esc=y.

Protevi, J. 2013. Affect, agency, and responsibility: The act of killing in the age of cyborgs. In K. McSorley (ed.) War and the Body: Militarisation, Practice and Experience, 128-37. New York: Routledge.

Puolustusvoimat. 2021.Ohjesäännöt ja Oppaat. https://puolustusvoimat.fi/asiointi/aineistot/ohjesaannot-ja-oppaat.

Purnell, K., and Danilova, N. 2018. Dancing at the frontline: Rosie Kay's 5SOLDIERS de-realises and re-secures war. *Critical Studies on Security*, 6(3), 370–75. https://doi.org/10.1080/21624887.2018.1432535.

Raynor, R., 2019. Speaking, feeling, mattering: Theatre as method and model for practice-based, collaborative, research. *Progress in Human Geography*, 43(4), 691–710.

Reed, H.P. 1946. The development of the terrain model in the war. Geographical Review, 36(4), 632-52.

Rehtonen, T. 2021. Personal communication 21.3. 2021.

Reis, V.H., Hanrahan, R.J., and Levedahl, W.K. 2016. The big science of stockpile stewardship. Physics Today, 69(8), 46-53.

Richardson, L. 1992. The consequences of poetic representation: Writing the other, rewriting the self. In C. Ellis and M.G. Flaherty (eds.) Investigating Subjectivity: Research on Lived Experience, 125-37. London: Sage.

Robinson, J.P. 2012. Invisible targets, strengthened morale: Static camouflage as a 'weapon of the weak'. Space and Polity, 16(3), 351-68.

Robinson, J.P. 2013. Darkened surfaces: Camouflage and the nocturnal observation of Britain, 1941-45. Environment and Planning A, 45(5), 1053-69.

Rogers, A. 2018. Advancing the geographies of the performing arts: Intercultural aesthetics, migratory mobility and geopolitics. *Progress in Human Geography,* 42(4), 549–68.

Rose, G. 2000. Practicing photography: An archive, a study, some photographs, and a researcher. Journal of Historical Geography, 26(4), 281-94.

Rosen, H. 1998. The landscape of autobiography. In *Speaking from Memory: The Study of Autobiographical Discourse.* Stoke on Trent: Trentham Books.

Rothstein, A. 2015. *Drone*. New York: Bloomsbury.

Sage, L. 2000. *Bad Blood: A Memoir*. London, UK: Fourth Estate.

Said, E.W. 1978. *Orientalism*. New York: Pantheon Books.

Satchwell, C. 2018. Collaborative writing with young people with disabilities: Raising new questions of authorship and agency. *Literacy*. DOI:10.1111/lit.12146.

Scott, S.T. 2019. "Georgia O'Keeffe's "Black Place," *The Art Bulletin*, 10188–114.doi: 10.1080/00043079.2019.1564178.

Schrader, B. 2014. Auto-archaeology and the political affect of war. *Journal of Narrative Politics*, 1(1), 4–23.

Sebald, W.G. 1999. *On the Natural History of Destruction*. Translated by Athena Bell. Munich: Carl Hanser Verlag.

Sestito, S. Rodriguez, K. Saba, K. Conley, J. Mitchell, M, and Gordon, A. 2017. Homeless veterans' experiences with substance abuse, recovery and treatment through photo elicitation. *Substance Abuse, 38 (4), 422-31.*

Sharp, J. 2020. Materials, forensics and feminist geopolitics. *Progress in Human Geography.* Online first at https://doi.org/10.1177/0309132520905653 (accessed 26th March 2021).

Shaw, M. 2003. *War and Genocide*. Cambridge: Polity Press.

Sherril, G. and Wasserman, J. 2006. *Theatre and Autobiography: Writing and Performing Lives in Theory and Practice.* Vancouver: Talonbooks.

Siegel, D., 2015. *The Developing Mind: How Relationships and the Brain Interact to Shape Who We Are* (2nd eds). New York: Guilford Press.

Sinding, C., Gray, R. & Nisker, J. 2008. Ethical issues and issues of ethics. In G. Knowles & A. Cole. (*Eds.*). *Handbook of the Arts in Qualitative Research: Perspectives, Methodologies, Examples and Issues*. Thousand Oaks, CA: Sage.

Smith, A.K. and Weiner, C. 1980 *Robert Oppenheimer: Letters and Recollections.* Cambridge: Harvard University Press

Soeters, J., Shields, P.M. and Rietjens, S.J.H. (*Eds.*) 2014. *Routledge Handbook of Research Methods in Military Studies.* London: Routledge.

Solnit, R. A Field Guide to Getting Lost. New York: Viking Penguin.

Sosa, C. 2017. Campo Minado/Minefield: War, affect and vulnerability—a spectacle of intimate power. *Theatre Research International, 42 (2), 179-89.*

Sparkes, A. C. 2002. Autoethnography: Self-indulgence or something more? In C. Ellis, & A. Bochner. (*Eds*.). *Ethnographically Speaking*. New York: Alta Mira Press.

Speedy, J. 2005. Using poetic documents: An exploration of poststructuralist ideas and poetic practises in narrative therapy. *British Journal of Guidance & Counselling, 33 (3), 283-98.*

Speedy, J. 2008. *Narrative Inquiry & Psychotherapy*. Houndmills: Palgrave Macmillian.

Spratt, D.A (*Ed*.). 1982. *Prehistoric and Roman Archaeology of North-East Yorkshire*. CAB Series 104.

Spry, T. 2001. Performing autoethnography: An embodied methodological praxis. *Qualitative Inquiry*, 7(6), 706–732. https://doi.org/10.1177/107780040100700605.

Stahl, R. 2010. *Militainment, Inc.: War, Media, and Popular Culture*. Abingdon: Routledge.

Sting. 2016. "Pretty Young Soldier." New York: EMI Music Publishing Limited.

Stocking, G. (*Ed.*) 1984. *Observers Observed: Essays on Ethnographic Fieldwork*. Madison, WI: University of Wisconsin Press.

Story, B. 2016. *The Prison in Twelve Landscapes*. New York: Grasshopper Film.

Stubblefield, T. 2020. *Drone Art: The Everywhere War as Medium*. Oakland: University of California Press.

Sword, H. 2012. *Stylish Academic Writing*. Cambridge, MA: Harvard University Press.

Taber, N. 2005. Learning how to be a woman in the Canadian Forces/unlearning it through feminism: An autoethnography of my learning journey. *Studies in Continuing Education*, 27(3), 289–301. https://doi.org/10.1080/01580370500376630.

Tawney, C. 2015. *Grey Funnel Lines: Traditional Song & Verse of the Royal Navy 1900–1970.* Abingdon: Routledge.

Taylor, J. 2016. *Dazzle: Disguise and Disruption in War and Art*. Oxford: Casemate.

Taylor, P. 2016. Unforgettable Potent. Independent. 6th June 2016. https://www.independent.co.uk/arts-entertainment/theatre-dance/reviews/minefield-royal-court-london-theatre-review-unforgettably-potent-a7067196.html.

The Armed Forces Covenant Trust. n.d. 'About the Trust.' Retrieved from https://covenantfund.org.uk/about-the-trust/#:~:text=The%20Armed%20Forces%20Covenant%20Fund,Departmental%20Public%20Body%2C%20or%20NDPB.

Tidy, J. 2015. Forces sauces and eggs for soldiers: Food, nostalgia, and the rehabilitation of the British military. *Critical Military Studies,* 1(3), 220–32.

Tiechert, E. 2020. Lola Arias' Campo Minado/Minefield 2016: Exploring Dramatherapy in Documentary Theatre. *Bulletin of Hispanic Studies, 97 (10), 1031-46.*

Tobing Rony, F. 1996. *The Third Eye: Race, Cinema, and Ethnographic Spectacle*. Durham, NC: Duke Univ. Press.

Veal, C. and Hawkins, H., 2020. Creativity as method: exploring challenges and fulfilling promises?. In A. de Dios and L. Kong (eds.) Handbook on the geographies of creativity, 352-369. London: Edward Elgar.

Veal, C. 2020. The art of parachuting: Embodied geopolitics, aerial aesthetics and dance-based combat training at Ringway Aerodrome, 1940–1946. *Transactions of the Institute of British Geographers,* 45 (1): 139–54.

Veal, C. 2021. Embodying vertical geopolitics: Towards a political geography of falling. *Political Geography,* 86, 102354.

Vertesi, J. 2015. S*eeing Like a Rover: How Robots, Teams, and Images Craft Knowledge of Mars*. Chicago: Chicago University Press.

Vertesi, J. 2020. Sh*aping Science: Organizations, Decisions, and Culture on NASA's Teams.* Chicago: Chicago University Press.

Vince, N. 2015. *Our Fighting Sisters: Nation, Memory and Gender in Algeria, 1954–2012.* Manchester: Manchester University Press.

Virilio, P. 1989. *War and Cinema: The Logistics of Perception.* London: Verso.

Von Benzon, N., Holton, M., Wilkinson, C. and Wilkinson, S. (*eds.*) 2021. *Creative Methods for Human Geographers*. London: Sage.

Voss, D. 2013. The philosophical concept of meat and flesh: Deleuze and Merleau-Ponty, *Parrhesia,* 18. 113–24. Parrhesia18_voss.pdf (parrhesiajournal.org)

Walker, D. 2016. Putting "insider-ness" to work. In A. J. Williams, K. N. Jenkings, M. F. Rech, and R. Woodward (*Eds.*), *The Routledge Companion to Military Research Methods, 256-66.*. Abingdon: Routledge.

Ware, V. 2016. Biting the bullet: My time with the British Army. In A. J. Williams, K. N. Jenkings, M. F. Rech, and R. Woodward (*Eds.*), *The Routledge Companion to Military Research Methods, 251-62*. Abingdon: Routledge

Weber, S. 2008. Visual images in research. In G. Knowles & A. Cole. (Eds.). *Handbook of the Arts in Qualitative Research: Perspectives, Methodologies, Examples and Issues*. Thousand Oaks, CA: Sage.

Weinberger, S. 2012. How ESPN Taught the Pentagon to Handle a Deluge of Drone Data. *Popular Mechanics*, June 11, 2012.

Wenger, E. McDermott, R and Snyder, W. 2002 *Cultivating Communities of Practice: A Guide to Managing Knowledge*, Harvard Business School Press.

West, H., & Antrobus, S. 2023. 'Deeply odd': women veterans as critical feminist scholars. *Critical Military Studies*, 9(1), 24-39. https://doi.org/10.1080/23337486.2021.1907020.

Wilcox, L. 2014. Making Bodies Matter in IR. *Millennium*, 43(1): 359–64.

Williams, R. 1976, 1983. *Keywords: A Vocabulary of Culture and Society*. New York: Oxford University Press.

Wilson, B.C.F. 1983. History of Fylingdales. Unpublished manuscript, Fylingdales Archive.

Winner, L. 1980. Do artifacts have politics? *Daedalus*. 109(1):121–36. http://www.jstor.org/stable/20024652 (accessed May 28, 2021).

Winton, T. 2014. *Land's Edge: A Coastal Memoir*. London, UK: Picador.

Woodcock, C. 2016. The listening guide: A how-to approach on ways to promote educational democracy."*International Journal of Qualitative Methods, 15(1), 1-10.*

Woodward R, Jenkings K.N. 2018. *Bringing War to Book: Writing and Producing the Military Memoir.* London, UK: Palgrave Macmillan.

Woodward R. 2003. Locating military masculinities: Space, place and the formation of gender identity and the British Army. In: Higate, In P.R. Higate (ed.) Military masculinities: Identity and the State, 43-56. Westport: Praeger.

Woodward, R. 2000. Warrior heroes and little green men: Soldiers, military training, and the construction of rural masculinities. *Rural Sociology*, 65, 640–57.

Woodward, R. and Jenkings, K.N. 2018. *Bringing war to book: Writing and producing the military memoir.* London: Palgrave.

Woodward, R. and Jenkings, N.K. 2012. Military memoirs, their covers and the reproduction of public narratives of war. *Journal of War & Culture Studies*, 5(3), 349–69.

Woodward, R., & Jenkings, K. N. 2012. "This place isn't worth the left boot of one of our boys": Geopolitics, militarism and memoirs of the Afghanistan war. *Political Geography*, 31(8), 495–508. https://doi.org/10.1016/j.polgeo.2012.10.006.

Woodward, R., Dawes, A., Edmunds, T., Higate, P. and Jenkings, K.N. 2020. The possibilities and limits of impact and engagement in research on military institutions. *Area*. first at https://doi.org/10.1111/area.12629 (accessed 26th March 2021).

Woodward, R., T. Winter, and K. Jenkings. 2009. Heroic anxieties: The figure of the British soldier in contemporary print media. Journal of War & Culture Studies, 2(2), .211-223

Woodward, Rachel. 2005. *Military geography.* Oxford: Wiley-Blackwell.

Woodyer, T. and Carter, S. 2020. Domesticating the geopolitical: Rethinking popular geopolitics through play. *Geopolitics*, 25(5), 1050–74.

Woodyer, T. 2012. Ludic geographies: Not merely child's play. *Geography Compass, 6(6), 313-26.*

Wright, K., Hurley, M. and Gil Ruiz, J. 2019. *NATO, Gender and the Military: Women Organising from Within.* London: Routledge.

Yarwood, R. 2015. Miniaturisation and the representation of military geographies in recreational wargaming. *Social and Cultural Geography, 16(6), 654-74.*

Baldwin, J. 2012. *Notes of a Native Son*. Boston, MA: Beacon Press.

Yusoff, K. 2007. Antarctic exposure: Archives of the feeling body. Cultural Geographies, 14(2), 211-33.

# Index

# About the Authors

**Alice Cree (Newcastle University)**

Alice Cree is a NUAcT Fellow at Newcastle University, UK. Her research expertise lies at the intersection between Critical Military Studies and Feminist Geopolitics, with a particular focus on creative methods in military research. She is PI on the ESRC funded project "Conflict, Intimacy, and Military Wives: A Lively Geopolitics," and she has published work in *International Political Sociology, Gender, Place & Culture*, and the *Journal of War and Culture Studies*, among others.

**Chloë Barker (Newcastle University)**

Chloë Barker is co-investigator at Turning Fylingdales Inside Out: making practice visible at the UK's ballistic missile early warning and space monitoring station. She is on the NSquare advisory panel;—NSquare is a collaborative funder for issues on nuclear threat and arms control—and leading on the Fylingdales Archive, which is based on new materialist thinking using online and paper archive to interrogate questions on nuclear deterrence and its material cultural legacy.

**Susanna Hast (University of the Arts, Helsinki)**

Susanna Hast is an associate professor in artistic research at the Theatre Academy of the University of the Arts, Helsinki. She is also a writer, and her debut non-fiction novel, *Ruumis/huoneet*, was published in 2022 in Finland. Currently she works on a project that studies the relationship between militarised language and democracy.

**David Jackson (University of Exeter)**

David Jackson is a former Royal Marine, and during this time, he served in Northern Ireland and the Falklands War. He was diagnosed with PTSD from his experiences of war. After a medical discharge from the Royal Marines in 1995, he trained as a psychotherapist. He now specialises in working with veterans and their families. He graduated from the University of Bristol in 2010 completing his EdD. His research interests are about how the research community can better the lives of veterans and families through creative research methods and using co-productive methods to find alternative voices and new knowledge. He is an honorary research fellow at the University of Exeter working on the Military Afterlives Project and the Stories in Transition Project. He is also a performer in the successful documentary theatre play *Minefield.*

**K Neil Jenkings (Newcastle University)**

K. Neil Jenkings is a senior researcher at Newcastle University, UK. He has authored and co-authored numerous publications on various social phenomena in military and society, health and medical organization and decision-making support, and rock-climbing. Recent co-authored books include *The Value of the University Armed Service Units* (2015), *The Routledge Companion to Military Research Methods* (2016), and *Bringing War to Book: Writing and Producing the Contemporary Military Memoir* (2018). He is also co-editor of the Routledge book series "Directions in Ethnomethodology & Conversation Analysis."

**Michael Mulvihill (Newcastle University)**

Michael Mulvihill is co-investigator in the School of Geography, Politics and Sociology at Newcastle University. He leads on creative practice research for Arts and Humanities Research Council's (AHRC) funded project *Turning Fylingdales Inside Out: making practice visible at the UK's ballistic missile early warning and space monitoring station* (AH/S013067/1) in partnership with RAF Fylingdales and English Heritage. He explores electromagnetic military encounters through electronic music in the band *One Key Magic* that have released the album *Worldly noise and electronic atmospheres* (2021) on Cruel Nature Records (CN173). In addition, he was associate producer on the BBC Four Arena film *A British Guide to the End of the World* (2019), which is based upon his doctoral thesis, "The Four Minute Warning Drawing Machine: Revealing the Assemblages of Nuclear Deterrence."

**Sara Matthews (Wilfrid Laurier University)**

Sara Matthews is associate professor in the Department of Global Studies at Wilfrid Laurier University. Her research and teaching are interdisciplinary and consider the dynamics of conflict and social change. Working primarily in the field of research-creation, her projects explore the relations between visual culture and martial politics as well as how communities craft creative modes of relationality and survival in response to practices of state securitization. In addition to her scholarly writing, Sara curates aesthetic projects that archive the ways in which encounters with conflict and loss emerge as new forms of futurity, materiality, and placemaking. Her critical art writing has appeared in *PUBLIC*, in *FUSE* magazine, and in exhibition essays for the Robert Langen Gallery, Circuit Gallery, the Ottawa Art Gallery, the Doris McCarthy Gallery, and as a blog for Gallery TPW.

**Laura Mills (University of St Andrews)**

Laura Mills is a lecturer in international relations at the University of St Andrews. Her research explores how everyday life and culture co-constitute global politics through examinations of cultural diplomacy, (the afterlives of) war, militarism, and security, and (the possibilities of) aesthetics and creative methods. Her work in these areas has been published in interdisciplinary journals such as *Critical Studies on Security*, *Contemporary Voices in International Relations*, *Survive and Thrive*, *International Feminist Journal of Politics*, and *Cultural Studies*. Her first monograph—*Post-9/11 US Cultural Diplomacy: The Impossibility of Cosmopolitanism*—is forthcoming with Routledge New International Relations Series. Her current projects engage with the Invictus Games and US military and veteran artwork through (auto)ethnography, visuality, narrative, and poetry.

**James P. Robinson (Manchester Metropolitan University)**

James Philip Robinson is a cultural-historical geographer at Manchester Metropolitan University. His research looks into the cultural geographies of camouflage, with a specific focus on the camouflaging of the British industrial landscape between 1936 and 1945.

**Rebecca Steel (University of Central Lancashire)**

Rebecca Steel is a doctoral researcher and educational practitioner with an interest in widening participation. Much of Becky's research focuses on the barriers the military community may face to educational attainment and progression. In addition to her research, Becky regularly works with the armed forces community to support skills development with a focus on raising confidence and aspirations and championing educational pathways. Becky is experienced at supporting community development and leads the College for Military Veterans and Emergency Services at the University of Central Lancashire. Becky is a member of the research team from the University of Central Lancashire and University of Salford's Forces in Mind Trust project, "Understanding the transition pathway for ex-service personnel discharged due to physical injury," a qualitative study aiming to capture the experiences of wounded, injured, and sick service personnel as they leave service and rejoin society as civilians.

**Alexander Thomas T. Smith (Warwick University)**

Alexander Smith is an Australian-born writer and academic who teaches sociology at Warwick University, where he is an associate professor. He holds a PhD in social anthropology from Edinburgh University and an MFA in writing from Warwick. Alex's literary and scholarly interests focus on democracy and political culture; war, memory, and national identity; and ethnography, life-writing, and memoir. His current book project is *Last Op*, an experimental project in creative non-fiction that interweaves elements of the autobiographical novel and personal memoir with family mythology, ethnography, post-military history, and a psycho-geographical journey through some of England's forgotten wartime airfields. Alex's research has been funded by the British Academy, British Council, Economic and Social Research Council, Leverhulme Trust, and the New York–based Wenner-Gren Foundation for Anthropological Research. He is the author of *Devolution and the Scottish Conservatives: banal activism, electioneering and the politics of irrelevance* (2011, Manchester University Press) and *Democracy Begins at Home: Political Moderation in Red State America*, which is due to be published with the University Press of Kansas in 2023. He is also co-editor of *Sociologies of Moderation: problems of democracy, expertise and the media* (2013, Wiley Blackwell) and *Science and the Politics of Openness: Here Be Monsters* (2018, Manchester University Press). Alex edits the New Ethnographies book series for Manchester University Press.

**Charlotte Veal (Newcastle University)**

Charlotte Veal holds a postdoctoral fellowship in landscape in the School of Architecture, Planning and Landscape at Newcastle University. Charlotte works in the interdisciplinary space between political geography and performance. Her research examines the art within the art of war and of the role of dance performance in responding to questions of landscape and security. Her research has spearheaded dance-led methods in the study of issues of security, geopolitics, militarism, and violence.

**Hannah West (Newcastle University)**

Hannah West is a research associate at Newcastle University working on the ESRC project "Conflict, Intimacy and Military Wives: A Lively Geopolitics," with military partners through online participatory theatre workshops. Her PhD explored women's experiences of "front line combat" through the British counterinsurgency campaigns of Malaya, Northern Ireland, and Afghanistan. Hannah has used creative methods to reflect on the gendered aspects of her own military service (hannah-west.org) and is the co-chair of the Defence Research Network (defenceresnet.org).

**Rachel Woodward (Newcastle University)**

Rachel Woodward is professor of human geography in the School of Geography, Politics and Sociology at Newcastle University, UK. She is the author of *Military Geographies* (2004), co-author of *Bringing War to Book* (2018, with K. Neil Jenkings), editor of *A Research Agenda for Military Geographies* (2019), and co-editor of the *Palgrave International Handbook of Gender and the Military* (2017 with Claire Duncanson). She is a co-editor of the *Journal of War and Culture Studies.* Her research interests include military landscapes and research methods in military research contexts, and she is PI on the AHRC-funded *Turning Fylingdales Inside Out* project.

Milton Keynes UK
Ingram Content Group UK Ltd.
UKHW021350220823
427292UK00008B/62

9 781538 160978